DRINKING MARE'S MILK
ON THE ROOF OF THE WORLD

DRINKING MARE'S MILK ON THE ROOF OF THE WORLD

WANDERING THE GLOBE
FROM AZERBAIJAN TO ZANZIBAR

TOM LUTZ

OR Books
New York · London

© 2016 Tom Lutz

Published by OR Books, New York and London
Visit our website at www.orbooks.com

All rights information: rights@orbooks.com

All rights reserved. No part of this book may be reproduced or transmitted in any form or by any means, electronic or mechanical, including photocopy, recording, or any information storage retrieval system, without permission in writing from the publisher, except brief passages for review purposes.

First printing 2016

Cataloging-in-Publication data is available from the Library of Congress.
A catalog record for this book is available from the British Library.

ISBN 978-1-68219-056-2 paperback
ISBN 978-1-68219-057-9 e-book

Text design by Under|Over. Typeset by AarkMany Media, Chennai, India. Printed by BookMobile in the United States and CPI Books Ltd in the United Kingdom.

In short, I have only two possibilities: either I can
be like some traveller of the olden days, who was
faced with a stupendous spectacle, all, or almost all,
of which eluded him, or worse still, filled him with
scorn and disgust; or I can be a modern traveller,
chasing after the vestiges of a vanished reality.
— Claude Lévi-Strauss

Is it right to be watching strangers in a play
in this strangest of theatres?
What childishness is it that while there's a breath of life
in our bodies, we are determined to rush
to see the sun the other way around?
The tiniest green hummingbird in the world?
To stare at some inexplicable old stonework,
inexplicable and impenetrable,
at any view,
instantly seen and always, always delightful?
Oh, must we dream our dreams
and have them, too?
— Elizabeth Bishop

TABLE OF CONTENTS

THE MAGIC LAND AT THE END OF THE ROAD 11
    A Roadworker In Montenegro   14
    An Actor In Connecticut   21
    The Wide World Game   26
    Restlessness   32
    Wonder   37
    Inhaling The World   41

SCHOOLTEACHERS AND GUIDES IN MOROCCO ... 45
    Coming From Tangier   45
    In The Medina   51
    Pitying The King   61
    Stuck In The Kasbah   64
    Into The Sahara   70

THE FOOL ON THE HILL 81
    Boğazkale, Turkey   81
    In Love With History   85

FEAR OF AFRICA 90
    Johannesburg, South Africa   90
    Pretoria   93

TWO UZBEK WEDDINGS AND THE CULTURE OF
HOSPITALITY 99
    First Day Wedding   99
    Plov Day In Tashkent   103
    Wedding In Bukhara   112

HITCHING ACROSS THE ROOF OF THE WORLD ... 119
- The Silk Road Into Kyrgyzstan — 119
- The Road To Sary-Tash — 123
- Across The High Pamir — 132

THE CEMENT SALESMAN AND THE VILLAGER 139
- Blantyre, Malawi — 139
- The Lake At Chembe — 142

MUSIC AND NOSTALGIA IN UKRAINE 147
- Kiev — 147
- Mother Russia — 152
- A Wife In Kishinev — 155
- Power — 158

SINHALESE, TAMIL, HINDU, MUSLIM 161
- Colombo, Sri Lanka — 161
- Kandy And The Buddha's Tooth — 163
- Up A Tree — 167
- Without A Paddle — 173
- Julius — 177

STALIN AND THE POLICE 181
- Baku, Azerbaijan — 181
- The Azeri Boss Hogg — 185
- Learning To Negotiate — 191
- Crossing The River — 194

MULTICULTURALISM IN IRAN 201
- Tehran — 201
- Hipsters And Hospitality — 207
- Isfahan — 211
- Caught Cheating On The Visa — 216

OCCUPIED TIBET 219
- Lhasa — 219
- Pilgrims — 221

THE DOCTOR IN THE CASINO 227
- Dar Es Salaam, Tanzania — 227

BUDDHA AND THE ENGINEERS 233
- Yangon — 233
- The Cowboy And The Indian — 242
- American-Sized In Bagan — 248

IT IS FASHIONABLE TO KNOW ABOUT JEWS 252
- Sighetu Marmației, Romania — 252
- Bibi And The Cemetery — 257
- Snobs — 260

NOTES FROM THE ALBANIAN DIASPORA 265
- Tirana, Albania — 265
- Hoxha's Mushrooms — 267
- Coming From St. Louis — 271
- Crossing The Mountains — 274

PEOPLE JUST LIKE ME 277
- Kishinev, Moldova — 277
- Tiraspol, Transnistria — 279

HALFWAY TO PETRA 283
- Amman – Aqaba Highway, Jordan — 283
- Cosmopolitanism — 285

THE WOMEN AND THE KING 289
    Lobamba, Swaziland   289
    The Reed Dance   291
    Women's Work   295
    An Offer   303

COMING HOME 307
    Yes   307
    Observance: Argentina, Guatemala,
      Laos, India, My Desk   309

ACKNOWLEDGMENTS 315

Photographs keyed to each chapter are available at
ontheroofoftheworld.com.

THE MAGIC LAND
AT THE END OF THE ROAD

> I tramp a perpetual journey.
> —Walt Whitman, 'Song of Myself'

'I DON'T WANT TO JUST BE A TOURIST,' a friend once said to me, 'I want to get to know a place, I want to be there.' The tourist—standing adrift in shorts and sandals, a Hawaiian shirt and straw hat—is an object of ridicule, an unserious human, someone who doesn't know where he or she is. My friend's idea was that a sojourner should stay in a foreign land for months, become part of a local community, learn it from the inside. A tourist is the opposite, an outsider, someone the locals either pity or despise, and for good reason: the tourist is oblivious, the tourist is rude, the tourist profanes, the tourist doesn't get it.

But what else would I be, other than a tourist, dropping, as I always do, in and out of far-flung lands at a breakneck pace, well over a hundred countries and counting? I don't have a job that brings me to these scattered places around the globe. I'm not a missionary, not part of an NGO project, not an anthropologist, not a diplomat. I don't go to Luang Prabang or Quito or Maputo looking to settle down, or even to stay for very long. I am not going to visit archives as a historian, I'm not there to interview the local dignitaries. What could I possibly be but a tourist? People ask me, on the road, what I do for a living, and I say I'm a writer, the implication being that I was traveling to write, I was writing about my travels. But until now, I wasn't. I was just traveling.

There are other options, most of which sound better, or at least less bougie, than being a tourist: explorer, adventurer, wayfarer, voyager; rambler, gallivanter, gadabout, meanderer, rover, flâneur; gypsy, itinerant, migrant, nomad; drifter, vagabond, hobo, transient, vagrant, tramp; quester, pilgrim—but none of these words quite ring true. Or maybe all of them do.

And others, too: I am, I know, a voyeur, a collector (of experiences, of pins in my mental map, of cultures, of stories, of epiphanies), an amateur sleuth into the human condition, a sampler, a taster, and probably, at times, oblivious, thickheaded, rude, greedy, and profane.

I am inordinately proud of my travels and at the same time embarrassed by my pride in them. I feel alternately overflowing and empty, replete with gratitude for my good fortune, and abashed at the overentitled, obsessive nature of my need to continue. I feel sometimes like the most interesting man in the world, sometimes like the most obtuse. I am driven onward and yet, even as I chart my next adventure, I remain unsure why I should want to, unclear why I need to.

And I do need to. The road beckons me, and always has. Am I running toward something? Running away? Is there a difference?

Whatever the motivation, the essence of travel is to be somewhere else, to be somewhere distinctly not home—I don't travel to work, I drive to work; I don't even travel to see relatives 3,000 miles away. I just go to see them. Work and relatives: that's just everyday life; work is part of home, my in-laws' place in Baltimore just part of home.

As Pico Iyer says, we travel until we come home, and then, if we are lucky, at home, in stillness, we write.

BUT WRITE WHAT? What does the traveler know? We committed vagabonds know the weary road, we know the airline terminals, both the gleaming hubs and the small town strips without conveyer belts or shops or signage or even taxis. At one airport near the Uyuni salt flats in the Bolivian Altiplano, I got off the plane with four others; two of them were locals who walked away from the airstrip, and two Japanese tourists who were picked up by their tour guide in a 4x4. I went out looking for a cab. None were around, and none came. There was a pleasure in that. I was at a loss. I was lost. We journeyman journeyers know how to get places anyway. We know how to wrangle a ride in an unknown language, we know how to figure out the bus stations and train stations and how to push through what look like dead ends. Is that something to write about? We know the misery in the world, and we know its riches—but we know that at home, too. We have heads full of images—mountainsides and mosques, street vendors and empty roads. We read up and know some history, we can make some cultural generalizations that are true enough, we know a few words from everywhere—hello and thank you and where's a bathroom? in dozens of tongues. We see the wonders of the world—the monuments, the ruins, the waterfalls, the peaks. We know the visa requirements and the exchange rates and endless arcane facts. But none of that gets at what drives us, or at least what drives me.

What we carry, years later, I've realized, no matter what else, are memories of the people we somehow, despite all odds, fall into accidental intimacy with, the people we make some indelible, brief connection with. This book is a record of some of those meetings, as random on the page as they occurred in real time—unpredictable, brief, incomplete, true, and, for me, as profound as they are quotidian. For whatever reasons, they don't happen, very often, at home. In fact, they happen most often when I get lost, when I don't know exactly where I am.

A ROADWORKER IN MONTENEGRO

MY FIRST OVERSEAS VOYAGE, like many, was accidental, a fluke. As I was graduating high school—without distinction, to put it mildly—my girlfriend, Sandy, ended up in Switzerland. She had an errant minister for a father, a brilliant man with a ritzy congregation and a brutal sex addiction. After one of his many *Scarlet Letter, Damnation of Theron Ware* blow-ups, he was sent away for a year, to the Jung Institute in Zurich, to get his anima and animus worked out. I don't think he ever did. He brought his wife and four of his five children, including Sandy, along with him. I had both an excuse and an incendiary need to see her. Back home, I worked, oddjobbing around town for four months, putting together an Icelandic Airlines round-trip ticket, open return, good for a year, and a small pile of cash the size a kid working shit jobs and living at home can put together. Then I flew to Europe, as so many did in those years, by way of Iceland and Luxembourg.

I bought a motorbike in Zurich and swept Sandy away, down into Italy—how dreadful that must have been for her parents, watching her drive off on the back of the tiny bike, rucksacks tied to the side, with my barely conscious, ponytailed self at the handlebars! We had no more sense of what we were in for than toddlers. We were camping, but had no tent; during a storm, we crouched under a tarp, which we thought to buy only after sitting through the first horrible rain under a bridge. At a campground a few kilometers from Venice, a man from South Africa, who had spent his first year of retirement driving around Europe in a small English Ford van he had refitted as a camper, came over to us and asked if we wanted to buy the van. He was leaving for home in a few days and we clearly needed better shelter. I said yes, but that I had very little money. He said he could let me have it for very little, say $500. I said, well, maybe I could do $50.

It never occurred to me that he'd accept, but it soon became clear that he had no other buyers. He suggested we follow him to Trieste, and as his ship's whistle blew at the dockside, where he was still holding up his Van for Sale placard, he gave us the keys, signing the title at the last possible minute on the principle that $50 was better than nothing, and at least he wouldn't be fined for abandoning a vehicle. We were now happy snails, Sandy and I.

We sold the bike and lived on the proceeds for several months.

You might think that having a vehicle with a toilet and two-burner gas stove and sheets and blankets would be conducive to more leisurely travel, with lots of comfortable stops along the way. But some fever pushed me on. I drove like an alcoholic drinks. Clocking one hundred kilometers simply meant it was time for 150 more. We drove up and down Italy and then around the Riviera and up into Andorra. (Why Andorra? It was an intense experience, a mountain smuggler's den with plate glass showrooms full of smuggled electronics and luxury goods, completely encircled by peasant culture, milk still delivered in cans strapped to the side of a packhorse, and old women walking cows from one clump of roadside grass to the next. And it was another country to add to the list; I made sure to hit Monaco and Lichtenstein, too, already a collector.) From Andorra we dashed across the peninsula to Lisbon, then down to Cabo de San Vicente, the far southwest tip of Portugal, and that may be the first time I fully, consciously, felt the thrill of arriving at the end of the road. Cliffs of sharp brown stone dropped away on both sides of the narrow highway, and eventually, the road went no farther, and there was nothing before us but a white lighthouse and the ocean's loneliness. We stood at the brink and felt nostalgia for the very land we stood on, surging with Gatsbyesque longing, nostalgia for the present. The wind blew in from the endless ocean, and in that moment, we understood, as Che Guevara said during his own youthful travels, 'that our vocation, our true vocation, was to move for eternity along the roads and seas of the world.'

Then, ten minutes later—I know, it's comic, ten minutes later—we were off again, hugging the curly coast road all the way across the Algarve, along the Costa del Sol, twisting through the fractal inlets below Granada, up the Costa Brava, through the marshes of Aude, across the Riviera once more, back to Genoa, across the Italian plains, and, nonstop, through Austria and into Hungary and the horse-cart trafficked roads of Yugoslavia and ruined Greece, and immediately back up to Germany, Belgium, and Holland. Did we ever slow down? That turnout in the dry hills above Delphi, or a random downtown parking spot in Budapest, secured with a handful of Marlboros to the curious gendarmes—these were our accidental destinations, our homes away from home. We would sleep until the sun woke us. That was rest enough on our restless road.

NEAR PODGORICA, MONTENEGRO, my first time behind the Iron Curtain, still a very real thing, we found the Cold War very much alive. Having driven in from Greece across a gray land with gray skies, the vestiges of peasant life—shepherds walking their flocks across the hills—jumbled up with industrial wasteland, we went into a grocery store that had what looked like pointedly denuded shelves: six inches of empty space, then three cans of goulash, then ten inches of empty shelf, then a can of sardines. My first non-consumer society. Titograd, as Podgorica was called then, seemed particularly grim, all smoking factories and mining tailings, and it made me wonder why the Yugoslavian dictator would want this particular town to bear his name. I knew Tito as the guy who had kept disparate and eternally warring populations—Serbs,

Croats, Macedonians, Bosnians, Slovenes, Montenegrins—tamped down through force and charisma. I imagined him as a backwater Khrushchev.

But I didn't think of him much, really—I was young and unconcerned with facts until they were at hand. I was callow youth incarnate, awake to spectacle—look! oxen!—but otherwise the world was too big a puzzle for me to think I might put it together, might collect enough facts and frames to make sense of it. The world was still as endless and unknowable as my own future.

Between Titograd and the Adriatic coast, high in the flaky, iron Dalmatians at dusk, we pulled over onto a patch of gravel, either a rough scenic turnout or part of some slow construction project, and a perfect place to hole up for the night—flat, untrafficked, starkly beautiful. I set about cooking our dinner over the propane burners. Around us the slate mountains rose dark and wet, and below a small river frothed at the bottom of a steep ravine. A few pine trees clung to the rock. As the stars came out and our breath became visible, Sandy and I got into the bed I had built in the back of the van to replace the South Africans' single cots, and had sex with as little forethought or afterthought as we did everything. It was still spring, and still cold in the mountains. We bundled up and fell asleep.

In the early light I woke, attuned to some movement outside. An animal? The gravel was crunching, and whatever it was sounded large. I heard some other sounds: twigs snapping? A bear? A person?

Then the front window, on the driver's side, was opened from the outside—the van was built for deliveries, and had a driver's-side window that slid back on tracks rather than rolling up or down. Suddenly a man's hand appeared through it. I experienced a shock of adrenaline—I had my girlfriend to protect, but had no idea what to do, and as is always true at moments like that, everything happened too fast. But then it became clear the hand was holding not a knife or a gun, but instead, improbably, a bouquet of pine branches, arranged artistically and tied off with a piece of string. A wordless offering of friendship. I reached forward and took the bouquet, said thank you, got dressed quickly, and went out the back doors to meet the gift-giver.

He was a tall, thin man in his late thirties, wearing a uniform of sorts—a military-looking jacket, with epaulets and a name tag—and his face, like the thick, roughly finished wool of his coat, was out of date, a face from the past, long, thin, with gray eyes, and an American Gothic–like lack of animation. He was a Great War photograph come to life.

I CAME TO UNDERSTAND that he was Montenegrin, spoke Montenegrin as well as some Serbian, and that his job was to take care of the stretch of highway where we were standing. The main task this involved was walking his length of the road and removing the rocks that fell, day and night, off the sides of the cliffs. I asked how much road he took care of, and he explained it to me by pointing toward what I think were landmarks of some kind, out of sight to the east and out of sight to the west, but since we had no language in common, I couldn't piece it together—maybe a few kilometers, maybe more. He seemed content in the work.

Since we were close to Titograd, I asked if that was where Tito was from. No, he said, followed, perhaps, by the information that Tito came to this area to go fishing. He mimed casting a rod, at any rate.

He was interested in our van, our mini-home, and in the meantime, Sandy had gotten dressed and was making coffee. I opened the back doors, and he was appreciative of the layout, the small propane tank, the chemical toilet. We all had some coffee, and then we packed up the kitchen and shook hands goodbye. I couldn't tell whether it was sadness I saw in his eyes, but I thought it was, and I couldn't quite sort out what had made him sad, but some part of me decided, then and there, that I wanted to travel always and forever. He picked up rocks, and had a deep soul, and I was, and still am, glad I met him. His generosity and his openhearted gesture with the pine branches were part of it, but the sense of sublimity came from the way the experience fell through the cracks of everyday categories: we were strangers, yet instantly intimate; we had one word in common—Tito—and yet communicated worlds; we spent minutes together and yet I am still thinking of him decades later.

TEARING AROUND EUROPE in that van at eighteen, I was a happy animal, not very different than the puppy we picked up on a beach in Portugal. We adopted him, and he traveled as happily and carelessly as we did. Whenever we stopped, he would run as fast as he could, anywhere, anytime he had the chance—in the Alps, on the beach. It made him happy to go as far as he felt safe as fast as he could, then turn around and run back. Why? We fed him, watered him, played with him, scratched his ears. Why run away? It was nothing but his doggyness that drove him, and it was just my own wandering youth that drove me. I didn't worry about it any more than he did. As Pico Iyer said, 'Serendipity was my tour guide, assisted by caprice.' Nobody was there to say I was crazy, that this blind, incessant wandering—with no destination to speak of, no goal, no checklist of museums or famous buildings, no itinerary, no end date, no plans for going home—was a kind of madness. And I wouldn't have understood them if they did.

AN ACTOR IN CONNECTICUT

WHEN THE MONEY RAN OUT ten months later, Sandy stayed with her parents, and I went back to the States. Between short-lived jobs I hitchhiked, again almost randomly, fully bitten by the madness. Once I learned how, I started hopping freight trains, sometimes trying to get somewhere, but sometimes just to see where I'd end up. I got jobs delivering cars for a car service, took them wherever anyone wanted. The manager loved me. He didn't have many drivers itching to get to Topeka. I was determined (already, like a genetic illness, the bug had me) to get to all fifty states at the earliest possible moment. I got to forty-seven in my early twenties, and the other three irked me.

I was watching the movie of my own progress in my head as I roamed, and the movie always featured a heroic young man 'lighting out for the territories.' I hadn't read *Huckleberry Finn* at that point, in fact hadn't read much of anything—no Walt Whitman, not even Jack Kerouac yet. But I didn't have to, since the idea of leaving civilization behind, going on a voyage past its fringe, pulling up stakes and leaving town, chasing fortune by moving West (or South, or North, or East) runs through the fabric of American culture like the recurring patterns in a Navajo blanket. I didn't need to know the books to know the restless urge, didn't need to know the open road's literary avatars to feel its deep allure.

BECOMING AN ANTHROPOLOGIST, Claude Lévi-Strauss said, resulted from 'envisaging a way of reconciling' his professional life with his 'taste for adventure.' And he understood that he was treading in some dubious footprints: 'I felt I was reliving the adventures of the first sixteenth-century explorers,' he wrote, and he wasn't entirely proud of it.

Long before I had any professional excuse—I have it now, finally, with the writing of this book—I was acting out, like Lévi-Strauss, some bygone image of exploration and discovery.

As young delinquents in high school, my friends and I found our enthusiasm for exploration and discovery severely curtailed by the incarceration that comes with being a suburban high school student. Our only option was to hitchhike out of town. We did it randomly: we stuck out our thumbs, and when people asked us where we were going, we would say, 'Where are you going?' and go there. What we loved was getting beyond the edges of our mental maps, getting lost. It was a game. Head as far out as we could and then race home before we got in trouble. It may have only been fifty or sixty miles, but it felt like sailing the ocean before Columbus,

AN ACTOR IN CONNECTICUT

not knowing what monsters lurked, not knowing if our ship might fall off the edge of the tabletop.

Lévi-Strauss often finds the people he encounters on his travels to be a nuisance, as do some other great writers, like Paul Theroux, who seems to despise pretty much everyone he meets. But for some reason the people I've met on the road have been under some special dispensation, immune from even teenage dismissiveness. We young hitchhiking boys got picked up once by a man with the entirely unlikely name of Tom Sawyer. We thought he was a hippie, but he was fifty, a Shakespearean actor, his hair long for a role. He didn't really live anywhere, he said. He moved from show to show, working in regional theaters, in big cities, wherever the job was. I'd never met anyone like him. He stayed with us as we started a campfire off the side of the road and bought us some wine. He seemed to enjoy sitting with us for a while, regaling us with tales, listening to our chatter, and then he drove off. His talk expanded our sense of the world and the romance in it, our sense of art, of adulthood, in ways I was far from able to articulate. I wondered what it all meant, what I had just learned about life. Here was someone living in a way I did not know existed. I saw a world open up around him. Not a world I would enter, but one that would enter mine.

THIS BOOK is an essay toward understanding my obsession with such chance meetings on the road, where I remain, for some reason, more open to true encounter than I am in daily life. This has become central to my travel fixation, even if otherwise it is made up of the same elements that fuel any tourism—simple curiosity, a yearning for adventure and exoticism, the quest for enlightenment, scopophilia (a love of *seeing*—my namesake, Doubting Thomas, needed to see the wounds, which, the minute I heard the story, made perfect sense to me), wanderlust, a yearning for wonder—it is, I sometimes think, not odd after all. The desire to see everything, to know one's own world—isn't this not only perfectly reasonable, but also almost our human responsibility on this small planet? Someone went to a lot of trouble to lay the world out in front of us, to build all these cultures, to create astonishments like Angkor Wat, Macchu Picchu, and the Forbidden City, to stick those heads on Easter Island, to throw the cathedral at Chartres, as Henry Adams said, up at the sky. It seems ungrateful not to take a look.

Many of us also travel because we want to feel worldly, cosmopolitan, to know the world the way the worldly people know it, to not feel left out when someone mentions Paris or London or Rome (or Angkor Wat, Macchu Picchu, or the Forbidden City). Something like this eggs me along, too. It's less attractive as a motive, I know, and makes me feel like a social climber, a kind of status whore. But let me just go ahead and say it: I wanted to know the world as the well-traveled know it. I wanted to be like Graham Greene or Marco Polo, T. E. Lawrence or Amelia Earhart, like a foreign minister—or maybe a shadow foreign minister. Imitative, I suppose, and reeking of the snob, of one-upmanship, and childish pretense: Harriet the Spy wandering the globe pretending to be Hillary Clinton.

Karl Marx famously said that the need for new markets 'chases the bourgeoisie over the entire surface of the globe,' and in the process us bourgeois folks transform the world in our own image. Even in 1848, Marx saw the world's local cultures being swamped by the tide of cosmopolitan uniformity, the very sense of loss Lévi-Strauss shared a hundred years later. Fifteen years or so ago, a sailor in Greece told me that he loved his long-distance work in the merchant marine, and one of his favorite things, whenever he approached landfall, was to tune in to the port city's radio and hear the local music. But part of the thrill was gone.

Now, he said, Wherever you go—Africa, Asia, South America—always the same: Michael Jackson.

But he and I, of course, help spread that global culture, and perhaps the very desire to be worldly. To go to the ends of the earth and revel in its difference helps destroy that difference, helps flatten the world and extinguish the exotic. The bourgeois traveler literally consumes the world's diversity.

Indeed I often think I'm enacting some bizarre psychological imperialism: I run around collecting countries like a European monarch amassing colonies, and, I may as well admit it, I keep count (115). That's silly enough, but I also cheat. I drove to San Marino, a tiny country in the hills of Italy, just to add it to my list. There's not much to see. I don't think I was out of the car for more that five minutes. I include in my total three countries where I only had time to walk out of the airport; since I have a rule in this game that airport terminals don't count, I went through passport control, stepped out the doors, walked past the loading and unloading zone, into the most minimum of interiors—a thirty-second Magellan. What kind of foolishness is that? I don't plant flags, I take photos, but at bottom it is an unseemly kind of hoarding. Making possessions of other countries at a hundred kilometers an hour. I assure you, I know that it is odd.

But, as aliens are fond of saying, I come in peace. The stories here are not about countries but about people: the Amidov family in Tashkent, my driver in Mandalay, Francine the housekeeper in Pretoria, an old man in Albania, a young one in Jordan, my hapless guide in Sri Lanka. These are people I crossed some habitual boundary of reticence with—I did and they did—and I am the better for each, and there is even a chance that some of these people felt something similar. In each case the world shrank just a little, and sympathy expanded, understanding increased. Such serendipitous meetings mean the world to me, in every sense of the phrase, and they are the kind of connections that drive me toward more. Sweetness, and adventure, and awe, and revelation, and sublimity—doesn't everybody want these things?

And the simple fact is this: there is a lot to know, there are a lot of places to see, endless opportunities for wonder, and so I am in a hurry. Always. Those *Lonely Planet* itineraries that suggest that you should put aside three weeks to see the northern coast of Ecuador drive me mad. In three weeks I would reach all four corners of Ecuador and a couple in Colombia, maybe touch down in Venezuela. I am always hungry. I need to eat. I need to move. I need to go on.

THE WIDE WORLD GAME

MY WANDERLUST was installed long before I ever traveled. As a boy, I went nowhere, never more than a few blocks from my ticky-tack small-town New Jersey home. My father traveled for work a bit, but save a few visits to very exotic Fitchburg, Massachusetts, to see relatives, or once to Norfolk,

Virginia, where my father was stationed for a couple of weeks the summer I was twelve, we went nowhere. On that trip, the family made a visit to Washington, D.C., and then stayed at a motel for five days near the beach. There, much to my exquisite surprise, I made out with a girl my age on a beach towel, kissing for hours and hours, both of us still innocent as lambs. It's tempting to think some template was installed then, some software downloaded, that on that beach on that glorious day, love and the romance of the road were forever linked.

Yet I don't think so. My introduction to necking aside, those rare family excursions never felt like travel, they never felt like adventures. Our domestic situation transferred itself from the house to the car to the motel room, and the family's standard gravitational pulls and centrifugal pushes kept their tight, fraught balance, unchanging, as if we weren't shuddering through space in the Ford station wagon. We all got in the car and arrived somewhere, the days away a simple continuation of my very odd—but that's a different story—childhood. Even in Norfolk, with my sweet experimentalist, her name now long forgotten, I would escape to the beach the way I'd escape to the woods at home, or into one of the houses under construction in the next block, back for lunch and back for dinner, deposited in every case into the daily emotional inertia of my life as I knew it. My sandy-haired girl gave me a new relation to lust, but it doesn't feel like part of my deep and abiding need to wander. When she and I came to rest in each other's arms, in fact, I almost felt the opposite, as if for a moment I was truly home.

And so from where does this travel bug come from? Milling around my fragments of early memory, I come across the day I headed off, in one of those years before kindergarten, with my little red wagon, never to return—what kind of supplies had I packed? Why did I need the wagon? I don't know. Where had I heard the phrase 'running away from home'? I don't know. I headed toward the edge of the known world, the intersection of Longview Road (yes, Longview) and Harper Terrace a half block away. As best as I can figure, there was an attention span malfunction, and I more or less forgot I was running away. I do remember the crossroads, remember being afraid and the anxiety caused by the decision I faced. Left or right? But then there's a blank. Ten minutes or so later, I knocked on Dennis Albanese's door, a few postwar houses up from ours, already halfway back home, to see if he could come out and play.

I also remember this: adventuring past the end of our housing development, a few years later, past the rows of new houses being built from the same GI Bill blueprints as ours, past the new cul de sac, its plots not yet sold, we followed a small stream into the deep woods, well beyond where we were allowed to go—how those boundaries were communicated I have no idea, but I knew we had transgressed them quite seriously, we were way off the rez. For the first time, we went far enough that we came to the remote end of this patch of woodland, surprised that the woods ended at all—up until then they were like a medieval map, with no far border. Before we hit the edge of the world, in the deep of our journey, under a full hardwood canopy untouched for decades, the temperature had dropped and the light softened. Jack-in-the-pulpits, awe-inspiring plants unlike any other, and swamp cabbage, as we called it, although it looked nothing like cabbage, sprouted out of cool, fetid loam. We picked up salamanders and tried to get them to change colors. And then, when the woods opened up, we were back into the bright, hot summer everyday. In front of us, magically, a field full of pumpkins appeared. Acres of pumpkins, and while I must have known that pumpkins grew, somehow, I had no idea they grew like this, with immense dark green leaves along spikey, curling vines. Just past the field we saw warehouses, or perhaps factories—buildings outside our ken, enormous, anonymous, industrial. We walked among the pumpkins and I began to worry; I imagined, with a start, a farmer, coming at us with a gun, angry at our trespass. The gun I imagined him pointing at us was a blunderbuss—I suppose the image was from a TV cartoon—but it spooked me, and we frantically turned back and ran. The woods stretched monolithically in front of us to both horizons, without a gap, without a landmark. We could see no way in. We were lost. We might never get home.

An exciting day, but we all get lost as kids, don't we? And every kid ineffectually runs away from home at some point, right? Neither seems to explain my overweening, gluttonous wanderlust.

MY FAVORITE BOARD GAME as a kid was *Hendrik Van Loon's Wide World Game*, which came in a standard Monopoly-sized box, with a thick cardboard playing board, folded in half, that opened onto a glossy world map, one with no political boundaries, only the names of cities, mountain ranges, oceans, and deserts. The map was presented in a style closer to the sixteenth century than the twentieth, with mountains drawn in, and sand dunes, even a camel or two, and the sea alive with creatures and ships. The rules were simple: you got an 'itinerary' card and rolled the dice to hop your little steamship or plane or train around the globe, from city to city, on dotted routes that I didn't for a second doubt were the routes actual ships and planes and trains followed. For some reason all trips started in San Francisco, headed east, and ended in Manila. First one to Manila won.

Hendrik Willem Van Loon was an encyclopediac, born in 1882, a historian and journalist, originally Dutch, who came to the United States first as a student at Cornell. After a German PhD (as most PhDs were in those days) and a stint covering the Russian Revolution for the Associated Press, he became an American citizen. Van Loon managed, somehow, to write over fifty books, and although some of them were for children, he never shied away from the big topics: *Ancient Man: The Beginnings of Civilization* (1920), *The Story of Mankind* (1921), *The Story of the Bible* (1923), *Tolerance* (1925), *The Story of America from the Very Beginning to the Present* (1927), *The Story of Inventions* (1934), *Ships and How They Sailed the Seven Seas* (1935), *The Arts* (1937), *A Short History of Painting* (1938), *The Story of the Pacific* (1940), a dozen biographies, more focused histories, books about music and musicians and artists, passionate pleas for the United States to join the war against Hitler, and a number of other works of geography. It is exhausting just to think about them. His sixth book, *The Story of Mankind* (1921), made him famous; it won the first Newberry Medal in 1922, was a bestseller for years, and jumped to the top of the list again each time he updated it. He had become a brand name: *Van Loon's Lives: Being a true and faithful account of a number of highly interesting meetings with certain historical personages* (1942) and *Van Loon's Geography: The Story of the World We Live In* (1932) are instances, and, in 1933, Parker Bros. brought out the first edition of *Hendrik Van Loon's Wide World Game.*

Van Loon illustrated all of his own books, and the image of Krakatoa on the box lid of his game was his work, as was the hand-drawn map on the board inside. I didn't care about Van Loon at the time, of course, didn't really wonder who he was. My deepest memories of the Wide World Game are the playing pieces, the metal boats and trains, the pure tactile pleasure of sliding them around the glossy board. And the names of the cities. It wasn't new, our copy of the game; I don't imagine it was from the 1930s, but it was a hand-me-down from somewhere, and its patina was part of its appeal. So were the palm trees—as exotic as could be in New Jersey in those years—adorning the bottom corners of the board. It was an initiation into what from then on seemed a wide world.

The more I played it, the more the names of the cities grew totemic. Timbuctoo, as Van Loon spelled it, was the first. We kids thought it was funny sounding, of course. We'd heard it as a punch line on Bugs Bunny or Daffy Duck. There was something about the way it sat there, alone in the Great Sahara with its exceptionally foreign-sounding name, that was provocative. The sense that it was at the end of some road tugged at me. Not even its river, rising and disappearing in the dunes, managed to get far past it. Timbuctoo was the end of the line, the middle of nowhere, the place nobody wanted to go. Except, I immediately intuited, me.

The "bucket list" hadn't been invented yet (and besides, I was a child, I was never going to die), but Timbuctoo was already on mine. Every time I came across images of a desert, in *The Black Stallion* books or *Lawrence of Arabia* (one of the first films I ever saw), or Bob Hope and Bing Crosby's *Road to Morocco*, watched while home sick from school, I was, however vaguely, plotting my way. And the same with Rangoon, Calcutta, Buenos Aires, Moscow, Shanghai, Cairo . . .

RESTLESSNESS

THE NOTION OF RESTLESSNESS, my own and others', includes these interlocking tenets: the belief that to move is to escape the confines of life as you find it, the belief that to escape constitutes some kind of superior quest, and the belief that to thus escape issues a critique, a Holden Caulfield–like rejection of the falsity, the paltry conventionality, the soul-crushing small-mindedness of wherever you happen to be. The belief, in other words, that freedom is not just the goal, but a knife to stab the past, to strike it dead, to cut all restrictive tethers, to slice into the future.

So the writers tell us. The open road, Whitman sang out loud, is liberation from all things petty, and deliverance into potency:

Healthy, free, the world before me,
The long brown path before me leading wherever I choose.
Henceforth I ask not good-fortune, I myself am good-fortune,

RESTLESSNESS

> Henceforth I whimper no more, postpone no more, need nothing,
> Done with indoor complaints, libraries, querulous criticisms,
> Strong and content I travel the open road.

Zen before the age of motorcycle maintenance. The road is where, by leaving your old indoors behind, you become a healthier, freer, stronger, and more content version of yourself. The urge to run away is transformed, on the way down the front steps, into the accomplishment of authenticity. By getting on the road, one escapes into the genuine. By leaving one's real life, one enters something much more real.

And along the way nothing, the poets suggest—if somewhat more ambivalently—is lost. Carl Sandburg:

> I shall foot it
> Down the roadway in the dusk,
> . . .
> The broken boulders by the road
> Shall not commemorate my ruin.
> Regret shall be the gravel under foot.

You hear him protesting. You hear the self-doubt grinding in the gravel. You feel the dusk descending. But he also is full of the quotidian romance of watching the earth go by:

> I shall watch for
> Slim birds swift of wing

> That go where wind and ranks of thunder
> Drive the wild processionals of rain.
>
> The dust of the travelled road
> Shall touch my hands and face.

His fellow Chicagoan, Vachel Lindsay, walked 600 miles from Florida to Kentucky in 1906, trading poems for food, a true poet of the open road, exactly halfway between Whitman's *Leaves of Grass* and Kerouac's *On the Road*.

When I got around to reading Kerouac, I found him speaking what I already felt. When Sal Paradise and Dean Moriarty first arrive in Mexico toward the end of *On the Road*, Sal goes into one of his many raptures:

> Behind us lay the whole of America and everything Dean and I had previously known about life, and life on the road. We had finally found the magic land at the end of the road and we never dreamed the extent of the magic.

As a young man, not entirely causeless, I rebelled—coming out of my teens I was a bit of an outlaw, although not much more than many of my generation, the hippies, the latest scourge of civilization. I was swimming most days in a cocktail of weed, speed, and wine, selling a bit now and then, in the way people did in those days, running a kind of drug-buying co-op, picking up kilos of pot or ounces of meth or coke wholesale and sharing the savings, an extra taste for my troubles. Riding that train – and eating some mushrooms and LSD once in a while—magic and death were everywhere. I accepted rides from strangers in the middle of the night, and took odd jobs where I could find them. I was on the lam, with no respect for law or convention. And today, however far all that has been left behind, some outlaw impulse to go AWOL still powers my wanderings, a desire to escape the shrinking confines of my everyday self, to get away from my life, to disappear.

But why? I have a good life. A comfortable living. A job I love. A beautiful family. Wonderful friends. I don't want to give any of it up. So why these fantasies? I once saw a book on the dollar rack outside a used bookstore: *How to Hide Your Assets and Disappear.* I bought it. I told myself it was for research, for a novel or a screenplay. I didn't have any assets to speak of, but I did want to disappear, and I still do.

Other complicated motives surely play a part, like the idea that I am on some heroic quest for enlightenment. Not to mention my politically incorrect pursuit of the exotic. And that scopophilia—trying to see everything, snapping pictures everywhere—what is that about? And the lack of an itinerary, ever? What am I trying to prove?

I could just cite the great travelers:

Robert Louis Stevenson: 'I travel not to go anywhere, but to go. I travel for travel's sake. The great affair is to move.'

St. Augustine: 'The world is a book and those who do not travel read only one page.'

Lao Tzu: 'A good traveler has no fixed plans and is not intent on arriving.'

Edith Wharton: 'One of the great things about travel is that you find out how many good, kind people there are.'

G. K. Chesterton: 'The traveler sees what he sees. The tourist sees what he has come to see.'

Bashō: 'The journey itself is my home.'

Ryszard Kapuściński: 'There exists something like a contagion of travel, and the disease is essentially incurable.'

Elias Canetti: 'Travelling, one accepts everything.'

Freya Madeline Stark: 'To awaken quite alone in a strange town is one of the pleasantest sensations in the world.'

Susan Sontag: 'I haven't been everywhere, but it's on my list.'

T. S. Eliot: 'The journey not the arrival matters.'

Pico Iyer: 'We travel, initially, to lose ourselves; and we travel, next, to find ourselves.'

Mark Twain: 'One must travel to learn.'

> Pam Houston: 'I am happiest when I have one plane ticket in my hand and another in my underwear drawer.'

> Greil Marcus: 'How could an honest man be satisfied to live within the frontiers he was born to?'

That all sounds good. I agree with each of them, as I read them, so I am not sure why saying them gets caught in my throat. Perhaps, for me, such sentiments sound self-serving, self-glorifying, even—as if we who travel the globe have something over all the benighted folks who stay at home. I don't feel that that is true. My traveling does not make me feel particularly wise or noble, or even, oddly, that adventurous.

Still, even on the loneliest nights in the most grotesque flophouse, or asleep on an airport floor, I feel lucky. Tonight I am in the only hotel in a small city in Belarus, and my $13 a night room smells like an artificial strawberry flavor from 1962—insecticide? cleaning fluid? But lying here, writing on my tiny bed, I feel very, very lucky.

WONDER

I HAVE A FRIEND, not exactly immune to the exotic but unafflicted by the travel bug, who loves to remind me that Wally Shawn, in *My Dinner with Andre*, chides Andre Gregory for not being able to appreciate the sublimity of what happens in the cigar store around the corner. Why, my friend asks, as Shawn did, must you search the far corners of the globe for miracles, when marvels await your recognition in the quotidian world, on your own postage stamp of soil? Why can't you appreciate the wonder that is right next to you?

In response, I can only say: why do we have to choose? Walking on Sunset Boulevard, on a Saturday, less than a mile from my house, I heard music, followed it to its source, and wandered into a storefront church. I was pulled into the middle of an ecstatic Pentecostal service, a band on stage that would have done well in a David Lynch movie, with two teen girls standing perfectly straight, arms at their sides, uncanny expressions, like carnies or savants, singing to a roomful of Central American immigrants, and no pastor in sight. The music was loud, moving the thick air, pulsing, double minor scales in an endless rotation; people were weeping as they sang along about their love for Jesus. The room was full of a deep, sorrowful, communal joy, making it feel more like a rave than any church service of my youth. A woman rocked her baby back and forth in a stroller, patting a tambourine against her thigh, facing sideways, tears streaming down her cheeks. She turned and smiled at me, then turned back to the wall and closed her eyes, still weeping. The minister finally appeared. He was a plumber during the day, and welcomed me with a hug as he introduced himself. The music induced a trance in everyone, including the musicians.

I was in awe of the congregants' ability to find this sweet spot of ecstasy every Saturday, in this abandoned shop, in their work clothes, with nothing more than a drum set, a bank of keyboards, faith, and the will.

I was blocks from my home. I was full of wonder.

But so I was, too, coming around a corner to see a family of giraffes loping away in Zimbabwe with an elegance that breaks my heart, scanning the magnificence of the thousands of temples on the plains of Bagan, approaching the ice-packed Himalayas or Pamirs or Andes, lying in a pirogue while an arm's reach away a herd of thirty elephants fords a stream in the Okavango Delta, watching the somber saffron monks start their early dawn walk in Luang Prabang, first encountering the sublime blue domes of Samarkand or the tutti-frutti onions of St. Basil's Cathedral in Moscow's Red Square, seeing a naked sadhu praying in front of a massive construction crane or tens of thousands lined up to place flowers on a gurney in front of Mao's formaldehyded body in Tiananmen—the occasions for wonder are endless in this world. The spectacular ones, like these, are unsurprisingly sublime. But so, too, are the more mundane moments: the five-year-old girls and boys in Burma with the most exquisite golden sandalwood-paste designs on their chubby cheeks. Or the unremarkable Persian families having their daily picnic in Imam Khomeini square. Or the superb dignity of the street-food cooks in the slums of Chennai. We who are addicted to travel know that it is a shortcut to wonder. We are, I suppose, addicted to wonder.

And I will admit it, I am not as good as I should be at finding it on a trip to Trader Joe's, or on a drive across town on the 10. Too much of the time, in my daily life at home, I stop paying attention, I go internal, I am as good as blind.

Maybe travel is a form of laziness, for those of us who need our wonder dropped in our laps. Perhaps it is just our church, the road—the place we know we will find, with nothing more than the faith and the will, our ecstasy.

I HAVE WRITTEN THIS, or much of it, on the road, but rarely as it was happening. I've always said I write because I don't think fast enough to just say what I think. I write because I am, in any given moment, inarticulate, and so writing helps. It takes me too long to understand the stories I see to even be a very good journalist; things always have to gestate. So as I travel, I write, but I am always writing about a previous journey. In Quito I wrote about being in Burma. In Cartagena, I spent a week writing about Dar es Salaam. This introduction was written in a half dozen places.

Every writer knows the experience of going deep, of being completely submerged in the writing, of surrendering all of the present to the moment being written about. Historians live in the past, science fiction writers in the future, mystery writers elude the police, romance novelists have their bodices ripped. And anyone writing their memories, whether it is from decades ago or just earlier that day, travels to that moment, to that place—writers abide in their own former selves as they write. To return to the present can be as disorienting as waking from a vivid dream, leaving us confused about what is real, confused about time, geography, self.

It's like an extreme version of travel itself, writing—the sense not just of relocation, but of dislocation. Often I emerge, having spent hours once again wandering the streets of Vientiane at night and finding a street marionette show, with the smell of the Mekong River still in my nose, only to walk downstairs and, blinking in the bright noonday sun, be perplexed not just by the daylight, but by the colonial Portuguese architecture, and find myself thinking, *These buildings do not look Laotian! It almost looks like the*

Spanish were here, or the Portuguese, and I am for a moment truly lost in time and space—and only then, slowly, I return to the present, and realize, *Of course! I am in Zanzibar! Of course the buildings look Portuguese!* Still, things do not feel resettled, the dream lingers, and the world continues to feel and look strange and new, as if this new moment is imaginary, too, and not entirely to be trusted.

Being lost can be, of course, a fundamental pleasure—were that not the case then heroin and other drugs that make one lose one's bearings would have much less appeal. And so perhaps it is all as simple as that: I love to get lost. I love that moment of slight panic—the feeling that I don't know the way back, that I don't know the way home. I love being lost in wonder.

INHALING THE WORLD

One day, in southern India, I came across a group of boys playing soccer in a torn-up field. They came over to where I stood and I took pictures and showed them the thumbnails. Then I had them pose—told them to make a serious face, like this, without a smile. They did it, ran up to see what I had taken, laughed, and reassembled for the next shot. Okay, now look sad, I said, and showed them, my shoulders slumped forward, clown frown on my face. They laughed, but then did it, and again rushed to encircle the camera and crack up again. Now a boxing pose. Now a salute. They were having a great time. They were not interacting with me, so much as with my camera, playing with its images almost as if I was not there. I am full, I thought, and I am empty.

I am what Ralph Waldo Emerson called the 'transparent eyeball,' pure perception.

I am everything, nothing, everywhere, nowhere.

I am like water, running without will, and yet relentlessly toward its level.

But I get ahead of myself. As Whitman ends his great poem:

> All seems beautiful to me.
> Allons! the road is before us!

Perhaps Whitman is right, that the road is the place where one experiences 'the profound lesson of reception, nor preference nor denial,' and perhaps this pure, Zen-like acceptance of the world, of the world as it presents itself—perhaps this is a good thing. I of course wonder: is this just a throwing up of hands at the mess? Is all of this open road talk itself some kind of denial? Whitman says, parenthetically, in the same poem:

> (Still here [that is, on the road] I carry my old delicious burdens, I carry them, men and women, I carry them with me wherever I go, I swear it is impossible for me to get rid of them, I am fill'd with them, and I will fill them in return.)

And I know, from my own travels, that nothing can free me from myself for long, from my old delicious burdens. I spend time worrying about other things, too—about my horrible carbon footprint, about fiddling while the world burns, about treating the world like it was built for my entertainment. Here again Whitman:

> I inhale great draughts of space,
> The east and the west are mine, and the north and
> the south are mine.

Like Whitman, I want the whole world, I want to inhale it all.

> I am larger, better than I thought, I did not know I
> held so much goodness.

Such a crazy conclusion, in a way, the idea that by inhaling the whole world I find my own goodness. But I'm not sure it's wrong. Something in all great travel experiences accomplishes just that. Is it possible to love a trip, a voyage of discovery, a plunge into the unknown, without a sense that we have become larger, better than we thought? Isn't that what we mean when we talk, in ideal terms, about any real education?

I scroll through the images I carry in my head from my travels, the scenes I am about to describe, and I think yes, yes, whatever goodness I have inhaled in this life, it has something to do with my having spent this time on the road, something to do with getting conned in a mangrove swamp in Sri Lanka, with throwing my fate to strangers in the high Pamir, wandering into underground tango clubs on the outskirts of Buenos Aires, getting cornered by émigrés in Albania, salesmen in Fez, drunken Boers in South Africa, drivers in Osh, "art students" in Shanghai. In the center of every experience is a conversation, a relationship. In each of the stories that follow, I have tried to leave the open road open, the wondering unconstrained, the sublime and the beautiful as I found them.

SCHOOLTEACHERS AND GUIDES IN MOROCCO

COMING FROM TANGIER

IN TANGIER in 1995 I felt the most foreign I had ever felt—seeing the men in their coarse, woolen, hooded djellabas, donkey carts hauling not just farm produce but appliances and cinder blocks, women in headscarves and chadors—it felt remarkably alien and thrilling, a planet away from anything I'd known. Heading south, I moved farther and farther from the familiar, deeper and deeper into the unfathomed. By the time I had made my way across the mountains, down through the desert to Merzouga, on the Algerian border, and then slowly found my way back, Tangier looked like Europe.

I pulled over at one point, and got out of my car—I had rented it in France and come over on the ferry—to stretch my legs and buy some clementines at a stand. I was accosted immediately by a half dozen people trying to sell me rugs, a hotel room, a taxi ride, any number of knickknacks—and it didn't seem to matter how I said no, thank you, or that I pointed out to the taxi driver that he had just seen me get out of a rental car; it didn't matter how sincere or polite, or brusque, or irritated, or uninterested I acted—nothing changed. All along the road, every negotiation, whether I bought something or not, ended badly, with nobody satisfied. Most tourists to Morocco, unless they are constantly insulated by drivers and guides, have to figure out how to respond to this onslaught, and for anyone who likes to think of themselves as respectful and open and generous, it causes a wave of complex emotions, none of them pleasant.

I stopped, a couple hours south, in a small-town café. A ten-year-old boy on the street pointed at my car, then at his eye, at the car, at his eye—offering to take care of it while I ate. I had parked right outside the door and could watch the car myself, so, without thinking, I said no, thank you. He didn't take that for an answer, of course, and kept pointing at his eye, the car, his eye. Eventually it seemed best to say okay. I ordered the same meat dish that I saw a man next to me eating, and it was fine, though the bill was clearly three times what it cost the other patrons; my bad for not asking the price in advance. I paid, then went out and gave the boy a couple dirhams; he did the car-eye, car-eye gesture again and held out his other hand. I gave him a couple more dirhams, much more than made any sense, and he went through the same routine again, seeming to get angrier each time. I tried to wave him off, but he wouldn't budge. He stood, blocking my way, his empty palm thrust at me again, car-eye, car-eye. I finally had to open the door, letting it push him out of the way, and he shouted imprecations as I drove off.

Why did these interactions feel so disconcerting, so uncomfortable? It wasn't the petty extortion—he and I both knew that I had paid him much more than I needed to—it was the impossibility of saying okay, nicely done, we're good here. I didn't begrudge the kid trying to make a little money. It's a poor country and it's perfectly reasonable to demand I share my wealth. I always tried to buy a little something from hawkers, even if I just left the gewgaw behind later. Still, every transaction seemed to end in anger and escalating demands, never in gratitude or common courtesy. I was baffled.

By the time I got to Fez, these mutually irksome moments had already become the norm. Every offer to have tea turned into a hard-sell in a rug showroom or silver shop, and I had started just saying no, on reflex, head down, refusing to engage. That felt horrible, too—all the other negative emotions now washed with anger at my own cultural incompetence.

I DROVE ALL DAY and arrived in Fez at night, checked into a hotel in the new part of the city, showered, and went out for a walk. In about a mile or so, I hit the gates of the medina and walked a short way into it, just a couple of turns, but I was mobbed by helpful people with services to offer, and there was something a little sinister in the air, shopkeepers looking at me with a question in their glances as they locked their gates, and it started to seem as if shops were closing because the nights were tough, too dangerous for people to be out and about. I decided to head back to the new city for dinner. As I was trying to find my way back out, I came up to a bunch of soldiers. An officer stepped out and asked me, in French, where I was going. Since I had already run into plenty of police looking for bribes, for baksheesh, I tried to act sure of myself, pointed straight ahead, said I was going back to my hotel in the new city, and tried to walk around him. As I did, the rest of the soldiers converged on me and halted me in my tracks. I was stymied. I was surrounded. I mumbled something about my hotel.

Ici, the officer said, Ceci, mon ami, c'est le palais royale.

I had just tried pushing my way around the royal guard, into the royal palace. As it dawned on me, the soldiers could see I was just an oblivious idiot, not some madman or regicide, and had a good laugh. They pointed to where I wanted to go. After a few more wrong turns, and inquiries to more soldiers posted along the walls, I figured it out and walked back to the new city.

For the first time in a while I ate at a restaurant with proper menus and a waiter and tablecloths. At the end of the meal, after writing up my notes and drinking a fair amount of wine, I was the only table left except a couple young guys across the room.

One of them said, in a heavy Moroccan accent, You are American!

I said, Yes.

Come, my friend, he said, Come join us for a drink, on the house! This is my family's restaurant, come, my friend, and have a drink! He said it like Joe Pesci in *Casino*. He was sitting with another guy who turned out to be an Australian traveler, a smart raconteur who, from the looks of things, had been hanging with this half-clown, half-gangster kid for a while: They were bleary. I kept a hand on my wallet and sat down with them.

The gangster-clown went on about how the restaurant was just a front, since his family was really into the drug business, and they had three large ships with which they transported hashish all around the world.

Oh, yes, my friend! he said. If you go to Amsterdam? If you go to New York? You will see our kif! It is the best in the world! It will have our stamp, the stamp of Rifwasis! Yes, my friend! You must have some!

I didn't know what the guy's deal was, since if he was, in fact, a major hash smuggler, he wouldn't be bragging to absolute strangers about his operation.

Thanks, I said, I don't smoke. Maybe, it occurred to me, he was a police informant and was setting me up for a bust. Otherwise he appeared to be a pretty harmless fool, and was full of high spirits, as was the Australian guy, who ran wilderness and other sport adventures for businessmen—everything from rock climbing to white-water rafting to bungee jumping.

Yeah, he said. I'm just like Crocodile Dundee. They're all big executives, my clients, but when they're with me, they are, like, children, y'know, 'cause they donnow what's up and I do. I like to spin them out a bit, y'know, and say things like, 'well, I've never seen the water up quite *this* high!' and watch them lose their shit a little. But, y'know, I bring 'em back, and they tell their friends, it was the highest the water's ever been and th'like, and everybody's happy!

Come, my friends! the Hash King said. We go to club! Women! We drink! We smoke! I have car!

Right-o! the Australian said. Come along, Stateside!

I begged off, promising to come back to the restaurant the next day, but I never did. Two days later the gangster magically appeared in front of me in the street. He had that scary energy of a drug addict panicked to find himself in the sun. He said I had to come back to his restaurant and go the club with him, I would not know Morocco unless I did. I told him yes, of course, great, I will come tonight, but I was a bit spooked, and steered clear of his part of town until I left.

BEFORE THAT, early in the morning, I was leaving the hotel to walk to the medina when, in the hotel lobby, a portly, slightly dissolute, hunched man of sixty offered his services, showing me his official guide license and promising an educational experience of the highest order. He didn't try to hide the fact that he was deeply bored, which I respected.

No, thank you, I said.

Sir, if you will forgive me, you cannot tour the medina of Fez without a guide, it is impossible.

I'm sorry, I said. I need to see that for myself.

He bowed slightly, and seemed happy enough to be able sit back down in the lobby.

Out on the street, I was immediately approached by two young guys who tried to sell me their services as guides while fighting with each other about who saw me first. Neither of them spoke English. Both refused to take no for an answer. I stopped at an outdoor café for coffee and bread and they sat at the next table and continued to argue, I assume about who had dibs on me, unflagging.

I paid my bill, and as I left, they jumped to either side of me, speaking to me in French, and telling each other to shut up or fuck their mothers in Arabic, and I said look, I need someone who speaks English, and you don't speak English. I said it in French.

Speak English, one said.

You speak English?

Yes, they both said.

What is your name? I asked.

Yes, the quicker one said. And the other followed: Yes!

They followed me the entire mile to the medina, yapping at me all the way in French, pushing each other, and eventually I flipped out and yelled *NO!* at the top of my lungs. *NON! Je n'ai pas besoin de guide!* and then two of my five words of Arabic: *AFAK!* (please). *IMSHEE!* (go away). This they pretended not to understand and kept flanking me, still insisting, in French, that they spoke English. They followed me right into the medina, and there a bunch of other guides descended, clamoring for the job.

IN THE MEDINA

AT THE GATES to the medina of Fez, my double shadows tried to fend off the new competition, and one of the new young men asked me, in English:

Is it true? Is one of them your guide?

No, I said.

This was a mistake, because now all fifteen were after the job. I kept walking toward the gate.

I will show you leather factory, one said. Very nice, leather factory.

You need guide! several said. Only twenty dirham!

I held up my guidebook.

No good! they said. Some were walking backward in front of me. Map is no good.

I marched ahead, ignoring them. One by one they gave up and dropped off as I kept pushing forward and said nothing. I thought, finally, I have found a way; don't engage, don't even say no, just keep walking. A street or two later I had marched up a dead end. The medina is a medieval city, the cobblestoned streets the width of a shower stall, a messy cobweb of wires above, and improvised additions jutting over the street, making the alley into a tunnel. I retraced my steps and tried the next turn. It also came to a cul de sac. I looked at my map, but nothing was on a level or straight or parallel. The paths curved up and down, in every direction, and nothing was marked. A third route looked promising and then died. I tried some of its tributaries, and started to lose track of where I was.

Men with pack donkeys went by, making deliveries to the shops, some carrying wrapped packages, one with sacks of vegetables, one with a cargo of thirty or so heads of freshly slaughtered sheep, still dripping blood, tied onto its back. After a half hour of trying to make headway, I gave up. I couldn't navigate the medina alone. I found my way back to the entrance. The fifteen guides were smiling, waiting for me. They knew I'd return.

They surrounded me again, making their pitches. I asked how much, and they started shouting prices. One, who had a kindly face and a relaxed presence, standing back a bit, looked me in the eye.

Nothing, he said quietly. Free. If you don't like me as a guide, you pay nothing. If you like my work, you pay me whatever you want.

Really? I said. You won't then ask for more? The others kept jostling for position in front of me and making offers.

No, he said. I understand. It is completely up to you. What you think is fair.

His name was Youssef. We walked into the medina together. He was an out-of-work plumber. At night he was a singer for an Egyptian-style pop band, and in the day he took tourists through the medina. He had tourist English, French, German, Japanese, Italian, and Spanish.

I will show you everything, he said. We will go to my uncle's tannery—his English was very good—and I also have a cousin who does metalwork.

I said, Okay, but I don't want to buy anything.

I understand, he said. Please, though, if you don't mind, this is the way things work here. You will give me a little money, if you like, my uncle will give me a little money, my cousin will give me a little money, not because you buy something, but because I bring all the tourists to their shops, and some buy something. You do not have to buy anything, but I have to take you. I hope that is okay.

Are they really your uncle and cousin? I asked.

Only in a manner of speaking, he said.

How could I refuse? As we walked I asked about his life. He had done well as a plumber, had worked on bathrooms even in the royal palace, but the economy was very bad, and so he only had sporadic work. His band gigged once in a while, playing a little European pop and rock, but mostly Egyptian. Egyptians had the best music in the Maghreb, he told me, and to prove it he sang me a song as we walked, playing a kind of beat box on his chest. He was very entertaining, and told a few jokes.

Listen, he said. A man gets on a train and falls asleep because he has a very long journey. A woman gets on at the next stop with her little dog. They ride along and the whole time she is very unhappy, because the man has kicked off his shoes and his feet and the shoes smell very, very bad. So, after a while, while he is sleeping, she picks up his shoes and throws them out the window of the train. Then, with only half the smell, she, too, can fall asleep. After a while, the man wakes up and sees his shoes are missing, and looks all around for them. Then he goes over to the sleeping woman and takes her little dog out of her arms and throws it out the window. When she wakes up she is in a panic, calling for her dog, and she asks the man if he saw where it went. And he says, 'Oh, it's okay, he's just gone to look for my shoes.'

I told him that I, too, played in bands, so he took me to the musical instrument streets, where people made drums and flutes and ouds, all with hand tools, themselves with handmade handles. As promised, we went to his uncle's tannery, where, up on the roof, dozens of vats marinated animal skins in stinking fluids. The skins that had been hoisted from the evil liquid were spread out to dry on rooftops. I wondered about the average lifespan of the workers, as it smelled the opposite of healthy. We went to an obligatory rug shop, where women were weaving carpets by hand. I tried to talk to one, but she wouldn't respond, and Youssef let me know it wasn't done; women would not speak to strangers. In another shop women were weaving cloth—beautiful shiny, satin-like cloth with brightly colored stripes—on old rickety, manual looms. In the carpenters' street, a man worked a foot-powered lathe, turning pieces while sitting on the ground in a shop that was the size of a large closet. His great-great grandfather might have sat in the same spot with the same tools making the same things. Youssef said yes, trades were handed down through the generations. His father had been a plumber.

He then took me to a shop of a friend of his who sold antiques, but who, he said, hid all the best ones and only showed them to people like me who didn't want to buy anything. I said this sounded like a bad business model, and Youssef laughed. The shop owner looked like an old hippie, in a worn army jacket and a scraggly beard. He apparently smoked dope all the time. He asked if I wanted a hit, and I said sure.

I'd like to quit, he said. Some day. I think.

His shop was dusty and overflowing, and did not look like he had had customers in years. He was, in fact, hiding his favorite pieces. When it was clear I wasn't buying, he reached behind a set of wood carvings, and pulled out one that was exquisite. The silverwork was fine, but underneath it, in a covered box, he had some better pieces.

Why do you hide these things? I asked.

Because people will want to buy them, and they are not for sale.

But you sell some things?
Oh, yes.

Just not these?

If I sell these things, he said, Then I have money, and so I get women and whiskey and then it is gone and I have nothing. But this way I have all these beautiful things. Heh? All right!

He had a boom box going and loved all sorts of American music from the sixties and seventies. As we were talking he would punctuate the conversation by saying, very happily, and with a heavy accent, the name of some band, and then laugh loudly and pat me on the back and give the thumbs up sign and nod, happily.

Yes, yes, Jimi Hendreex! he said, with a big thumbs up. Yes. Trets and Mootels (Toots and the Maytalls, thumbs up!). Paul Sigh-Mon! he said stretching the vowels out, and again thumbs up!

He put on *Rhythm of the Saints*, thumbs up, and we took another hit and listened appreciatively. Then he said, *Leenerd Skeeenerd! Yeah!!*

He kept a guest book in which travelers from all over the world had written little blurbs. I added mine.

Do you want tourist lunch? Youssef asked.

No, local.

Good, I hope you will like my place.

We turned several corners and came to an indentation in a wall the size of a short closet. A man was set up with a grill and there was a tiny table. I sat with Youssef and three other people around what I though was the proprietor's workspace, but was in fact our dining table. He brought us tea, made by pouring boiling water into a glass pushed full with fresh mint sprigs. The six of us, five customers and the owner-cook-waiter-dishwasher, shared a space about five feet by seven feet with his grill, equipment, and stores. We had two different kinds of skillet-fried fish, one that looked like a bluegill or sunfish about eight inches long and tasted like bluefish, and the others the size of big sardines that had some kind of hot pepper on them. We had fried potatoes, fried slices of eggplant, fried mildly hot peppers, a hunk of deep-fried dough filled with mashed potatoes and onions, a big round loaf of bread much fatter and richer than pita, and a bowl of sauce made out of tomatoes. We shared everything, eating with our hands, picking away the fish from the bones, sopping up the sauce with our bread.

As we ate, we could see the life of the medina rushing by the little opening that was the front of the store: kids carrying a board with two rising loaves of dough down to the bakery to get baked, mules carrying loads of oranges or animal skins as they were slapped at and yelled at in Berber and Arabic by their drivers, the men in their striped or monk-brown djellabas, the women in their brightly colored silk or black wool robes, almost always with a headdress, sometimes with a veil as well, the Tuareg and Berber and Bedouin women with tattoos on their foreheads and chins if they were married, the artisans—rugmakers, carpenters, drum makers, leather tanners—carrying their wares to stores, a man pushing a cart with thousands of bright red, pure white, and orange carrots, people going on their daily rounds.

After a while we were joined by a friend of Youssef's, who looked like a cross between a Dickens villain and the Mad Hatter. He was wearing stained but flashy hippie clothes, a loud brown and white checked sport jacket with very wide lapels, none too new, an extra-large Arabic scarf around his shoulders, and some kind of funky almost–top hat thing on his head. He played the edgy clown.

He's a very funny person, Youssef said as he introduced us. His name was Walid. He didn't speak English, just Berber, Arabic, and French. The three of us went around for a while and then we stopped near the gate to have a glass of mint tea. Pretty overwhelmed by the day, I was glad to sit down—they just grabbed some stray pieces of wood and boxes for seats on the ground. Around us, people were selling fresh eels and other odd-looking fish. Donkeys and horses passed and people too, carrying home sundries and live chickens hanging by their feet. I was flooded by a sense of how easy, and friendly—because Youssef had many friends, always stopping to say hi to him and sometimes to Walid, as well—was the life they lived. Walid saw me watching Youssef and said something in Berber; I asked Youssef to translate.

It is a saying, 'when a man is pure in his heart, he has many friends.' He then seemed embarrassed that he might seem to be bragging.

I said to Walid, in my horrible French, This is just a wonderful place.

He looked at me hard—Youssef was the romantic, Walid the realist—and said, Pour vous, peut-etre, pas pour moi.

His French wasn't much better than mine, so we couldn't get very far with direct conversation, but he was very quick, and very people-smart. In French, I asked:

You don't like it here?

No, this place has nothing for me. I can never do anything here but what you see me doing now. It is fine, I suppose, but it is not good for me.

You can see why for me it is interesting, right?

Yes, of course, he said. You will go home to America. Maybe I would like it too if I could go home to America!

The day was winding down, and I asked them to come with me to the new city and and let me buy them dinner. They had told me that they both liked whiskey, but never got any in the medina, and so I said we could have a whiskey at the hotel bar and then go out to eat. But they begged off, saying that they didn't like the new city, and the new city didn't like them, that they preferred to stay in the medina.

This was a surprise, in a way, especially since Youssef was very Western-looking in dress and bearing, and Walid, while he was not, had just finished telling me how stuck he felt there. They asked me to come back to the medina, instead, and they would show me how to eat a good dinner here, and that it would be much cheaper, and we could buy some wine. I accepted.

I LEFT THE MEDINA and still had a little energy, and was still a bit stoned, so I decided to walk up to the top of a big hill that overlooked the city. Toward the top a group of boys were running around playing games along the hill. Maybe twenty of them between the ages of six and ten or so converged on me and started demanding dirhams. They were all pushing each other against me and were clearly trying to pick my pockets, though foiled by zippers. They were smiling but a little scary. It felt like a scene from *Lord of the Flies*, these wild boys on the edge of the city, and there was nobody else about. The sun was starting to set, and as I tried to walk away from them they kept getting in my way and finally started throwing pebbles at me, irritated by their lack of pickpocketing success. Partway down the hill, I came across a small park, and there were six or eight young adults sitting there. I went up to two young guys who looked like intellectuals, bright eyes, wire-rimmed glasses. They had been watching my descent, bemused by my predicament.

Hi, I said. These kids are a bit intense.

They are what history has made them, one young man said. The other gave a curt laugh.

I looked around at the other people in the park, and realized I was on my own.

You must admit this is true, the other young man said. Look at them.

The boys had calmed down to see whether these young men would intervene. I looked at them. They were just kids. They were poor, shoeless, far from clean. I was incapable of imagining their future.

Please move on, the first young man said. He had a prayer cap on and was well groomed and tailored. A college student, I decided, or graduate student. We are having a conversation, he said. Please do not continue to interrupt us.

I started back down the hill, and the kids gave a whoop in acknowledgment of the permission they had just received. I started to run. The boys laughed and threw a last volley of pebbles in my direction. I was surprised at how unsettling it was, to be attacked by tiny jackals. And how unsettling to be rejected by the young intellectuals. To be the representative of the oppressive colonizer. To stand alone on the wrong side of history.

PITYING THE KING

I WENT BACK to the hotel and had a twenty-minute nap before going back to the medina to meet Youssef and Walid for dinner. They were clearly a little surprised but very pleased that I had actually shown up. We went around from little booth to little shop, first buying a hunk of beef, then, at another stand, having it ground with spices and herbs, then taking it to a third place where a man put it on skewers and cooked it for us for a few dirhams. We bought bread, and a couple kinds of olives and some bottles of wine, and a bunch of clementines, and went to a room, up a couple flights on a very tight stone circular staircase, where many people obviously slept, with their beds rolled up against the walls, and sat on rugs at a low table and ate and drank wine and smoked some hashish, and had long, serious and not-so-serious talks about life in Morocco.

How do you feel about living in a monarchy? I asked. How do you feel about the king?

I wish him all the luck in the world, Youssef said, benevolently, which struck me as funny, partly because of the hashish, I'm sure, partly because of the idea of an out-of-work plumber being magnanimous to a king.

When a man has nothing, Youssef explained, serious, If he makes nothing, if he does nothing with his life, there is nothing wrong. But if a man has everything, and so much power and riches, and he does not do great things, it is a tragedy for him, and, most important, it is a sin. I smoke, and I drink wine, and these are not right, but Allah knows that I am poor, and he understands that my life is hard, and he forgives me. But the king, he has everything, he has all money and servants and the most easy life. If he does anything wrong, it is a sin. I would hate to have that burden.

I was touched by the idealism, the young, poor man empathizing so strongly with the richest, most powerful man in his world, feeling sorry for him. Walid kept his own counsel. It seemed to me he recognized, respected, but very much did not share these sentiments.

Youssef asked me what kind of work I did, and I started by saying I had done some plumbing myself, that I had been a remodeling contractor and had done all the jobs, carpentry, masonry, plumbing, everything.

Walid said in French, My job—and then he waited to make sure he had our attention, deadly serious—My job is to smoke and to drink. We laughed, but I also really wanted to know how he got by, and he could see this, and so he said:

No, to be completely serious—he leaned in, confidential—my real work is to listen to music. I work very hard, sometimes all day I do nothing but work and sleep, work and sleep. Yes. It is very difficult work, but it must be done—music must be listened to, or why is there music? I feel that I am the best person for this job. It is my calling.

But you are not a plumber now, Youssef said to me.

No, I said, Now I am a teacher, a professor. In a nanosecond, Walid launched into *WE DON'T NEED NO EDUCATION!* in a perfect British accent, a superb miming of the original. The last syllable of professor wasn't out of my mouth when he started it. Very funny, and very swift. Later, when he was singing reggae, he showed he could do whole raps in perfect Jamaican dialect. I suspected that his English was much better than he let on.

I asked what they thought of the poverty in the country, and about the disparities of wealth, about the future of their society and country, and they both shrugged at such questions. Youssef was very religious, and his basic take on the world was that of the Koran filtered through Moroccan culture.

Allah knows all, but we humans can never know very much, he said, somewhat apologetically, like I was old enough that I should know these things already. Whatever happens is Allah's will, and good people live forever in heaven.

He shrugged. This was enough for him. It meant that wealth and poverty were God's business. And other things: it meant that you always had to be prepared to die, that you always had to live the best life you could, that you had to be good to those around you, had to be true and honest. Walid made a little bit of fun of Youssef when he laid down these religious ideas, but he, too, clearly had some respect for the truly thoughtful, compassionate and humble wisdom of young Youssef's belief.

On the other hand, when I asked him whether he prayed five times a day as a good Muslim is supposed to, he said that no, he didn't, in part because he was not pure, because he drank and smoked.

But Allah understands, he said again.

Yes, I replied, You said that Allah understands your life is hard. But there are systemic inequities—I stopped myself;

we had been smoking and drinking, and I had been careful with my vocabulary until then. But I needn't have worried; the phrase didn't faze him.

Yes, he said. That is why rich countries have more to answer for than poor countries.

Aha! said Walid, without waiting for a translation.

And then Youssef signaled that the time for serious talk was over, and sang us some songs, beating on his chest softly for percussion.

STUCK IN THE KASBAH

ALONG THE WAY from Meknes to the Sahara, many small village-like clusters of buildings punctuate the long line of canyons, or surround the ruins of an old Kasbah, or castle, sitting atop a hill. It is hard to conceive, seeing these piles of rubble scattered across the near-barren country, what tribute or taxes could have been exacted from the local population by the medieval warlords who built them. Whenever I see castles, ruined or not, I can't help imagining the horrors of medieval warrior culture, of living in such fear of marauding hordes that you had to build forty-foot walls around your house—stupendous shields to keep people from killing you, raping your friends and family, and walking off with your stuff, monstrous stone shields with holes just big enough to shoot out of but not very easy to shoot into. You can read the people's daily fear in their architecture, in their tiny windows. Such a mean, nasty way to live. Not that nuclear holocaust, metal detectors, open carry, and IEDs are a great advance, but we're always more shocked by other people's forms of violence and, in my life, so far, war has always been on television.

Since these Kasbahs were originally built, somewhere between the eighth and fourteenth centuries, they have been in the slow process of crumbling into the sand and clay from which they were made. Almost at random, I pulled off the road to take a closer look. I picked one that seemed completely abandoned, but as soon as I got out of my car, a couple of small kids appeared and asked for dirhams. They were cute, dirty, very interested in seeing a stranger, and looked hungrier than the kids I had seen in the north. I greeted them in French but got no response. I started walking toward the castle, when out of a small, nondescript side building a man emerged, parting the rugs functioning as his front door, wearing a djellaba and slipping into his sandals. We exchanged *salaam aleikums* and *bonjours* as he walked rapidly toward me. He looked a lot like the shepherds along the road, and I assumed that's what he was. It turned out, however, that he was the local schoolteacher, the only schoolteacher for this small community—because there were many families living in and around the ruins, as it turned out—and for the other four or five similar communities in the vicinity. His schoolhouse was about three kilometers away, and some of his students had to walk two or three times that, each way, to get to school. He rode a bike. The kids following us not only didn't go to school, he told me, but probably never would. Their families couldn't afford it. The Moroccan government paid his salary, and paid to keep a roof on the schoolhouse, but students had to buy their own paper and pens and textbooks and other supplies, and many of the families couldn't manage even part of that expense. Besides, he said, many of the fathers resented his authority, and thought that they should be able to give their children all the knowledge they need, as their fathers had done for them. Ignorance and poverty, he said, formed a never-ending cycle.

And is that so wrong? I wondered for a moment. The engine of modernity that Lévi-Strauss lamented, degrading and erasing local cultures—wasn't this schoolteacher its primary agent in the village? Why shouldn't this community go on the way it had for a thousand years? The place was a kind of hippie paradise, people banded together to live a simple life, close to the earth, shielded from the commercial hollowness of modernity, no exploitative jobs, just some gardens and some animals and occasional bartering for things they couldn't make themselves. I asked the teacher if he ever thought this way, that perhaps allowing traditional life to continue was not a terrible idea. By way of an answer, he took me into the Kasbah. It was the image of entropy, becoming dust, and as we came around a corner, a woman was squatting in a square, roofless room, hacking away with a short-handled axe at some firewood. When she saw me she jumped up and ran away in terror. Passing another of these broken-down rooms, with pieces of scrap wood and metal and cloth patched into an ineffective roof, a woman poked her veiled head out to see who we were, and yanked it back in. It was like a Hollywood Western, when the bad guy arrives in town, and everyone goes into hiding. I caught glimpses of families significantly poorer than any I'd seen so far, scratching away at a living like their own scrawny chickens.

Even more surprising than the disappearing women—because they were undoubtedly steering clear of any shariah infractions—was the fact that their children hid, too. The few ruffians who greeted me were ready to mix it up for dirhams, but most of the kids, and all the girls, were cowering in corners. These people were far enough off the road that some of them may never have met a person from another country in their lives, certainly had never seen a foreigner inside their own dilapidated walls. Was there any pent-up curiosity about the larger world, or only fear? They weren't behind doors, because there were no doors. From what I could see there was no furniture to speak of, either, just a few soiled rugs. Of course there was no electricity, much less plumbing. In one room without a roof, a campfire was petering out, surrounded by stones. Sheltering themselves required constant improvisation, and the difference between the way these people lived and the way the homeless in America get by was minimal.

The teacher said nothing, confident that the precariousness of the lives I was witnessing would be obvious. He asked if I would please share his lunch. I tried to refuse, thinking that whatever food was available in this deprived community was clearly needed, but he insisted; I refused, he insisted; I begged off, he insisted, I had no choice.

Yes, of course, I said finally, I would be honored—this in French, undoubtedly largely incorrect on my part. He was a very calm and gentle man, with a teacher's relation to my ignorance. He spoke slowly, patiently repeated himself until I understood, and helped me get said what I was trying to say, looking for all the world like a saintly shepherd from a Christmas pageant.

I followed him into the hut he had come out of, which looked like it had two rooms, the one he led us into and another behind it that I assume was a kitchen area. It had a solid roof and glass in two windows. When we came in, a low table was already set, the centerpiece a big bowl of steaming couscous, with a few boiled vegetables and one piece of meat about the size of a quarter on top. There were two spoons and two glasses and a teapot on a tray. This was just a little mysterious, because I had been walking with him for twenty minutes or a half hour, and this stuff had obviously been laid out no more than thirty seconds before we walked in, everything freshly hot. He must have a wife, I realized, who never showed her face, and he must have warned her that he was going to ask me to lunch. And she must have kept an eye on our progress around the village so that she could put out our food just before we arrived and disappear. He never mentioned her and never acknowledged that she might be there. A wife? A servant? We talked about many things over lunch, including the question of feminism—yes, he said, in the cities there are feminists, and some of the girls here will grow up and move to the city and change, but in the small villages people are very, very traditional. I asked if his wife would like to join us, and he said she had already eaten. It may have been true.

The room we sat in had a packed dirt floor, a small desk the size and sturdiness of half of a card table, a minimal chair, a twin-sized mattress, a low table about three feet in diameter where we were eating, and the rug we were sitting on. And that was all. On the desk were his papers, a couple of books, and an old radio with an improvised antenna. He was educated, he was very observant and sensitive and intelligent, and he had been living like this, doing his best in this impoverished and sometimes hostile environment, to help some of the children learn to read and write before they left for the city or at least for larger towns. He seemed heroic, in part because he wasn't happy. He had been teaching there for seven years. I asked if he would stay and he shrugged his shoulders.

I have asked for a transfer, he said, I ask for a transfer every year. This, you can see, is no place for a young man, no place for me to have a family. There is nothing, no cinema, no library, no people for me to talk with, really. Only the radio, which does not work very well. Again he shrugged.

And why won't the government transfer you? I asked.

I have to wait. Sometimes seniority, sometimes favoritism makes the difference. I need to wait until a spot opens up somewhere better, and there are many people like me, hoping to move to a better place.

We sat and shared the bowl of food, each eating with our own spoon from the same bowl. Neither of us touched the piece of meat. It teetered on top of the tower of couscous.

Many of the men here, he said, keep some sheep, and that is not enough. And many can find no work at all. They go to Erfoud or Rissani looking for something to do, and sometimes come back having found a few days' paid labor, sometimes without having found any. It is a desperate place, he said. Like many.

As I left I told him I wanted to give him *un petit cadeaux,* a gift to be used for his school, however he saw fit, and I handed him a hundred dirhams. He thanked me, on behalf of the students, and I felt I had finally got the swing of the gift economy. I thanked him for the lunch and shook his hand and said goodbye. He seemed to have been glad to have some conversation, even if in halting French, and I felt honored to have met him. As I drove away, all the children who had been hiding ran out and chased the car, hollering, desperately, for dirhams.

INTO THE SAHARA

DRIVING SOUTH on the two-lane road from Azrou toward the Sahara, I was on a mission to get to the *Lawrence of Arabia*-style dunes that, in Morocco, appear about eighty kilometers past the end of the last road south. I had come from Tangier, the city of Burroughs and Kerouac, through Larache on the coast, inland to Meknes and Fez, over the Atlas mountains, through Azrou and Midelt, past a couple of small military garrison towns—Errachidia and Erfoud—after which the road devolved into a series of pistes, before disappearing altogether.

The Atlas mountains were blotched with snow but the weather was warm, and the views were spectacular, especially as I drove down through the Gorges of Ziz, canyons that seemed named by a pulp SF writer. All along the banks of the Ziz river there were villages with waziz, or oases. At each waziz, the earth had been leveled and parceled into tiny plots, and irrigated like shallow rice paddies. The waziz were only an acre or two in size, and almost entirely covered with a canopy of palm branches, so that from above, as one comes came down into the valley, they looked like palm groves.

Woven reeds made into fences kept out blowing sand and perhaps animals. They were a marvel of iron-age engineering, children's sandbox play turned into survival mechanism, vegetable farms shrunk into the smallest possible footprint.

At the bottom of the mountains lies the Sahara. Unlike the immeasurable and endless dunes of wavelike sand, the stuff of my dreams, much of the Sahara is flat, made up of rubbly volcanic rock, flatter than Kansas, stretching as far as the eye can see. In other spots the bedrock is exposed for miles, some of it yellow, some of it red. Mountains like the colored buttes of Utah crop up, and in yet other places it just looks gray as the moon. There were a few towns still, like Errachidia, attached to a military base and thus full of soldiers, many of whom looked to me like Saddam Hussein, I think in part because the army is made up mostly of Arabs, who stand out in this Berber and Tuareg territory. Fifty or so kilometers south was Erfoud, which had the look of a frontier town, with streets made of dried mud and full of potholes. There was nothing like a sidewalk, and broken down machinery and abandoned vehicles were everywhere. I found no sign of any social services—no road crews or garbage men or police. In each town farther south, the characters wandering around looked more and more battered and shifty. The farther south you go from Tangier, the more the women's faces are tattooed when they marry; the farther south you go from Fez, the more women wear the niqab, their faces completely covered except for a slit for the eyes. There was trash in the streets and animal dung everywhere. People stared at my little French car like I was from outer space. I was a rare and seemingly unwelcome occurrence.

Another thirty kilometers to the south I came to the last town on the map that was shown to be on an actual road. Rissani was beyond the frontier, full of desperadoes, the roads with potholes as large as my car. Even on the main drag the traffic was more animal than automotive. The few trucks were all from World War II, and the kids were all shoeless and dirty. The women here were without exception in the full burqa, some with the crosshatched mask approved by the Taliban.

This was it, Rissani, the last stop. Before me, across the bare, stony, roadless ground, lay the promised big dunes on the Algerian border. Maybe it was watching *Lawrence of Arabia*—uncomprehending, spellbound—on the big screen at the age of eight that gave these dunes their magic. Maybe it was the cumulative effect of hundreds of other exotic images over the years—the Tuareg on their horses and camels, the caravans, the endless, trackless, moving peaks. Maybe it was that they are, simply, sublime—a mix of beauty and terror that everyone feels. Whatever it was, I was pulled toward that desert image in the way some people, standing on a tall building, feel compelled to jump into the street below.

THE ROAD, which was already comically bad, became worse after I left Rissani. I looked out at the blank flatness, the tire tracks leading off in dozens of directions, and had no idea which way to go. As I sat staring into the distance, a kid on a bike pulled up to my window. His name was Mohammed, and he was wearing a shesh, the traditional Tuareg turban, and had bad teeth, like everybody down there. He looked to be about fourteen or sixteen, spoke French well but had no English at all. He offered to guide me into the desert.

For some reason, I was convinced that I could find my way—surely this maze of tracks would coalesce, shortly. Where else could they all be heading other than to Merzouga? And wouldn't the colossal dunes appear on the horizon any minute, anyway? My map showed the tiny settlement, sitting at the edge of the dunes only sixty or seventy kilometers away, and leading to it a series of dotted lines, with the legend *piste*. Down the hierarchy of byways from 'secondary roads' and 'unpaved roads,' piste meant path, basically, but since it was on the map, I thought I should be able to follow it without a guide. I asked the boy to point me in the right direction and gave him a few dirhams for his trouble. He insisted I needed a guide, but I was used to that game, thanked him and kept driving; I noticed him riding after me on his bike, determined. I headed out across the gravel in the direction he pointed out to me.

I soon found out that what looked like a flat surface was in fact full of washes, cracks, ridges, and other impassable spots—invisible from a hundred yards but deep enough to bury the wheels of my Peugeot. The vastness spread in front of me without any landmarks to head for, and no consensus among the tread lines. I tried moving forward only to have to back up and try another route that didn't require a four-wheel-drive jeep, my sense of direction getting fuzzier with each tack. It was clear I needed help, and I turned around to find the guide I had left behind. He knew I wasn't going to make it and was bicycling toward me.

He dropped his bike, got in the car, and for the next sixty kilometers directed me, every ten yards, saying *a la gauche*, *a la droite*, *tout droite*, and, repeatedly, *doucement*,

doucement—slowly, sweetly. Up and down grades, always picking one of the many options outlined by previous cars and trucks, reading indecipherable clues, knowing his own particular trail by heart. Without him I never would have made it before dark, if at all.

Even on a more or less straight line it took about three hours. It was two before the dunes arose in the far distance, and nothing else as far as we could see in any direction, not a hill, not a building, nothing. As we approached Merzouga, the oasis slowly replaced the heat shimmer along the horizon, as it was supposed to. A couple dozen mud buildings emerged from the haze. Mohammed asked me to stop and wait *un moment* just as we entered—I could tell by the way he kept suggesting I go more *doucement* that he thought of me as one of those crazy, driven Americans, and felt both bad that he was making me wait a minute, and a little nervous that I couldn't do it and would plow ahead without him. He skipped between two buildings and went to report to someone—a relative?—that he had arrived. I left the car and wandered into the oasis. It was a work of absolute sublimity, not an errant blade of grass, not a crooked line anywhere. Mohammed found me and told me that the men in the village tended to the oasis when they got too old to do other kinds of work. It was divided into hundreds of little gardens, all covered with a canopy of palm, each garden about twenty or thirty square feet, with perfect eight-inch mud walls for keeping in the water. One tranche was full of kohlrabi, and several were growing wheat. Imagine. Wheat fields no bigger than a dining room. The whole oasis probably grew enough wheat for fifty loaves of bread, hand watered a couple of times a week, even in the winter. The town had no plumbing at all. Everybody came to the central well for water.

This was my goal, the last outpost, a tiny village of assorted drifters and Tuareg camel drivers and horsemen, with at most a few dozen houses, only one of which had electricity, provided by a gasoline-powered generator. Truly off the grid, at the end of the road. After Merzouga it was a thousand miles of sand if you wanted to get to anything green, to the middle of Burkina Faso, where sub-Saharan Africa begins.

Mohammed took me to a house that a couple young guys ran as an inn. It had three rooms, each with two cots, and each about the size of a bathroom. I was given a candle stuck in an eight-ounce Coke bottle but no key; the room didn't have a door, only a rug hanging over the opening. There were also cots along the wall of a bigger common room; these were rented out in high season. While I was there a French couple and an Italian couple showed up, along with the guides that had brought them. In the common room an old man sat, in a djellaba and shesh; he must have been eighty years old, very black, he or his family from the far side of the Sahara, and he played an oud, a kind of two string guitar made with a sheet of hide stretched across a banjo-like round frame, that could be drummed on while the strings were picked. He played it the whole time I was there, quietly, without ever stopping. The innkeeper was about twenty years old, strikingly handsome and romantic looking, Tuareg, and he had a helper who was thirteen or fourteen. Also present were a quiet and intense Berber guy who had several camels on which he took tourists like myself into the dunes, and another guy in his twenties who lived locally and whose connection to the inn was unclear.

At night we all ate couscous together and then they started playing Berber music on the oud and assorted drums and singing doleful nomad songs. We all—tourists, guides, locals—joined in playing drums made out of pottery with hides stretched across the tops, finger cymbals, and crude maracas. The rhythms are very different than those in the West, and very complex. I did my best to join in without screwing it up, and I think I did all right, seconding some parts without making a mess of things.

But the French tourist was hopeless, and he played very loud—he was smoking hashish, as we all were, so he was a bit out of it. Every time the group would get in a groove and really start feeling it, we could hear the Frenchman getting more and more excited, banging louder and louder, with no sense of rhythm whatsoever, like Steve Martin in *The Jerk*. His off-groove walloping would eventually distract and disrupt the group. Unable to ignore the maelstrom of random sound coming from his drum, the rest of us would drop out, the music would fizzle, and then, out of the ruins of the song, the Frenchman would have a few last loud, spastic whacks at his drum, look up, and yell, at the top of his lungs, SU-*PERB!* He was so happy and enthusiastic that we had to forgive him.

Then the Moroccans asked me to perform a song, I started 'Hand Jive,' because I thought a Bo Diddley beat would be interesting for them to jam on. They all joined in, and when we were done—that is, when the Frenchman ruined it and yelled SU-*PERB!*—the Moroccans all nodded their heads to each other and said, *Bon chanson, oui, c'est un bon chanson,* like comedians discussing whether a joke was funny, and they clearly thought it was not much of a song, reasonable, maybe, but a bit simple. I went into 'Iko, Iko,' and again, pursed-lip, mild approval. Then we did a bunch of their songs until we just couldn't fight the Frenchman any more.

These kids wore traditional Tuareg headgear. They were proud of their traditions, and of their horses and camels, of the life they were making. Fighting the desert for food every day, they were trying to live in the ways of their ancestors. It may be that many of them chose this because it was clear to them how slim their chances were in any other direction, but their pride was beautiful, their determination to take the best of their culture and perform it to the best of their ability struck me as noble. The oasis was a model of efficiency and productivity in the most brutal of possible environments. A couple of the young men were putting up a water storage tank from handmade bricks and mortar, using the tools of their ancestors, slowly building and rebuilding their fragile world. The whole area had no law except the word of the village elder. There was not a single car or truck owned by anyone in the whole town, just a few motorbikes among the thirty or forty families. The full range of hardship—living with tooth pain all their lives, dying from small, easily treatable infections, with intermittent hunger, or the more subtle but equally real hardship of knowing the possibilities of the world and yet having no way to ever access them—none of this was as visible to me at that moment as the romance of their lives, a romance they recognized and prized.

Just before sunrise, as agreed, the camel guy came into my room and woke me up. It was very cold and still dark, although dawn had made its first change, as I couldn't see the stars anymore, just a couple of planets. It was quiet, nothing but a slight wind. I put on every piece of clothing I had, a couple of pairs of pants and several shirts and two sweaters and a jacket and used a t-shirt for a burnoose and got up on my camel, and he walked me into the dunes. The sand was absolutely pure, and very fine, with each grain like a minute piece of glass. As the sun rose, they became billions of tiny prisms, and the colors changed minute by minute as the sun's angle steepened. After we had wound into the dunes for an hour or so it started to get light, and as we climbed higher and higher I kept expecting to see the sun. The camel, as it walked, rocked me forward and back with each step, rather than the way a horse makes you go up and down, and I had a sense of what it would be like crossing the desert in a caravan, riding for hundreds of kilometers from oasis to oasis, in a vast silent ocean of sand. We stopped just below the highest dune. The camels would go no further and slowly came down onto their knees, front knees first, and we slid off. I started walking farther up as the camel guy waited below, resting against the side of one of the animals. I reached the summit as the sun rose in its daily spectacle. The dunes stretched out as far as I could see, and in the near distance below us the village of Merzouga looked liked a series of tiny boxes made out of mud next to a clump of miniature palm trees. The sand went on, wave after wave, all formed by the wind into the most exquisite sculptural forms, with long curving ridges moving up and down and around, unbroken by vegetation or anything human. Down below I could see trails of desert rats running from one lump of camel dung to the next, but up top there was nothing but my own new footprints, destined to be soon erased.

At the foot of the dunes, on our way back, maybe a quarter of a mile from the inn, my camel plunged forward and gave a little shove like a bucking bronco. I had been sitting with my hands in my pockets—it was still cold—and had stopped paying attention, since everything so far had gone smoothly. I found myself sailing through the air, so quickly that I was lucky to get my hands out of my pockets to break my fall. The camel was jumping and bucking, angry at something, and so, when I hit the ground, I rolled away as fast as I could, in a panic, fearful that the camel, roughly twice the size of a horse, would kick me to death. One hoof came down just past my face as I rolled, but I kept rolling. My back and left arm were sore for a couple of days and pebbles were lodged under the skin of my palm, but I was otherwise unscathed. The camel bucked and kicked a few more times, breaking the lead rope tied to the back of the saddle of the camel in front of him, and trotted back home. The camel guy asked me to wait while he went and caught his animal. I'm sure it isn't good for camel management to let them get away with throwing a customer, but adrenaline was still flooding my circuits, and I decided, however selfishly, that his camel was not my problem. I declined and walked the short distance to the inn.

The next morning Mohammed and I got back in the car and drove in a different direction through the desert, heading to Erfoud, again without the assistance of a road, At the last minute, another of the guys decided to come with us, happy, in that nomadic way, to head off somewhere else at the drop of a hat. Again, as we drove, Mohammed always seemed to know exactly where we were, and would warn me to slow down as we approached an especially hazardous spot, unseen by me—*doucement, doucement!* I asked them what their plans were as I dropped them in sleepy Erfoud, and fifteen-year-old Mohammed shrugged and smiled.

Au revoir, he said, and they walked off with nothing but the clothes on their backs and a couple days' wages in their pockets, miles from home. I headed north into the mountains.

THE FOOL ON THE HILL

BOĞAZKALE, TURKEY

IF YOU HEAD EAST in Turkey, whether from Istanbul or Cappadocia in the south or Ankara in the middle of the country, eventually you run into the homeland of the Kurds. It is a war zone, sometimes quiet, sometimes terrifyingly active. When I arrived in Istanbul in 1999, Abdullah Öcalan, the Kurdish leader, was on trial, in what was Turkey's 'trial of the century.' Pictures in the paper showed him sitting in a bulletproof glass booth, built in a special courtroom on the heavily guarded prison island of Imrali, eighty kilometers southwest of Istanbul in the Sea of Marmara. Kurds were protesting in many world capitals (in Athens a Kurdish man set himself on fire), and Istanbul was tense, afraid of bombings or worse. Roadblocks had been set up on all the highways heading east, and anyone heading west was searched, sniffed by dogs, and their car or truck tossed. In 2013, fourteen years later, Öcalan was still locked up on Imrali, where he was the only prisoner. From his jail cell, he proffered a political solution to the long-running conflict between his people and the Turkish state, one that was making ground on both sides until the Syrian conflict turned everything upside down. In 1999, as now, the Kurds maintained complicated relations with all the countries that make up what they call Kurdistan—Turkey, Iran, Iraq, Syria, and Armenia. The fight for an independent Kurdistan has been waged in many of these countries since the 1910s.

Ankara, Turkey's capital, sits about halfway between Istanbul in the west and the Kurdish zone along the eastern border. Two hours east of Ankara, on the way to Kurdistan, was Boğazkale, a tiny, one-street town below the ruins of Hattusa, an ancient Hittite city being slowly exhumed—digs have been going on for 120 years—by German archaeologists. Hattusa was the capital of the Hittite empire during the late Bronze Age, beginning in roughly 1580 BCE, when the Hittite king moved his seat there and changed his name to Hattusli I. This was about fifty years before his grandson, Mursili I, famously sacked Babylon.

I have no idea what drew me to Boğazkale, except perhaps that it was about as far east as the roadblocks permitted one to go. I drove directly from Istanbul, almost 700 kilometers, seeing how far I could get before circling back around to the famous Cappadocia, with its churches carved out of rock underground, its plains of penile rock formations, and its cave-based hotels.

Shortly after I arrived in Boğazkale, I met a local, a working-class Turkish man, who had a devotion to the Hittites beyond all reason, while I wasn't even sure who they were. I checked into a small B&B, run by a guy and his mother. In the morning I headed out to the ruins. There were no other tourists, the season long over. It was cold, the sky was gray, and for a while I had the melancholy hill to myself. A half hour in, a man spotted me, though, and came running up. He had a lot of tchotchkes and no English. The curios were carved soapstone in various Hittite shapes, 'Lydian' coins, and clay bulls. I bought one of each, which overjoyed him. I kept walking.

The hill covers about a square kilometer, and it is only partially excavated. Archaeological excavation holes were cordoned off here and there, and the four major cardinal point gateways—flanked by imposing twenty-foot stone lions—had been uncovered. I marveled at a couple of those, and the view out was also impressive. The top of the hill afforded panoramic 360-degree views, and I had to think, what an excellent hill for a warrior culture to call home. You could certainly see who was coming, and it was easier to throw things down at them than it would be for them to throw things up at you.

THAT MORNING the only invading army consisted of three men, all, I could see as they got closer, weighed down by the same assortment of tchotchkes and trinkets as the first guy. They surrounded me and started pressing their wares on me. I said I had already bought some, and showed them. I'm sorry, I said, I thought it was just the one guy, or I would have spread the wealth.

What guy? they demanded.

I don't know, I said, I didn't get his name. He was about yea high.

They puzzled together about who it could be, and then one figured it out.

Roma! he said, and then asked me, Roma?

I don't know, I said.

They shook their heads and continued to be astounded—I couldn't tell exactly why. Because the gypsy had never beaten them to a sale? Because he was undeserving? a bad salesman? lazy? because he had broken some code among the sellers?

Then one of them exclaimed, Look! Here he is.

My guy was making his way up the hill to us.

This one? one of the men asked.

Yup, that's him.

Roma! they all said, with that same mix of admiration, envy, surprise, and disgust. He was all smiles. He had, in fact, beaten them at their game. They all gave in to a great bout of laughter and camaraderie. Roma! You sly dog! I imagined they were saying. They slapped each other on the back and yelled happily at each other. He remained low on their totem pole, but a notch higher than he had been yesterday.

Then everyone, including Roma, tried to sell me some more tchotchkes. I said no, no, no, and started walking up the hill. They followed along, taking turns getting in front of me, walking backward, selling. Eventually they all dropped off, except one man, who put his wares down on a rock—safe enough now that the place had become entirely empty, save the two of us—and continued to walk along with me, chatting about the hill.

IN LOVE WITH HISTORY

MUHLIS WAS HIS NAME, he told me, and every summer he dug for the Germans who owned the hill, descendants of the German who had originally bought it in the late nineteenth century. It is a six-month digging season, and he was in his twenty-fifth summer. He had started alongside his father, now deceased, who had dug for the Germans for forty-seven years. His father had started alongside his own father.

The hill was first settled in 6000 BCE, and so the Hittites were really fairly recent, he said, here only about 4000 years ago, or halfway back. Before the Hittites were Hattians and Hurrians, and when Muhlis was digging, he was always most interested in finding evidence of these earlier civilizations—from 4000 BCE, 5000 BCE. This is what really interested him.

Some of these men, it is all the same to them, he said, referring to the other people in town. A Lydian coin, a Phrygian shard —

You aren't excited if you find a Lydian coin?

No. Too new.

So Greek or Roman things, uninteresting?

Hah! Roman! No. This is yesterday.

He took me through all of the different groups who had occupied the hill, told me what was found in various sites that were excavated in recent years. I asked if he made a decent living.

No! It is not good. We live poorly. I am not complaining for me. We all live poorly. We all need to supplement, with these tourist things, he said, referring to his souvenirs, now several hundred yards behind us. And giving tours. And—

He hesitated.

And? I asked.

We need to sometimes take something little from the digs and sell it.

Like a Lydian coin?

Like a Lydian coin! He laughed, but then became serious, confessional. He was a serious man. He knew his history in a deep and learned way, with the internalized intimacy of a hands-on archaeologist. He knew each of the civilizations and other marauders who had crossed this territory over the millennia, he knew their relation to each other and their neighbors, he knew their artifacts, of course, but he also knew their cosmologies and sciences, and how those had crossbred over time. It was impressive, but I don't think he had the least intention of being impressive. I felt like he had worn out every ear he knew and was extremely content to have an active listener, a blank slate. His enthusiasm and endless thirst were a lesson in the relation of university learning to generational oral transmission.

For me, he said, for me, living in history is—he struggled to find the right words—it is like the world is so much larger. The world has more space, more—and he hesitated again, moving his arms out sideways, then up and down. It has more—

More dimensions, I suggested.

Yes, like three dimensions, then four dimensions, then five.

So the Germans don't pay you enough to live year round? I asked.

They don't pay enough to live in the six months! My daughter, she needs medicine. We are very poor. Not me, like I say, all of us.

And so the hill pays, in effect, I said, When you sell something from the dig.

Yes, the hill pays! It should. Very smart, those Germans, to buy when they did, in the nineteenth century. Nobody cared then. The people here were very happy, I think, selling them a worthless hill, good for nothing but goats.

And will your children work for the Germans, too?

No, I hope! I hope they can go to school. I imagine what it would be like to learn history in school.

When did you leave school?

I was twelve. Always it is money. My family needed my work. Always money. Someday, he said, my children will say to me, 'What is wrong with you? Why didn't you go to Ankara for work like everybody else?'

I looked over at him. He had grown abruptly silent when he said that, as if surprised that he had articulated his own dilemma. His eyes had teared up. I wasn't sure what to say, and it was probably best I didn't say anything, because in a minute he raised his head and looked at me, and he was happy.

I can't help it, he said. I love this hill. I love these ancient civilizations. I love history! I just love history!

I WENT WITH HIM to his house, and met his wife, Fatima, and his young children. Fatima had a long-suffering, Dorothea Lange look to her at first, but beneath it as we sat and talked—she listened, and he translated at times—I could see the tender girl beneath the weariness. She was well suited to her serious romantic of a husband, and they required very little conversation to stay in sync. The house was medieval—mud that incorporated two-inch and three-inch branches in an eons-old method that required minimal materials and minimal tools. The roof had clay tiles. Everything was handmade, and it looked it. Nothing was very straight or very square. The mud had been patched frequently. The curves of the plaster inside remembered the hands that made them.

The children came in for a minute, and I could see they were not entirely well. One may just have had a cold, but the other was ailing somewhat worse, with a running nose, red, watering eyes, and chapped lips. They were presented, stared at the stranger with a reserved distrust, and were relieved to disappear when dismissed.

We had tea. The water was boiled on a propane stove, but otherwise, it could have been the same cup of tea Muhlis's great, great grandparents might have shared with the first Germans to arrive. I took a picture of Muhlis and Fatima; I have no idea what's become of it. And he took a picture, with my camera, of me with his wife. She about jumped out of her skin when I sat next to her. I had unwittingly broken some law of contact, sat too close, and as soon as the picture was taken she stood up, a little flustered.

Her cosmopolitan husband was torn between making things right by apologizing—he had agreed to the picture, so it was in a way his fault—and wishing his wife wasn't so provincial, wishing that she wasn't so easily rattled by the ways of Americans.

She doesn't know, he said to me, in that tone of sorrowful resignation he used when thinking about getting a job in Ankara.

She has only lived here, he said. This is all she knows.

FEAR OF AFRICA

JOHANNESBURG, SOUTH AFRICA

AS MY PLANE APPROACHED Johannesburg in August 2012, I felt a familiar creep of fear, a mild madness of apprehension brought on by the imminence of the unknown. I had been to Egypt, Morocco, and Tunisia, but sub-Saharan Africa was something else. I knew almost nothing about it. I had paid attention to the continent the way Americans do—when the news had managed to smack me in the face with some horror, or some new violence erupting. I was a PBS American, not a Fox News American, but still, I didn't know much. I could name most of the fifty-five countries, I had watched a number of documentaries, knew of the more notorious leaders, had read the canonical authors like Achebe and Coetzee and a dozen others. I had studied the

Nigerian constitution in a political science class one year, knew my Fanon and DuBois, and PEN had made me aware of the plight of journalists in Ethiopia and the Nigerian delta. But these thimblefuls of knowledge aside, I was entering a strange land, and expecting it to be a bit illegible.

My fears weren't completely unreasonable. I'd read the State Department's travel warnings, and, even allowing for their typically alarmist tone, the brutality of life in South Africa was undeniable. The average murder rate was 37 per 100,000 (compared to 5 per 100,000 in the United States), while in parts of the Western Cape it soared to more than 100. The country, inured to violence and riven by a vicious distribution of wealth, also had more rapes per capita than anywhere else in the world. I had another kind of fear as well, a kind of social anxiety. I had worked in black clubs, eaten in black restaurants, been to black neighborhoods and black cities. I had black friends, black students, black colleagues, a black president. But, until this trip, I had never been in a black country. The fact that I was embarrassed to find myself anxious only made it worse.

THE STEELY POSTMODERNITY of the Johannesburg airport did the opposite of settle me down. I floated through the Olympic-wattage gleam of the airport in a deep lag-state and endured the usual rental car hassle. I had planned to do a big loop through the southern third of the continent, but no rental company would allow their car to cross into Zimbabwe, which was going to be my first stop. I went from desk to desk, Avis to Hertz to Budget to Sixt (seven or eight companies in all, three or four assistants per company: all white), but no, no, no. Then I did a second lap, desk to desk, to ask, what happened if I flew to Harare, or Bulawayo—could I rent in Zimbabwe and drive back into South Africa? Some called their head offices for me and reported back a simple no; others said no without checking. Admitting defeat, I agreed on a tiny car—I would figure out Zimbabwe later. I then purchased expensive permits that would, I was informed, allow me to cross into the other countries on my route: Mozambique, Swaziland, Lesotho, Botswana, and Namibia. No one, in any of those countries, ever asked to see them.

For some reason, Johannesburg was the epicenter of my fear. I decided to drive first to Pretoria, to ease into things. I would hit Jo'burg on the way back, when I returned the car and took my flight home. It was cowardly, maybe, but I was tense enough just driving out of the airport—on the wrong, English side of the road—and only started to relax once I was on the eight-lane, Olympics-quality highway to the capital, which was an hour or so to the north. Many of the other drivers were white, I noticed—twenty percent of Johannesburg is white, but eighty percent of the drivers seemed to be. I arrived in Pretoria late that afternoon.

PRETORIA

I WANDERED AROUND, getting a sense of how the city was laid out, and then went to find a B&B. They were clustered in gingko-leafy, big-lawned neighborhoods on the edge of the city center; formerly exclusive areas now feeling the creep of downtown. Their residents had responded to the advance of the urban poor with walls and remote-controlled gates at the top of their driveways. Some had then moved farther out, and converted their ancestral homesteads into inns. I pulled up to one I'd found in a guidebook and rang the intercom. I was buzzed in and parked. The door was opened by a wide, slightly wary black woman wearing a frilled apron and a maid's cap. She showed me a small room, priced on the low end. I said I'd take it, but Francine was not to be hurried. Before I could collect the keys, I had to hear the rest of the rules—nothing of note—and confirm that I understood them. She double-checked that the room I had spoken for was the room I wanted. Although she didn't give much away, I had a feeling that, having sized me up sociologically, she thought I should be interested in one of the larger rooms.

The house had once been a beautiful, upper-middle-class home, that of a mid-rank government official, maybe. It featured gorgeous woodwork, a soccer field–sized backyard, and a pleasant terrace. The only off notes were the locks on all the interior doors, installed when it had been hacked up into rooms for rent, and the tire marks from cars parking on the back lawn. My room was on the ground floor off to the side; I took it to have been a study of some kind, or perhaps a servant's quarters.

Francine ran the place almost single-handedly. She registered me, gave me the key, showed me where to park, did the laundry, made the beds, managed the alarm system, did the shopping, answered the phone, swept, mopped, dusted, and cleaned—did everything, in fact, except handle the money. That had to wait for a white woman: the owner's niece. When she arrived, she ignored Francine completely and proceeded to list for me all the house rules I had already heard from Francine—who now stood to the side, impersonating furniture. The niece took my cash, wished me a hurried, frosty goodnight, and left, still betraying no knowledge of Francine's existence.

Driving in I had noticed a restaurant—a take-out place, really—in a mini-mall five or six blocks from the guesthouse, where the residential district became commercial. I asked Francine if it was a good restaurant and she was unrevealing—it was clear I was making some kind of mistake, but I couldn't tell what it was. Her answers to my questions had none of the play of African American conversation, no gesture to help me out of my ignorance, not even the kind of 'mm-hmm' that means 'well, I'm not saying *anything*, but . . .'—enough to give a person a clue. She maintained a straight poker face, one that spoke of a lifetime in which no good could come from letting an opinion air in a situation like this.

Apparently basic safety was part of her job, though.

It's close, right? I asked, I can walk there and back?

Yes, you drive, she said. Not 'no, safer to drive,' but 'yes, you drive.' Even in contradicting me she wouldn't contradict me.

And then she explained again that she had to buzz me back in through the gate, and how to ring her.

I drove out, as the sun was setting, to the restaurant—checked and saw steady traffic in and out, a good sign—and then went another few blocks to a liquor store, where I bought an inexpensive red. The store and its parking lot were entering the evening. A few red-eyed black guys, a couple of road-killed white guys in the depths of alcoholic disease, lots of foot traffic, the air starting to tingle with desperation. Working girls began to show up on the corners. One approached me as I got in my car; I politely declined and made my way back to the food stand.

I walked in, and luckily a number of people pushed right past me and ordered, so I could see the drill, which couldn't have been simpler. There was a menu on the wall with a dozen items, but everyone ordered mieliepap—the South African staple, a big wad of rough polenta—and gravy, which looked more like a stew, with hunks of beef and bone. 'One' got you one Styrofoam container of mieliepap and gravy, 'two' got you two containers, and everyone added greens. I ordered one with greens, paid my two dollars, and got back in the car. In the fifteen minutes I'd been out, the dusk had solidly settled and the Night of the Living Prostitutes had begun in earnest. Women began to appear everywhere, mostly on the corners in groups of three and five, converging on the passing cars, peering into them, flaunting their wares. A white guy in a rental car was of predictable interest, and at lights and stop signs they approached me. I waved them off, with what in retrospect must have been a fairly condescending sad smile, though I didn't mean it as such. I just kept thinking AIDS, AIDS, AIDS, AIDS, AIDS. Some of the women were black and very young, and looked healthy and bright; others were black and older and looked weary; still others were white and looked older than they probably were, with the sore-scattered skin of junkies and tweakers. HIV infection, one assumes, approached 100 percent.

There were a remarkable number of them. It was early, of course, but I didn't see any cars pulling over and picking anyone up—a very bad seller's market. As I got back into my neighborhood, only a block or two away from the employment line, I slowed down to pull into my driveway and a couple women appeared out of nowhere. By the time I was punching the intercom to have Francine buzz me back in, they were at my car door. The more forward of the two was white, around thirty, and dying. I was trying to say no, thank you to her and ask Francine to open the gate at the same time. I said, It's Tom! And the prostitute said, Hi, Tom! And the intercom said Hello? I said, Francine! It's Tom! And the intercom said, Who? and the black prostitute, correctly assessing my lack of interest in her poor dying white partner, pushed her out of the way and presented herself, nonverbally, and smiled. I said, It's Tom, and the intercom said, What do you want? The second prostitute said, Yes, what do you want, Tom?

I realized, hearing the voice on the intercom, now saying something in another language, that I had pulled up to the wrong house. I looked to see if I could back out, which meant being a little rude to the woman leaning on my roof, and where did the other one go? The intercom said, again, What do you want? Nothing, thank you, I said to the intercom, wrong place, and the second prostitute said, You go with me? And I said, No, thank you, I'm sorry, and started to back out, worried about running over the dying white woman, who I could see nowhere. I was flustered, unreasonably so. Other women were now approaching the car, intuiting a problematic negotiation they felt they could handle better, and I just bit my lip and started backing out into the street slowly, too late remembering I was on the English system and had checked the lanes wrong, almost smashing into a fast car barreling down a lane I hadn't checked yet, its horn blaring and tires screaming, the driver staying on his horn angrily for a couple blocks. The prostitutes laughed. I tried again, backed out, pulled away, and six houses down found the right B&B. In my defense, it did look very similar—in that it was a house, and had a sign, and had a gate. Otherwise it was very obviously different. I hit the intercom, and Francine buzzed me in.

I brought my mieliepap and gravy and greens and wine out to the garden, and Francine brought me a plate, fork, napkin, glass, corkscrew, and placemat. As I shoveled some of the contents of the Styrofoam box onto the plate, she allowed herself the slightest smile. I was eating poor people's food. She was neither shocked, nor interested, nor impressed by my offer that she join me, if not for dinner—there was plenty—then for a glass of wine. She shook her head, with a tilt to the side to signify the mildest thank you for asking. She stood by the door for a couple of minutes, just behind my range of vision, to make sure I had whatever I needed, and then silently withdrew. The food was good. The garden was quiet, oversized, and odd. My car was parked in it. The wine I had had before, back home.

IT WAS JUST BREAKING DAWN when I left in the morning, to head farther north. I didn't see Francine. I left my room key on the front table, and drove out the gate, as if I had never been there. In the early morning light nobody else seemed to be stirring. Francine would wash my sheets, remake my bed.

TWO UZBEK WEDDINGS AND THE CULTURE OF HOSPITALITY

FIRST DAY WEDDING

SAMARKAND, BUKHARA, TASHKENT. The intricate mosaic madrasas, the ornate tombs. The exhilarating blue of the mosque domes, the delicious, delicate curves of thirteenth century arches, the deep glazed colors—green, red, yellow, gold, lots of blue. The turbaned falconers, the dashing horsemen, the hidden harems. Hashish and hookahs, camels and carpets and caravansaries. The Silk Road. Can anyone not feel the allure?

    I landed in the blistering summer sun of Tashkent, after a five-hour flight across the mountains from Delhi, and rode in from the airport with a taciturn cabby. We passed through collectivized farmland scattered with dumpy industrial buildings, then strips of apartment blocks mushroomed with satellite dishes, and then into the nondescript streets of the Russian part of town. The avenues were broad and sparsely built and sparsely populated, in ways that are good for military parades and unencouraging to free assembly. In the middle of the turnabouts stood monuments to medieval Uzbek heroes that had, I assumed, been put up in the 1990s to replace the statues of Lenin and Stalin that watched over the Soviet occupation.

My first night I stayed in an architecturally ridiculous hotel, some misbegotten compromise between an ambitious student of mid-century modernism and the Central Planning Committee, its bravura ungainliness characteristically Uzbek SSR. Nowhere else did the Soviet distaste for whimsy and embellishment battle so strenuously with its host culture. Even each of the brutal gray USSR apartment blocks from the 1960s and 1970s wear some minimal but striking geometric fascia with colored paint. Though most are now faded and chipped, they are still unmistakable, and like nothing you'd find in Moscow: mournful, minimal nods to the millennia-long traditions of Uzbek architectural adornment.

I had picked a hotel off the web in the lower-middle of the price range, somewhere between the expense-account inflated top and the unpredictable bottom—usually a safe bet for a first night. I was entirely unprepared, therefore, for the crazy opulence of the entryway, all blue marble and mirrors, with its prodigious, baroque—and, it turned out, unused—sweeping circular stairway leading somewhere, two stories of plate glass displaying it to the street. The front desk was a large, polished, curved affair, with a single computer monitor in the center, around which three young attendants hovered. I checked into a serviceable, unremarkable room on the eighth floor.

The lobby said something about the Uzbek sense of architecture as drama, of design as declaration, however compromised by the use of standard prefabricated modules, probably manufactured in China, or perhaps North Korea. The countries along the Silk Road demonstrate in many ways the fierceness of their cultural commitments, with everything from their headdresses and hats to the shape of their minarets, to their willingness to kill each other. But here, as everywhere, tradition gradually succumbs to volume discounts. In the room, the discounts won, which just meant it was the international norm.

Looking out my high window ready to see the town, I found there was little to see—just the barren boulevard and the statue of Tamerlane. But I heard something: through the unopenable glass came the distinct sound of brass instruments and drums. A band was playing. In the hotel? On the street? I went back down the elevator and asked the young people at the desk, in one of my fourteen words of Russian—*muzyka*?—and they pointed outside. As soon as I hit the searing air, I heard them; they were just across the way, at what turned out to be the entrance of another hotel. I walked the city block between the two adjacent buildings and pulled out my camera just as a limo was disgorging the bride.

Four drummers and four horn players were the entire band, each of the latter holding aloft a ten-foot valveless tube ending in a trombone-width bell. Snapping pictures as they followed the bridal party into the hall, I was ushered in along with them and encouraged to continue photographing. The band, in particular, was hamming it up for me, and in a pause in the proceedings they posed for me backstage, as directed by their leader. I thanked them, again using Russian—*spasibo*—since there was no English anywhere. I started to leave, but they dragged me into the hall with them. Everyone acted oddly happy to see me. I photographed the guests, photographed the Vegas-coiffed his-and-hers MCs wielding their microphones, the little kids running around, and the solemn bride and sad groom sitting mute at the head table. The groom looked particularly uncomfortable—not about me; I don't think he noticed.

It was my first Uzbek wedding, so I didn't realize I was expected to stay, eat, and drink. I left to explore the town. The slightly confused looks from the revelers as I departed were not, I only later realized, them thinking, *Who was that and why was he here?* but, *Why is he leaving already? Doesn't he realize the importance of unknown foreign guests to any wedding?* I was unprepared for the power of hospitality in this part of the world. I had read *The Odyssey,* and wondered how the suitors made such a mess for Penelope and Telemachus, wondered why Odysseus was welcomed as a guest everywhere, even when disguised as a shepherd, the way he was offered rooms, food, baths. The Greeks called it *xenia*, and in Uzbekistan I felt its sway.

As I ambled away I kept thinking about the bride and groom. He looked so frightened, and she so somber. They both stared straight ahead, as if into the horror of their future together. Everyone else seemed to be having a good time, but they had some other jobs to do. Hers consisted of bowing her white net-veiled head slowly every few seconds. His was to not move, at all. Was it culture, or was this a shotgun wedding? Was it expected of them, or did they just happen to be dour people? Had he just found out she had slept with the best man? What special, local emotions enveloped them? Nobody else paid any attention to them—the wedding, as weddings often do, had its own trajectory, and they were bit players. I sometimes look at those pictures and think, these two kids—what terror they beheld, what resignation they evinced in the face of their doom!

PLOV DAY IN TASHKENT

ON MY SECOND DAY I went to find the *eski shakkar*, the old city. Laid out on a human scale, it was just east of the big Chorsu market, a pre-Soviet, pre-automotive, premodern city center. I stopped to chat with boys and men along the way, getting no further than my tiny Russian vocabulary would allow. But one guy, around sixty-five or so, five feet tall and 130 pounds, spoke English. He had one wandering eye and both of them thyroid-large and lively, his sparse hair slicked back. I said I had a hard time finding the old city.

Oh, yes, he said. It is a very exclusive neighborhood! Like Hyde Park! Dearborn!

I laughed and he winked at me. A half dozen boys had gathered around us.

Yes, very much like Dearborn! he said.
Good English, I said.
I lived in Chicago, Detroit, he said. Ten years.
I asked him where the center of the old city was.

Oh! You want the center of *eski shakkar*, he said, with a big smile. No problem! Here, follow me! And he strode three steps. I followed. He stopped short and held out his arms. Here we are! he said. The boys all laughed.

You are a comedian, I said. A comedian and a cosmopolitan.

He laughed and slapped me on the back.

Exactly! he said. That is what I tell everybody! That I am a cosmopolitan comedian. Still, they don't believe me!

We tipped our hats and I walked on. The past 1,000 years had, in many ways, simply passed the old city by. Much of the construction was medieval straw and mud braced with saplings, and some of the alleys were just wide enough for a donkey. Carcasses hung unrefrigerated at the butcher shop. Craftsmen banged away with hand tools on leather, wood, and metal.

Along one quiet alleyway a woman and her daughter were standing at their front gate. I asked if I could take a picture. They giggled and waved me off, but the daughter asked in English where I was from. I said America, and the mother excitedly shouted into the family compound, something that included the word America, while she waved her hand up and down at me, meaning, *wait here*. A man of fifty-five or sixty came out, in nothing but shorts, wool socks, and sandals, his naked, paunchy torso sweating—he had obviously been working at something. He said, Ah, America! and they all seemed extremely pleased. He ushered me into the family compound.

Please! he said, and that seemed to be about all of his English. The daughter told me that she had an older sister living in Washington. Washington! the man said, proudly. He put his arm through mine, speaking to me in Russian—every once in a while he asked if I spoke Russian, and when I said no, *nyet*, he went on anyway. He pulled me into their courtyard, and told the daughter to let me know I must stay for dinner. America! the father kept saying, beaming.

The father—Mr. Amidov—had been starting a batch of plov. As with barbecues in the United States, tending the backyard plov cooker is a man's job in Uzbekistan. Shaped like a wok the size of a small Weber grill, and attached to an LP gas burner, the plov cooker is a permanent fixture in the courtyard. Mr. Amidov was busy cleaning it out in preparation for a new batch. It was Saturday, plov day, and they apologized for the need to keep working. They had no English, the daughter had left for work, and I had used up my little Russian instantly—but I managed to make it clear that I hoped they would continue, and that I wanted to know how to make plov myself. He encouraged me to take pictures.

Plov is the Uzbek national dish, and, as the name suggests, it's a version of the pilaf found all over this part of the world, from the Balkans to Kenya and from the Middle East to South Asia and beyond. Alexander the Great first encountered it in Bactria, in present-day Afghanistan, the first major valley south of where I was. It is more than a food, it is an institution, it is health, it is hospitality.

The first step is to cook the fat. The best, I was assured, with some creative mime-work on the part of Mr. Amidov, was the tail fat of the sheep. He did not limit himself to mime, but talked a mile a minute. He was one of those guys, a talker, and he produced a constant patter of Uzbek and

Russian, supremely unconcerned by the fact that I understood none of it. His wife knew to talk over it now and then rather than wait for an opening. He was an enthusiast, and his indomitable energy carried us across all the linguistic chasms. Sometimes, after he asked me a question in Russian and I answered in English, he translated my answer to his wife, who nodded that she had already got it.

He turned the heat up under the great curds of tail fat in the pot until the grease was partially rendered, then threw in piles of peppers and carrots and onions that had been peeled and chopped by his wife and daughters beforehand, along with some incompletely cooked—he made me try one to see that it was still partially hard—dried yellow split peas and a liberal palmful of cumin seeds. This was followed by strips of mutton, a dozen or more whole heads of garlic, pepper, coriander, barberries, and another palmful of cumin seeds. At each step a standard marital comedy was acted out—everything the husband did, he did wrong. His wife corrected him. He waved her off, muttering, and did it the way she said to. Too much of this! Not enough of that! A spat, an argument, and then he did what she wanted, trying at the same time to insist that it wasn't because it was what she wanted, that he had known all along. Meanwhile the pot bubbled, and he gave it an occasional, proprietary stir.

Mrs. Amidov brought out a large, light-blue plastic bowl of uncooked rice, wet from rinsing. By now there was a half-gallon of grease, simmering a *confit* of meat and vegetables, redolent and rich. With the rice, the marital battle commenced again: he dropping spoonfuls of rice into the fat one at a time, she motioning that he should just dump the whole bowl in; he stirring and carefully considering the proportions, she motioning to take the rest; he objecting to her tone and adding a couple more ladlesful; she snorting her disapproval and saying (I assumed), *oh, come on, just dump the rest in*; he stirring the pot and contemplating, then scooping out a few more gobs, explaining to me that it was important to get the proportions just right; her sighing heavily and pushing the bowl back at him, him rocking his head side to side, taking half of what was left in her bowl and mixing it in, and again turning to me and saying something about the right ways to do things.

In the end all the rice had been put in the cooker, with a final eye roll by Mrs. Amidov. He made a dozen steam spouts in the rice mixture with the handle of his wooden spoon, then covered it with a porcelain bowl that didn't quite come to the edges. He then went inside to fetch a second, bigger metal bowl to put on top of that. While he was gone, his wife poured an extra bowl of water in, and put a finger to her lips—our secret. He returned, dropped the second bowl on top of the first to act as a lid—I'm not entirely clear on the purpose of the smaller bowl—and then we waited for the rice to cook.

He called into the house, and a young son came running out, scrambled up a large tree in the courtyard, and came back down with a big plastic bag of cherries, which we sat and ate. The son disappeared back into the house. Another daughter came out and started peeling hardboiled eggs and slicing them. We went into a kind of breezeway—not quite inside, not quite in the courtyard—where the daughters, it seemed, had laid out a table. It was already stacked with big loaves of round Uzbek bread—another point of ethnic pride—and a salad of shredded carrots and pickled long-stemmed mushrooms.

Picnic! Mr. Amidov said, happy to have found another common word. The kids never joined us. I asked why, saying their names, but their parents waved it off. We then had a very spirited discussion about our respective presidents. Theirs, Islam Karimov, was a Soviet functionary who, by extending his terms and holding bogus elections, has ruled since independence in 1991. He got thumbs down all around. Then we went through the U.S. presidents, and Obama got thumbs up from all of us—they were being a little cautious, gauging my reaction, and Obama was still pretty new on the job. Next up was Bush II, who Amidov called *Leetle Boosh*. They looked to me, and when they saw both my thumbs go down, they laughed and heartily joined in. Then Clinton got big thumbs up from them, the elder Bush a mixed, but mostly up reaction. Clinton was clearly the guy they loved, and I wasn't exactly sure why.

The plov was done. We went back into the courtyard, where the lids were pulled off, a final batch of cumin seeds was tossed in, and the mixture was lightly disassembled—the heads of garlic were removed, and then the hunks of meat were pulled out and sliced. We kept talking about the U.S. presidents. They thought that my description of *Leetle Boosh* as the devil (I made horns on my head with my fingers) was going a little too far, but not that much. But *Beel Cleenton!* He was the best. They made a big bed of the basic plov, on which they nicely arranged the heads of garlic, strips of meat, and slices of egg,

Sitting back down at the table, we moved from politicians' names to place names, proper nouns being the safe haven for languageless sociality. The plov was spectacular—wonderfully deep flavors and, with all that fat soaked up by the rice and peas, incredibly rich. I managed to mime a description of Los Angeles, and they praised Samarkand and Bukhara, places I was headed. I brought up Andijan—in 2005, the government's security services had opened fire on a demonstration in Andijan, and while the government claims 187 were killed, other estimates reported more like 1,500. There are disputed versions of what happened—the government itself floated multiple stories, at one point claiming that it had merely quelled a prison break and then settling on the idea that Islamist radicals had attacked the police. Some regime critics suggest it was an attempt to put down a color revolution; others that there was an internal struggle within the government that was played out in the street. The U.S. condemnation of the attacks led to the closing of a major American base in the country and nudged the regime toward China, which, fearful that Hizb ut-Tahrir and similar groups might spill over from the Stans into Uyghur-dominated western China, approved of the police action as a necessary response to Islamist terror.

The Amidovs agreed that Andijan was a shame, *but*, Mrs. Amidov said, holding up a finger—and she mimed putting a scarf on and then started bowing and praying, mimicking an observant Muslim woman with sarcastic salaams. She followed this with a *phooey* gesture. I asked if they were Muslim, and they said yes, of course, but—and again she put on the imaginary headscarf, then wagged her finger—they didn't like fundamentalism. They were—we somehow managed to get this concept onto the table—secular Muslims.

After dinner we moved into a kind of parlor, or perhaps formal dining room, its walls covered by rugs, or tapestries, with a chandelier and what looked like upholstered trim along the ceiling—all more sumptuous than I expected. The table held what seemed like an endless supply of threeand four-tier candy dishes. I had eaten so much plov I was afraid to move, and certainly afraid to eat any candy. It was a mix of homemade things, local brands, boxes of samplers, and international, mainly American, individually wrapped candy bars—Mars, Snickers, Kit Kat. We talked about currency problems, the way the economy was halfway dollarized. The problem, Mr. Amidov said, was that the government won't admit there is inflation, and so now, at 3,000 som to the dollar, and the biggest available denomination being a 1,000 som bill, $200 had bought me a stack of som a foot high. Using dollars in Uzbekistan was technically illegal, as was trading dollars for som on the street, where you get twice as much for your dollar. In practice, both were the norm.

Mr. Amidov was either a mechanical engineer, I learned, or he was a retired mechanical engineer. He was also, in his spare time (or full time now that he was retired) a maker of hats. He had a dozen frames out to dry on a rack in the corner of their courtyard, each the base level for the hat to which he glued and (or?) stitched wool and fur on the outside, and a silk lining and leather headband inside. The frames looked a bit grotesque at first glance—I thought they were some kind of animal bladders, something visceral about the pale stretched material. He explained how he made them, some of which I followed, and then showed me the finished versions, the kind of hats a Russian prime minister or dandified

Afghan president might wear, with several textures of wool—including that very tight curly stuff, shiny and black—some with fur as well, all extremely well made. He sold them, he told me, to a fancy shop for $20 apiece, which I could tell was quite a lot of money for a wholesale hat in those parts by the way he basked in glow of the number. I said, because I wanted to make it clear that he couldn't give me one as a gift, that I wanted to buy one from him before I left.

For the first part of the day, I was fascinated by Mr. Amidov's relentless talking, as he did his interpretive dance to make himself understood, and thought his constant garrulity charming and naïve. Over time, though, I realized it was more than that, that it actually worked. Somehow—maybe because of deep phonemes? deep grammar? deep homonyms?—I started to feel I understood what he was saying. So I started, too, to speak aloud everything I was thinking, as did Mrs. Amidov, who, although she observed normal rules of decorum in relation to me—she only talked when I wasn't, and vice versa—treated her husband's flow like an ambient television soundtrack, something you could attend to or ignore at will. He never seemed to notice that she was talking, unless he objected to what she was saying, at which point he would turn and correct her. We chattered away, and by the end of the day it felt like family, and we were communicating as if we were all limited by nothing more than heavy accents.

He, as I had suspected he might, insisted I take a hat as a gift. None of them fit, which was a bit embarrassing, all just a little too small—I have, for some reason, a massive head, I think from my mother's side (I remember noticing as a kid, with some distress, that my Uncle Gerald's head was twice the size of my father's), and I think Mr. Amidov felt it a lapse in the milliner's art not to have the right size hat available—but none of that mattered. He insisted that I not pay, I said, no no no no, the plov, that was from the heart, and I appreciate it from the heart, and there were great protestations of mutual love and respect, lots of gesturing to the actual heart, but this, I kept saying, this hat, this was separate, this was just business (*bizness* being, of course, one of the most universally understood words we have). All the way out the door, he kept insisting that it was his gift, pushing away the proffered payment. The children had magically reappeared to see me off, and I was shaking their hands, and giving a hug to Mrs. Amidov, and at the last moment, Mr. Amidov let me slip the bills—two twenties—into his hand at an angle his family couldn't see. We had a gentleman's agreement, all of a sudden, as he took the money, but I wasn't entirely sure what it was. His daughter wouldn't have seen the handoff anyway, being as engaged with her phone as any teenager in America, and the son had already disappeared again. It was his wife, I realized, that he was shielding the transaction from, and I suspected I had become a pawn in the Great Game of Mr. and Mrs. Amidov. She made it clear he knew not as much as he pretended about plov. He made it clear she would see nothing of my money. And, as is often the case in politics, it was already too late to be neutral.

WEDDING IN BUKHARA

WE EACH HAD a shot glass. The vodka was plentiful, and every ten minutes or so, someone would boisterously decide it was time for a communal chug. I was at a wedding dinner in Bukhara. Wolf, my new friend, was getting blearier. *TOM!* he would shout again, and the whole table shouted it in answer. He pulled me close, his hug now much more like an aggressive headlock. *Wolf!* I would respond, somewhat less enthusiastically than the time before. I hoped he didn't notice.

Be careful, my new schoolteacher friend had said, The men, they drink too much.

I had met the schoolteacher, and Wolf—that wasn't his name; his name, Bori, also meant *wolf* in Uzbek—the night before, out wandering through Bukhara in the dark. I had stepped out of my hotel and was strolling through the neighborhood when I heard music. I followed the sound through unlit streets, getting a little nervous about losing track of my hotel, and came across a large party in what was either a small park or a large empty lot, in which twenty tables had been placed. The music was from a PA set up for the occasion, and eighty or a hundred people were eating and drinking. At first I thought it was an outdoor restaurant, but then it became clear it was a private party. I was about to turn away when an almost scarily beautiful woman—very dark hair, very light skin, very colorful eyes—approached me and said hello. She was around twenty-five, and had honed a girl-next-door demeanor that pretended you weren't in a panic. It almost worked.

English? she asked.

American.

Please come join us. My cousin is getting married. It is good luck to have strangers at a wedding, you will do us a favor.

She took me by the arm, warmly, and pulled me in. She led me to the table of the mother and grandmother of the bride. This was the rehearsal dinner, and people did not seem entirely relaxed—not split into camps, exactly, but certainly careful with the new in-laws. A few women in their forties and fifties sat at one end of the table, laid out with cold and hot mezes, and a cohort of sturdy women in their seventies and eighties were gathered at the other. One of them could have been a hundred, with paper skin and clouded eyes. I was introduced to the older women first, so the matriarchs could approve of my presence. I wasn't sure what the cousin said to them, but they looked at me blankly, like they didn't expect anything particularly good or bad to come of my showing up like this. The middle-aged women and I all smiled at each other, and I bowed to them, thanking them for their hospitality, and one of them, the schoolteacher, responded in perfect English; she was a very nice and perceptive woman in her late forties, dressed the way nuns dress now, with a mustache and very heavy eyebrows, and extremely intelligent eyes. My strikingly beautiful new friend took me by the arm to another table or two and introduced me. In between she talked about the trouble she had, because her boyfriend was Russian, which meant that her father would kill him if he knew, but she didn't care, and then she pointed to an open spot on a bench and said, Please, sit, eat!

The table included a number of other foreigners plucked off the street—a Japanese student, a Canadian couple in their thirties, and a Danish man in his sixties. They all were dying to get away, except the Danish man, who was thrilled to be there, and kept saying, almost under his breath, *This is quite amazing!*

Wolf came over to the table, and saying, *Amerika!* grabbed me—he was a big man, well over two meters, and built like Paul Bunyan—stood me up, and hugged me. He said something in Russian, and saw that I didn't get it. He called out to the schoolteacher, and she came over to translate.

He wants you to know that he heard you were American, which is good with him, the schoolteacher said.

Wolf interrupted her. He wants, she said, that you know I am a schoolteacher, and that I am a good translator. She shrugged at this, like it was easier to say it than not, although she didn't see the point. And he says that you need to come with him to meet the fathers of the bride and groom.

Thank you, I said, and that was when she said to be careful.

Wolf walked me a half dozen tables down to a large round one full of men. The fathers of the bride and groom were introduced—I of course remained unclear who was who. The men were relaxed into a solid vodka buzz, smoking. Wolf was the ringleader and the drunkest, refilling people's vodka glasses at a fairly alarming pace, already in that part of the evening when a large amount of vodka was splashing over onto the table and nobody noticed or cared. Wolf objected loudly if anyone—including the star American guest he had one arm wrapped around—tried to drink only half of their shot after any of his innumerable toasts. As he got drunker, his grip around my shoulders slipped up to my neck, his embrace becoming more like a mixed martial arts move. TOM! he would toast to me. Wolf! I would answer. I was trapped, which made me more alert than woozy, despite all the shots. His clinch got tighter. He was sweating, eyes red. Was he drooling a little? He started yelling something at the table that made them laugh.

The schoolteacher came over and stood on my right side, and the beautiful friend came up on Wolf's right, and they said something to him, loud enough for the table to hear, and the schoolteacher said to me, in English, that they were going to take me to visit the bridal party. Although Wolf clearly didn't want to let me go, and had to give me one last chokehold squeeze around the neck, he let me leave with them. The blood started to return to my body. Wolf said something to the table that made them laugh nervously out of their own fog, but the women had already spirited me away.

Since this was the rehearsal dinner, the bride was sequestered with her retinue, which as far as I could tell was an entirely pro forma, ceremonial restriction, as a constant parade of visitors of all ages and sexes came through and did hugs all around. She wasn't hidden away so much as given a receiving room. A dozen or so people were there when Cousin Beautiful and the Schoolteacher brought me in. They all seemed blessedly sober and unthreatening, and the bride was even more beautiful than her cousin. She was dressed in some traditional clothing that I assumed was required for her part that night, all of it very *1001 Nights*, flowing, sheer silk with spangles and moments of embroidery, and with the encouragement of her girlfriends and relatives, she was hamming it up, performing for me and for them. I once again, although in a very different way, had a rush of feeling both very drunk and on high alert.

I snapped some pictures, which made her ham it up even more, and then I noticed that she was directing it all at me, not anyone else in the room. She *was* flirting with me—is this what the random visitors were for? The Schoolteacher and Cousin Beautiful were at the entrance to the room, in conversation with a man, paying us no mind. The bride encouraged me to take more pictures, and started hiding behind her veil, coquetting, ridiculously adorable, and flirting outrageously, flush, full of her girlish power. Was this what was supposed to be happening? A kind of bachelor party–like last chance to be unmarried? I had an image of Wolf crashing through the door and landing one those enormous fists in my face. The bride had coaxed a little sister over to take my camera and snap some pictures of the two of us, and she was now kissing me on the cheek for the camera, wrapping herself around me, crazily sexual it seemed to me, and I glanced up to find the Schoolteacher looking at me, but her expression gave no clue—was she disgusted, mildly amused, neither? Was she jealous? In which direction? The Beautiful Cousin came up and took me by the arm; the bride whispered into my ear one last impossible promise, in Uzbek, which of course I could not understand. I was very drunk. The Beautiful Cousin walked me out of the room, hustled me past the tables—Wolf seemed to be yelling at one of the men at his table, banging on it with a fist—and out through the gate where she had first brought me in.

Go now, she said, Go away. Good time. She handed me a small slip of paper with a phone number and gave me a gentle push.

I wandered drunkenly amid domed madrassas under the clear moonlight, and somehow ended up back at my hotel.

HITCHING ACROSS THE ROOF OF THE WORLD

THE SILK ROAD INTO KYRGYZSTAN

FROM TASHKENT, Uzbekistan, there are several overland routes into Western China, each tracing one of the many iterations of the old Silk Road. One, which would be more frequently used if things weren't so tense with Tajikistan, heads south into that country before crossing its disputed border with China and heading into Kashgar, the westernmost city in China. Another heads north into Kazakhstan and then east to Ürümqi, the capital of Xinjiang province, another twenty-four-hour, 1,500-kilometer drive east of the border.

The less fraught route, politically, is through Kyrgyzstan, running across the alternately industrial and pastoral Fergana Valley into Osh, Kyrgyzstan's second city, then up into the mountains through a 14,000-foot pass to a tiny crossroads town called Sary-Tash, sitting windswept at 10,500 feet. The road then forks south to Tajikistan and the Pamir Highway to Afghanistan, or east toward China, crossing the border at Irkeshtam, 200 lonely kilometers from Kashgar. Much of this is the same route used by Marco Polo when he traveled east into China for the first time, and by Genghis Kahn when he headed west. It is one of the most storied paths in the world.

The guidebooks warn that the China road is often washed out or snowbound, and gets so bad that at times it disappears altogether. The consensus advice is, *Don't do it.* No public transport tries to use the road. The only way across is to arrange a ride with a trucker. Trucks, and a very few jeeps, break down on the road regularly. If yours does, the online wisdom has it, your best bet is to bail and get in the next vehicle that will have you. You don't want to be unsheltered at night at 14,000 feet. It's a twenty-hour trip, and since driving in the dark is suicide, an overnight stay in Sary-Tash, population 1,427, is necessary.

IN 2010 I TOOK A BUS from Tashkent to the Kyrgyz border, where, after a couple of hours jollying along customs agents looking for 'presents' (Kyrgyzstan is ranked one of the most corrupt nations on earth), I finally got my stamp. I made my way into Osh, and took a room in small, monkish motel frequented by NGO staff. The Kyrgyz have known many rulers; the Mongols in the twelfth century, then the Chinese Qing dynasty in the seventeenth, then Uzbek khans in the nineteenth, and finally the Russians in 1876. Kyrgyzstan became independent in 1991 but remains one of the poorest countries in the world, with 40 percent of GDP coming from remittances migrant Kyrgyz workers send back from Russia, where you can see them, in Moscow, pushing wheelbarrows of wet concrete across construction sites. The city of Osh feels like it has not quite emerged from Soviet limbo, nor Kyrgyzstan as a whole from its pastoral, nomadic past. In most parts of the country, yurts are still more common than buildings.

The place people arranged rides across the mountains, *Lonely Planet* told me, was at a 'jeep stand' on a street corner at the northern edge of the city. I had never done this cross between hiring a driver and hitchhiking before, and wasn't sure what a jeep stand was supposed to look like. I got myself to the corner the guidebook suggested and nothing was happening. No jeeps, just a few bedraggled people wandering by. The sun was setting, and, so far, I had not met a single person who spoke English. I approached a couple of Kyrgyz guys with black bangs sticking straight out of their caps—gone were the careful, elaborate haircuts and coifs of the Uzbek cities, gone the look of indoor living; these guys had faces of brown leather, even though they were still in their twenties. I mimed a steering wheel, pointed off toward the mountains, said the name of the town at the top, Sary-Tash. Thank god for proper nouns. They pointed up the road and spoke a few sentences of gruff Kyrgyz. I thanked them with one of the four words I had learned and hurried up the road as the sky darkened and the air turned icy. Evidently the stand had moved, since the guidebook's last printing, a half kilometer north.

When I got to the right corner, I was immediately surrounded by young and middle-aged men. It felt like the hectic floor of a stock exchange, except that everyone was speaking an odd tongue and, as I learned fast, the Kyrgyz notion of personal space allows for much more physical contact than ours. Forty drivers were vying for my attention, pressing in like a rugby scrum from every direction. I don't know why, but, instead of panicking or worrying, I had one of those moments when grace descended, as when a car goes out of control and time slows. Calm as a spy, I took in the swarm, making eye contact with each would-be driver in turn, apprising them, not judging, in a detached, almost paranormal state. I noticed a forty-year-old guy a row back who was also calm, and whose eye was kindly. I nodded to him and we walked from the throng. The other drivers immediately accepted the decision and backed away, keeping an eye out to see if negotiations broke down, but otherwise out of it, resuming the conversations my arrival had interrupted. My pick and I started drawing figures in the dirt and agreed on a price. We discussed time by pointing at his watch. He estimated eight hours to Sary-Tash. I somehow got him to understand I wanted to go first to the market in Osh, and so we would leave at 7 a.m., spend an hour in the market, and get to Sary-Tash before sundown. I wrote down the name and address of my motel. He winced when he saw the words weren't in Cyrillic, but we agreed he would take me there now to ensure he knew the way. I pointed left and right until we got there, and communicated, again with gestures, *see you in the morning.*

THE ROAD TO SARY-TASH

HE ARRIVED the next morning with his sixteen-year-old daughter, who was studying English at school. She worked us through each of the details—he wanted to be sure we understood each other, that he was taking me first to the market, and then just to Sary-Tash, definitely not to China, at the agreed-upon price. She was a sweet, smart kid, and he was very proud of her. We got in the car, dropped her off at school, and went on to the market in the city center.

In the buzzy market Kyrgyz men wore their tall, white and black, traditional felt hats, a few Pashtuns were in their turbans, and the Uzbek and Tajik men wore embroidered caps—I wasn't sure I could tell the difference, although most were Uzbek, who are almost half the population of Osh. One man of forty-five or so wore a fedora. Lots of young men and even some middle-aged ones had adopted baseball caps. The women tied their headscarves in the Uzbek manner or the Tajik or the Kyrgyz, although a few modern women went bareheaded. The market was a beautiful bustle: tables heaped with dried fruit, nuts, and vegetables, and butchers' stands with whole animals hanging, blood dripping from the noses. One butcher shop built into a wall had four beef feet, each from the hoof up to the first joint, not all from the same cow, unmolested except where they had been separated from their legs, hooves and hairy hide pristine, standing straight up in a row out front like an advertisement for something dire. Big buckets of intestinal fat waited to be prepared into heart-jamming meals. At the kumis stands, women ladled out bowls of the fermented mare's milk to the men. My driver had a big bowl, suggesting I have some, too, but it seemed early for alcohol. I just had to assume he knew what he was doing.

Modernity is always uneven. As I came down the road from Tashkent to Osh, shepherds and horse mongers on foot and on horseback moved great herds of animals, forcing cars and trucks to a halt. Occasionally I'd see a shepherd talking on a cell phone. In the market, too, traditional products, unchanged for centuries, mingled with the mass-produced plastic wares of the Chinese manufacturing machine—like the orange bowl from which my driver downed his kumis. Women in quasi-traditional dress, with enough gold plating on their teeth to thrill a hip-hop star, had fun with my camera. One woman in her seventies motioned me over to take her picture, and posed with her chin sticking out defiantly. I snapped one, showed it to her, and she waved me back to take another. This time she stuck her chin higher in the air. She checked that one, and sent me back again, enjoying putting me through my paces. When she saw the fourth one, her chin now Mussolini-high, a big smile on her face, she stabbed at the readout, and nodded. *Okay, good.* Her friends laughed. Below the market, along the river, newly ubiquitous Chinese metal shipping containers were teetering in stacks. A couple of men, who had perhaps slept in one of them, were bathing in the river, a swift stream fed by ice that had melted moments earlier. Horses and donkeys moved some of the freight, tractor-trailers and trains the rest.

AS WE HEADED EAST from Osh, we quickly encountered the timelessness of herding life. Yurts, yaks, fields of wild Asian poppies, groups of noble horses ranging across steep green pasture. The round cream-colored yurts, with brightly colored carpets for doors, seemed to pop out of the ground randomly along the hillsides, like mushrooms. The road was rough. We rattled along at twenty kph most of the time, slowing for washouts, climbing ever higher, even though the grade had been evened out and the path widened by the Soviets in the 1930s. The road was slow, tough, but not at all scary. As we got above the tree line, even the yurts fell away, and the land got emptier, almost pure stone. Every once in a while, a person would ride by on horseback, but at 11,000 feet, and then 12,000, that ceased. The world had turned to shard and gravel and slab and ice on a monstrous scale. I tried to imagine an army of Mongols coming across, with camels and horses and wagons, or, a hundred years later, Marco Polo with his retinue. What incalculable lunacy. Their highest point had been another 2,000 feet up; Soviet dynamite had lowered the threshold for us and already it was hard to breathe.

Descending from the oxygen-deprived pass, we entered the high, tough Alay Valley, a one-hundred-mile by twenty-five-mile stretch of often frozen land. Nomads still bring their herds there each summer, but it is otherwise impenetrable, ringed by the most stupendous snowy mountains, Himalayan-looking peaks upward of 24,000 feet. It was late afternoon when we reached Sary-Tash, a wind-battered, sun-blistered crossroads that looked more like an unkempt set of outbuildings than an actual town. To the southeast rose the Pamir Mountains, called "The Roof of the World" at least since the Victorian era, a translation from the Persian, proof that they have been inspiring awe in travelers from afar for a long time. They are where the Hindu Kush, the Himalayans, the Karakoram, and other ranges collide.

THERE WAS NO REAL HOTEL in Sary-Tash. One woman had the word *inn* painted (in Cyrillic, in Kyrgyz) on the front of her house and rented out a couple rooms, and I took one of them; she also had 'Café' (КОФЕ) painted on the front, but she didn't have a café. There were two places that served food in town, but the one I went to for dinner had very little to offer. I mimed eating to the proprietress, and she pointed to a small basket with a dozen eggs and a half-stick of bologna on the counter. I mimed asking if there was anything else, acting as if I were peering into a cupboard and holding my hands up in question; she shook her head no. I had eggs and bologna. The café was also a shop, and had a dozen bottles of Coke, a dozen of beer, boxes of juice, and for some unfathomable reason six pints of Armagnac on a shelf.

My room was clearly somebody's personal bedroom; somebody, in fact, who seemed to have only just stepped out. His clothes were hanging on hooks, and his other private stuff scattered around the room. What looked like a bed when I poked my head in, before agreeing to the $2.50 room rate, was technically a bed—that is, there was a bed frame, and a bedspread—but under the spread was not a box spring and mattress, just a neat pile of folded clothes and socks and accessories; the bed was basically a dresser or closet (the room had neither), and the rugs on the floor were the bed. The room was six feet by eight feet or smaller, and, without stretching much on my bed-mat, I could touch all four walls. On one of them was a garish Technicolor photo of a sweeping circular staircase; a McMansion piece of madness, an image of opulence that was—what? Compensation? Motivation? A spur to revolution? Or was it simply aesthetic, an image of beauty?

For a bathroom there was an outhouse fifty yards behind the house, with a rickety wooden door and two seatless holes for squatting. At dusk it was fine, although the temperature was already dropping fast. But when nature, or the bologna, called in the middle of the night, it was misery. Without an electric light within a hundred kilometers and scarcely a star in the sky, I was blind, and, the temperature now well below freezing, I was shivering my teeth out. I prayed I would find the holes without stepping in one of them. I put on every piece of clothing in my pack, a half dozen layers in all, all three pairs of pants and as many socks, clean and dirty, that would fit in my shoes. I was underprepared, obviously; the guidebook had indicated much more temperate lows. A flashlight, though, would have been smart, or remembering to bring my phone, but the combination of urgencies meant I couldn't turn back for it. I had to reach around like a blind man on the floor to properly set up and aim. It would have been wonderful to have running water when I made it back inside.

WHEN I GOT UP the next morning I found the family already out back, cooking up a batch of thickened yogurt in a huge vat set over a wood fire. The father and daughter added milk or wood once in a while as the grandmother stirred and directed, smoke engulfing them all. I walked out to the corner—there's only one corner, really, where the road splits to go east to China or west to elsewhere—to see if I could hustle up a ride.

A man was there with a car, a very old Mercedes, and after some haggling he agreed to take me to the Chinese border for $30. This really pissed off the other guy standing there, who the driver had apparently agreed to take to Osh (presumably for less), and I left them screaming at each other to get my gear. When I got back to my room, there was a breakfast of porridge and yogurt waiting for me on the floor. I ate it, grabbed my stuff, and headed out.

My landlady was standing outside my door with a young man, maybe twenty-five, maybe thirty. She pointed to his car, which was also a Mercedes, and said the word for 'China.' I asked how much. The kid carried a stick, and scratched $75 into the dirt. He had a strange energy about him, an odd affectlessness, and what struck me as crazy killer eyes. He was about my height, but built like a wrestler. His lined denim jacket, baseball hat, jeans, and work boots all looked new enough, like he wasn't hurting for money. An operator. He held himself like a bouncer looking for trouble, but it didn't matter, since I'd made other arrangements.

Thanks, I said, but I have a ride—pointing up toward the corner.

The driver said something to the landlady—she had very little English, the driver had none.

He go, she said. *Gone?* I couldn't believe it. I went out to look up the road.

Indeed, my driver was nowhere to be seen. Either another rider or two had shown up to go to Osh, or the original guy had outbid me. Or maybe this new guy had interfered. He was intense, and just a little menacing.

But at the moment he was my ride.

I tried to argue the $75 price with him, borrowing his stick to scratch $30, implying it was the going rate. He shook his head slightly, no, staring at me. He didn't offer a new number. I scratched $40. He took the stick back and wrote $75. He wouldn't budge, just kept his scary gaze on my eyes. I made a big *okay, okay* fuss, took his stick, and scratched $50.

No.

He was completely unmoved, like a mob enforcer letting you know there is no pleading to be done. I took my suitcase back out to the road, and walked up to the corner to wait for another car. This guy followed me over, low key, knowing he held the cards. The empty road stretched out, 1,500 kilometers to Kabul, more than that to Ürümqi, capital of China's Wild West. No vehicles moved. There wasn't even a horse to be seen. It was still cold, but the sun was ruthless, with 3,500 fewer meters of atmosphere to tame it. I told myself that if it had been my driver from yesterday, the good father, the straight shooter, I'd have paid the $75. But I didn't like this guy's look. I didn't want to get in a car with him.

Then I noticed, just off the side of the road, a half block up, a man readying a large old truck. The engine was idling and he was topping off water and checking levels while having his breakfast, brought to him piecemeal by his wife at the front fence. He washed it down with kumis and wiped his mouth on his sleeve, the diesel chugging. I walked up with my bag and said hello. My malevolent shadow came with me, and the two of them started chatting in Kyrgyz—of course they knew each other, I thought, it was a tiny town. I assumed they would collude and the truck driver would suggest $75. Instead he told Crazy Eyes his price, and Crazy Eyes started scratching it in the ground; he was still carrying his negotiating stick—or rather, since he didn't negotiate, his invoicing software. He was very deliberate—like a serial murderer, I thought—but eventually a new price was scratched out: $40. I said okay, thinking the guy with the car would come back now with a better price.

I looked again at the truck. It was beat up, and the ride even in a fresh truck, with good shocks, would be jarring. I really didn't want to do ten hours of rough road in it. But Crazy Eyes not only didn't counteroffer, he started walking back to his car. I yelled out after him, Okay, *$60!*—counting it out with six sets of jazz hands. He shook his head. I said, Okay, okay, $75, with seven fingers, then five fingers, but he shook his head, motioning that I was to get in the death-mobile. He got in his car, and drove off.

I was clearly in the grips of some kind of high mountain transportation cartel. The driver took one last swig of kumis, packed a couple liter bottles of it in his door, and we both climbed up into the cab. He revved the engine, pushed the recalcitrant transmission into gear, and started driving down what was very clearly the wrong road. I pointed in the right direction, but he waved me off. He was slightly drunk, eyes red and a little fluttery, the mare's milk having taken a toll. It was 8 a.m.

There were only two ways out of town, and this was the wrong one. I kept pointing behind us, saying China in every accent and variant I could think of. He turned to me and smiled, shook his head, and made a hand sign like *wait*.

We were out of the town already, but instead of turning around, he veered off the road altogether and started driving across an open field. There were other light tire tracks, going every which way, but no clear path. We seemed to be heading to what had to be a farmhouse, a half mile away. By the time we pulled up to the house, we were a mile or two out of town, and I was in full-bore fight or flight mode. The only sense I could make of this scenario was that I was being kidnapped. As we rounded the corner, into the farmyard, sure enough, I saw the serial killer's black car, parked as if hidden behind a wall.

What was I to do? Jump out and run?

Crazy Eyes came out, walked over to his car, got some things out of the trunk (I couldn't quite see what), and threw them with a loud clunk in the back of our truck. Shovels to bury me with?

Then he came around, opened the passenger side door and started to climb in.

No, no, no, I said, and hopped out. He shrugged and got in the middle.

What could I do? Leave my pack in the truck and run back to town? Try somehow to yank it out of the back and hop out, and end up miles from nowhere? What if there was an innocent explanation? What if jumping out just meant they killed me here? They were looking down at me, and seemed unsurprised by my distress, even amused. The one thing I knew was that I wasn't thinking entirely straight. Altitude? Mourning the loss of language? Still in an altered state, I climbed, warily, back into the truck, with Crazy Eyes staring at me from the middle seat, and we headed back to the road, then back to town, and then onto the highway, this time on the right road. We were on our way to the Irkeshtam Pass.

ACROSS THE HIGH PAMIR

AT ITS BEST, the road was rough. At its worst, it simply disappeared. Tire tracks would fan out in all directions, and my driver would pick one seemingly at random, sometimes the most traveled, sometimes the least. At times, the road would die altogether, only to be reborn a mile later as all these disparate improvised routes converged back together, like a miniature version of the Silk Road itself, which fanned across the continent, some variants north into Russia, some south as far as India, shifting with conditions.

A couple hours out of town we stopped for no apparent reason, and the driver and Crazy Eyes hopped out. I panicked again, thinking we'd arrived at a good place to bury me. There was not a living soul, nor any sign of humanity save the track we were on, as far as the eye could see.

But the reason for the break turned out to be more mundane: there was a slow leak in the front tire, which meant we needed to stop every hour or two and inflate it with a portable generator, hooked up to the truck battery. I would rev the engine for them while they stood outside and smoked. The truck was empty—one of the reasons the ride was so horrible, since a little weight would have smoothed it out a bit—but I wondered how often the tire would go flat once the truck was loaded with Chinese goods. All the eastbound trucks were empty; the trucks coming back from China full.

The empty trucks bounced noisily like ours. The full ones swayed dangerously through the ruts.

Every once in a while we'd see people—a yurt and a couple of horses, a clothesline in the wind—and sometimes we would stop and a man would pop up out of nowhere for a chat. The social lives of these guys were as ad hoc as their work lives, subject to the combined randomness of the truck driver's life, the unpredictable road, and the itinerancy of yak herds. Always it was tough, the driver sometimes having to slam and skid to a halt, back up, and find a way not to bottom out. At one point we stopped at the top of a ridge, after traveling a while on one of the roadless routes. The driver and Crazy Eyes got out to survey the vertiginous slope, like reading a diamond route on a ski mountain, or like a golfer and his caddy planning out the best approach. Staring down the hill, we could read like a tracker the battle that had gone on before our arrival, infer from the mud and trampling where trucks had gotten stuck in the muck trying to cross a stream bed. Where the wheels and axles had sunk, and had needed digging out.

After some kibitzing, they selected a route and raced down the hill, hoping to gain enough momentum on the descent to plow through the mud and get going up the other side. I braced myself against the roof with one hand, feet spread, legs rigid, the other arm hugging the door handle, all to try to keep from having my head slammed into the roof or window.

All this fear! My driver and Crazy Eyes felt none of it; for them, this was just a job. And my panic about getting killed? Why would these guys kill me? What would they do with my stuff? There was no fence in Sary-Tash, no particular need, no market for a beat-up old Nikon or decrepit Dell laptop. And besides, these men weren't criminals, were they, even if one looked like he was? And if I did die, the truck flipping down the side of some gorge, well, wasn't that the gamble I had taken? If I didn't like the odds, why had I taken the bet? Wasn't I, after all, here for a bit of danger, a bit of adventure? The fearsome, alluring end of things: why not approach it with a bit more dignity? After a few of these kamikaze runs, I started to put my two cents in, pointing out what I thought the best option. It went into the mix, and once we even went the route I suggested. I started praying for success rather than praying not to be maimed. It was an improvement.

Jammed into my corner, though, spine compressed for the hundredth time, it seemed like this ride would never end.

EVENTUALLY, OF COURSE, it did. At about 2 p.m. that afternoon we arrived at the first Kyrgyz border station, a small stone box of a building with some ragged flags flying. The driver saw me snap a picture and became very agitated—evidently, taking pictures was a bad idea. Crazy Eyes smiled his *you'll get what's coming to you* smile. I stashed the camera and got out my passport. This was the first of three border stations we would have to negotiate, and I wondered how much time it would take—and how much cash. Between here and the second Kyrgyz border station was ten kilometers of no-man's-land, followed by another ten kilometers of it before the Chinese border station.

We got out of the truck, and the guys started handing down my bag. I tried to have a discussion about whether our agreement included them taking me through to the actual border. Having no language in common again put me at a disadvantage. So did the fact that they set my pack on the ground and walked away. They were drunk, and clearly this was, for them, the end of the road. They knew better than I did that my shakedown was going to take much longer than theirs, and they had no intention of waiting.

I grabbed my pack and followed them into the border station, a ten-foot-by-ten-foot stone building with the whitewash peeling off. It had a dirt floor and a small wooden desk and chair, at which a slightly overweight man sat smoking, a Kyrgyz Sydney Greenstreet. A meager array of papers was spread in front of him, like in a play with a lazy propmaster. My driver and Crazy Eyes and I all handed our passports to the man. He took mine with his left hand without looking at me, so engrossing was the piece of paper in his right. A flunky motioned for me to go back outside. Crazy Eyes and the driver stayed. A few minutes later, they came out laughing, waved to me, got in their truck and left.

Every fifteen minutes another truck showed up. The drivers would get out, look at me, turn and go in, come out, wait for five minutes, get summoned to pick up their papers, and leave. I nodded hello and goodbye to each. I was finding it all oddly relaxing after the tense ride.

Eventually, an hour later, I stuck my head in the door, and the fat man looked up at me wearily. He must have been thinking, *can anyone really be this stupid? Is it worth it?* He tossed my passport six inches from where it was. I walked over to pick it up, and he slammed his hand on it. He looked me in the eye and asked me, in Russian, if I spoke Russian. I acted like I had no idea what he was saying. He took his hand off the passport and waved me off like I was a pesky child. An Uzbek truck driver was outside, and I waited for him to get his papers approved and offered him five Euro to take me to the real border.

At the next station, in fact, this Uzbek driver showed me the ropes. You put a five-Euro note in the middle of your passport and hand it over with your customs and immigration forms. You sail through. I assumed it was a shakedown because, surrounded by rocky mountains, the nearest real town hundreds of kilometers in any direction, that station clearly served absolutely no purpose—what could happen here that couldn't just as well happen at the real border?— except to give officials an opportunity to suck money out of the truck drivers a second time in each direction.

WHEN WE ARRIVED, the real border was closed for lunch. Trucks were backed up in six or eight lines, eight or ten deep. I felt vindicated; I couldn't have gotten through anyway. I spent an hour or so with a group of ragamuffin kids who never tired of posing and seeing themselves in my camera. They were seven or eight years old, just hanging out. Imagine growing up there! What a window on the world it must have been, watching the caravans pass and freight slide by along the Silk Road, as people had done for millennia. When the gates finally opened, I walked through. The customs man was facing a long line of impatient truckers, all of whom knew the drill. He leafed through my passport, looked at me with disgust, but had no time for playing games. He stamped it and yelled something at another border official, who pushed me in turn toward a Chinese driver in a gleaming new tractor-trailer. He must have washed and polished it while waiting for the border to open. The driver nodded, I climbed up into the cab, and we started across the line into China. We didn't talk.

The Chinese border station was clinically efficient and thorough. Men with mirrors on poles checked under and on top of every truck; cameras were poised everywhere; agents went through every compartment and took notes. There seemed to be dozens and dozens of them. I'd been slingshot from the busted-down past to the totalitarian future. As I made my way through the polished corridors of the brand-new customs building to receive my stamps and have my luggage x-rayed and rifled through by latex-gloved hands, I marveled at the money, the infrastructure. It felt like I hadn't seen infrastructure for days.

A couple of hours later, I hit the first, nameless town on China's westernmost tip. There I found a driver to take me— five hours away, it turned out, even on excellent road—to Kashgar.

THE CEMENT SALESMAN AND THE VILLAGER

BLANTYRE, MALAWI

I MET A MAN from Malawi—a well-fed, sweet, meek and earnest, suit-and-tied businessman—in the elevator of my dingy hotel in Dar es Salaam. He had, I suspected, a healthy-minded religious practice and a home life of placid and pleasant conventionality. It was the first time in Tanzania for both of us, and I asked him what he thought.

I don't want to disparage, he said, and hesitated. He was, above all, a polite man.

No, please, tell me, I said, I'm interested in your impression.

It is, he said, A bit chaotic, and—he hesitated again, and lowered his voice, although we were alone in the elevator—I am surprised to find it quite so dirty.

Yes, I suppose it is, I said, like many cities.

Blantyre, he told me with conviction, Is not like this. Blantyre is quite sharp! He said this with real pride, a pride whetted, it seemed, by what he had been seeing.

I have no picture of it in my mind, I said. The only image I have of Malawi is the lake.

You have been to the lake? he asked, proud, patriotic.

No, I said. But I'm going soon.

To Blantyre? Then you shall see. We had stepped off the elevator on the same floor.

Were you born in Blantyre? I asked.

No, I was born in a small village, but I managed well in school, and I was offered a position in Blantyre, with a French company.

And so you are here on business?

Yes, he said, although I was excited to be able to see the famous Dar es Salaam, so I stayed, not on the company, of course, for the weekend, and I have brought my wife as well.

The company is a good one? I asked. You are happy with the position?

Yes, very much, he said. We are a cement company, and as you see, we have international business, with which I am just now becoming more acutely involved—he had a consciously flowery elocution, and it occurred to me it may have been what he thought was expected of an international businessman. And, he added, I very much like that it is a French company.

Why is that?

The French are very exacting, he said.

I GOT TO SEE Blantyre a few weeks later. The airport looked like those tiny ones in the Midwest, built to deal with one or at most two planes at a time, that are being abandoned by the airlines and the FAA. Stairs are rolled by hand to the doors. The luggage is unloaded onto the bare floor just inside the terminal door. And the city itself is not, in fact, particularly sharp.

Blantyre is a fraction the size of Dar, and the colonial remnants are more prominent. The center has two unequal parts, the larger gray and dirty and noticeably impoverished—not a slum, not a favela, just a characterless, somewhat run-down, sleepy third world city, its poverty evident in the sidewalk tables loaded with broken and used merchandise, the single cigarettes for sale, the empty, dingy shops, and the soot-stained concrete. On one edge, though, sits a self-contained, almost upscale suburbanish shopping area, where the money, such as it is, congregates, and I imagined my cement salesman and his wife having lunch there. Most streets devolve into dirt roads at the edge of town, lined with makeshift sundry and food stands.

The cement salesman had recommended the Malawi Sun Lodge, and I headed there in the car I had rented at the airport. It, too, had a very small-town feel, like an attempt at luxury by a management and staff that had never actually experienced it. There were a half dozen tourist restaurants, none of which had much to offer. A couple of street salesmen waited to pounce on anyone wandering out of the Malawi Sun, but they eventually took no for an answer. The best food in town was to be had in a pap-and-stew place run by an Indian woman who had spent twenty years in Canada before resettling. She didn't have much of a reason to offer for the move. She shrugged and said it was easy to do business in Malawi.

THE LAKE AT CHEMBE

I DROVE up toward the beautiful lake and tried to get a sense of the local mores, stopping here and there to buy fruit on the side of the road and a couple handmade baskets, more in order to take pictures and talk to people than for the merchandise. I had a minor problem in Zomba, the largest town between Blantyre and the lake, with a drunken man in his thirties, a sun-flaked man who had lived outside so long it was as if he had bark—like sycamore or eucalyptus bark, peeling off here and there—on his face and arms and bare feet, feet that by the looks of his splayed toes had never, ever been in a shoe. At first he seemed just friendly, and perhaps a bit slow; I said hello and engaged him for a moment before I registered just how crazy he was. He was chronically drunk, his brain fried. People in the market where he made his demurely threatening gestures, pawing at me and trying to give me bear hugs, just watched, but I had a sense they would have intervened if things had gone sour. A man sitting outside a barbershop called over to me to say, Be careful, he's a thief!

Tradesmen glanced over from their work on a Pentecostal church a half block away, then returned to it. Vegetables were being sold. Ancient trucks were having malfunctions attended to. People were friendly, open, and for the most part, of course, quite poor. None were particularly interested in the white man wandering through, except to notice that the brain-damaged thief had latched on to me. He followed me back to my car, and I needed to start driving before he would allow the door to close.

He was the exception, though. Malawi is a peaceful, slow-walking country, the kind of place where people mosey and saunter, and except in Blantyre there's a noticeable lack of hustle. On the road north I stopped to buy a basket from a man with his wares on a rack made of saplings and cane, and much of his village came to kibitz. It was something to do on an otherwise uneventful stretch of road, for me and for them. It wasn't a hospitality culture—there was no sense that I needed to be welcomed or taken care of—but it was very relaxed. I bought a few things, took a few pictures. Nobody was much enthused one way or the other.

PAST MONKEY BAY on a dirt road I came to the lakeside village of Chembe. From there it was 550 kilometers of pure blue, almost due north, to the far end of the lake. The dusty village was constructed of local bricks, some buildings with thatched roofs, some with tin, and there was a set of cabins for rent from a nasty old hippie who was so uncommunicative I couldn't tell if he was originally German or Australian. A couple of young guys, brothers it turned out, offered to take me out to a perfectly picturesque island less than a mile offshore in a wooden skiff fitted with a small outboard motor. They promised that eagles roosted in the island trees, and when we got there, they threw some baitfish into the water. Dutifully, the enormous birds shot down and grabbed the fish, elegant and efficient. It was to me a novel form of symbiosis—wild animals and young men working for tips, together. The brothers were charming, spoke English well, and waxed lyrical about their desire for higher education and their inability to pay for it. It was ridiculously clear that this was bait, thrown in the hopes I would swoop down and drop dollars in their hands. I asked where they had gone to high school and if they needed to take any exams to qualify for a university slot, and their answers were hopelessly uninformed. I debated whether to coach them, to set them up for the next tourists. I decided against it. We talked about Malawi, and they were very proud of how beautiful the lake was, and how good the people were.

Non-Malawians, they thought, were full of anxiety, and rushed everywhere. They don't walk! the younger brother said—we had pulled up to the rocks and climbed ashore—and he did a comic version of an uptight Westerner, eyes to the ground, every muscle tense, stomping full speed as if angry. His brother laughed. You seem nice, though, the comic offered in apology, perhaps noticing that I recognized myself in his impersonation. I asked if taking tourists to see the eagles was their main job. Yes, they said. This is why we need education, the older brother said. We need to become more professional. The younger nodded, eager, hopeful.

DRIVING OUT OF TOWN, I picked up a boy hitchhiking. Or perhaps he wasn't a boy. When I picked him up, I thought he was twelve, but he could have been as old as twenty-five. Each time I glanced at him he looked different. He was going to see his mother, who was in the hospital with malaria. I asked if he was in school, and he said no. Did he work? No, he took care of his mother.

Oh, I said. Because she is sick?

No, she is in the hospital because she is sick, he said. I take care of her since my father died.

And what kind of work do you want to do? I asked.

There is no work, he said.

Did you ever think of going into Blantyre, or Lilongwe, to look for work?

No, he said, and he looked younger again. I tried that. But then I needed to come home, to take care of my mother.

Oh, right, I said. Because your father died.

Yes, he said. Of malaria. So I need to help my mother now.

I'm so sorry, I said. When did he die?

Two years ago, he said. Or maybe not two years.

He was a good-looking kid, but—and maybe this was unfair—he seemed chronically ineffectual. Between my questions he thanked me for picking him up, but he didn't ask a single question, not even inquiring where I was from or why I was there. Of course, I had been in the village a couple days—perhaps he already knew.

What do other people in the village do for work? I asked.

I don't know.

Some people work for the little hotel, I said. And there are hotels in Monkey Bay.

Yes, he said. The women do that.

Some people fish. Have you thought of fishing?

No, he said, with a slightly pained look, like maybe he had tried that, too. No, he said again, and, after a beat:

Fishing, that is just luck.

I waited a while to see what he might say, which simply meant we drove in silence. As we came into Mangochi, where the hospital was, I followed signs to it. He didn't offer directions.

Did you ever think of going back to school?

I can't, he said.

I looked over at him.

I have no one to help me, he said. It was not a request, just a simple fact.

I dropped him off. He thanked me with little emotion.

I hope your mother is okay, I said.

Yes, he said. She will be okay. She is in the hospital.

MUSIC AND NOSTALGIA IN UKRAINE

KIEV

AS RUSSIAN TROOPS rolled their monstrous beat-up tanks into South Ossetia in the summer of 2008, I was some five hundred kilometers away, on the Crimean peninsula in Balaklava, Ukraine. I was overlooking what Tennyson dubbed the Valley of Death, the famous setting for 'The Charge of the Light Brigade.' In late October 1854, some 670 British cavalrymen, outnumbered almost ten to one, charged at their Russian counterparts, broke through their lines, did a U-turn and came back, hacking away at the enemy from behind. They returned to their original position with 118 dead, 147 wounded, and fewer than 200 horses remaining. 'It's magnificent,' the French Marshal Pierre Bosquet is supposed to have said as he watched the carnage from the opposite hill. 'But it isn't war. It's madness.'

It is impossible, in this part of the world, not to think about war and bloodshed. It is especially unavoidable in the Crimea, a storied part of what historian Timothy Snyder calls 'the bloodlands'—that swath of territory trapped in the twentieth century between Russia and Germany, and perfectly capable of wreaking its own mayhem in its own right. Every town, every village, just about every crossroads, has a memorial to their WWII dead. When I rented my car in Kiev, Alexei, who runs the Budget office apparently single-handedly (he answers the line if you dial the airport office, the downtown office, the corporate office, the emergency line, or his cell number, which he gladly gives you), explained that I wasn't allowed to take the car into any of the neighboring countries.

Once, he said, shaking his head ruefully, we let a man take one of our cars to Moldova. We never saw the man or the car again. When I later rented a car in Moldova, the agent had a similar story about a Romanian. My guess is the Romanians tell the same story about Belarusians, and that the Belarusians in turn assume Ukraine is full of gangsters, thieves, and chopshops. But whatever the local opinions about their other neighbors, the overwhelming force on the border, for all these countries, is Russia.

I had always called the country *the Ukraine*, keeping it part of the small definite article club—the Sudan, the Philippines, the Dominican Republic, the Netherlands. The difference between *Ukraine* and *the Ukraine* was a live one, though, the definite article associated with the pre-independence Russian occupation—suggesting, as it does, a region rather than a country. Only the ethnic Russians, the former top dogs, preferred the definite article. Many of them, like those I talked to who applauded the arrival of Russian tanks in South Ossetia that week, pined for the good old days of the Soviet Union, and still considered the Ukraine somehow a region of Russia. For Ukrainian nationalists, using it is akin to calling Burkina Faso by its colonial name, Upper Volta, like not knowing when to say Burma and when Myanmar. Ukrainian ultra-nationalists were quite visible in the north. The Russians, as we have all since learned, were dominant in the south and east.

Ukrainian nationalism takes many forms. When the weather permits, traditionally dressed folk singers in needlepointed smocks, with coiled braids or decorated fedoras aloft, perform on the streets and in public squares, staking out their stretch of sidewalk among the emo singer-songwriters, electric violinists, and accordion-anchored cover bands. The music they play, like all folk music, is difficult to distinguish from its fakelore variants—'fakelore' being the term used by the American folklorist Richard Dorson in the 1950s to describe invented folk art, stuff that bears the same relation to tradition as a message at the end of a game of telephone bears to the original. British historian Eric Hobsbawm called these quasi-erroneous folk expressions 'invented traditions,' which develop in periods of dramatic social change as a source of collective identity. The reinvention of Ukrainian folk music traditions has nineteenth-century roots, as part of a revival jump-started by classical composers, who used 'folk' motifs in their own work.

In the 1920s the Ukrainian Diaspora in Canada and the United States reinvigorated this folk revival, influenced by the North American interest in blues, bluegrass, and other roots music. The Soviet Union, as was its wont, carefully monitored music and art so that in the 1920s and 1930s, just as Ukrainian music was being regularly recorded in New York and elsewhere, the Soviets clamped down on most of it at home, especially that large part of the repertoire that was liturgical in origin, and Russified the rest. In other words, much of what is celebrated by Ukrainians as thousand-year-old village music was written in the 1880s in Kiev, where it was significantly crossbred with European art music and the hybrid ethnic musics of surrounding countries, then rearranged for recording purposes in 1920s New York, reconceived once more by the Soviets in the 1930s, and then 'purified' of Russian influences by Ukrainian new nationalists after 1991.

The resulting sedimentary music elicits strong feelings, though, whatever its provenance, and fans angrily defend its Ukrainian authenticity. When someone raved about the traditionalist band Dreva on a website, oohing and aahing about 'the Slavic soul' he heard expressed on their recordings, another responded, 'How about calling it Ukrainian, not Slavic! Ukrainian! Get it? We are sick and tired of being lumped into some Slavic nation. "Slavic" to a Russian means subjugating all other Slavs under Russian domination. This is not music to Ukrainian ears.' A clip on YouTube of a Ukrainian a cappella folk ensemble singing in Russian brought a flurry of condemnations of cultural imperialism, claiming it was a deliberate attempt to insult Ukrainians and their language.

Such cultural nationalism often surrounds folk music, and in the case of one folk group I saw in Kiev it did so literally. I stopped to listen to a trio of middle-aged Ukrainian performers in traditional peasant dress singing folk songs with gusto to a fairly large, appreciative crowd. For a new visitor to the Ukraine, unschooled in the conflict, this folk group had no political resonance; to me they sounded, well, Slavic. But I recognized both the impulse toward cultural preservation—the desire to capture a bit of culture about to be washed away in the global flood of new popular forms—and the artificiality of the performance. The costumes the singers wore looked more like every other folk costume made since 1970 than they looked like the clothes worn by actual peasants a century and more ago. And, perhaps most obviously, the accompanist with the circular braids (the semi-official hairdo of the Ukrainian nationalist, sported, for instance, by then–Prime Minister Yulia Tymoshenko) wasn't playing traditional instruments but synthesized versions of them on a Yamaha electronic keyboard.

Standing to the right of the performers, practically sharing the stage with them, was a group of young men, full of feeling, roused by this music to an oddly angry sense of community, almost daring passersby to ignore the significance of the performance. They were in their twenties and thirties, their heads closely shorn, with a few tattoos and facial scars, and in this land of genocide it was hard to miss the historical echoes in their incensed pride. They found in this regional folk culture an ideal image of their own place in history, not unlike the young men attracted to white supremacy groups or other terrorist organizations: underemployed youth who embrace isolationist right-wing nationalisms, resent the impositions of modernity, and blame their own plight on its arrival.

MOTHER RUSSIA

THE PRIME ENEMIES of the Ukrainian nationalists—perhaps explaining the embattled, truculent air of the folk performers and their angry fans—were the ethnic Russians in their midst, the very people who have since welcomed the annexation of Crimea and have been fighting alongside Russian troops in eastern Ukraine. Like the anti-Georgians in South Ossetia and Abkhazia, many of these ethnic Russians, almost a fifth of the population, have long felt they were better off under the Soviet Union and welcomed reannexation.

In Sevastopol, a seaport further down the Crimean peninsula, a woman tried to explain it to me. She was sitting in the patio bar in front of my hotel, cadging beers and perhaps looking for evening work. Her family had originally come from Russia, but had been in Crimea for many generations.

First, she said, Ukrainya—almost spitting out the Ukrainian pronunciation—is not a real country. We are Russians, ethnic Russians and everyone else; we are all Russian. The Ukraine, this bit of ground, has always been either Russia or Poland. I am translator, she said. I know! The language is not even a real language!

Since she was the only translator at the table I gave her the benefit of the doubt on this, and it turns out to have a sliver of truth. Russian and Ukrainian speakers only began needing translators to understand each other in the mid-seventeenth century. The Soviets tried to minimize use of the language, while the post-1991 Ukrainian government has instituted a series of measures to increase its centrality.

Which is stupid, my translator fumed. It is a pidgin. Half Russian, half Polish—but more Russian. We are *Russian*!

As she said this, she sat more solidly and proudly in her chair, arms folded across her chest in a pose that dredged up my own vague TV-news memories of the petulantly defiant yet self-satisfied Nikita Khrushchev and Leonid Brezhnev. She worked translating between Russian and Greek (Greece is only seven hundred kilometers away across the Black Sea, and the Crimea is closer to Athens than it is to Moscow), and she was one of a number of people I spoke to who yearned for the Soviet years. She looked to be in her thirties, which meant she'd been just a child when the Soviet Union fell and everything changed. Still, she had no doubts about how much better things had been.

Yes, life was better in Soviet Union. I know. My mother tells me. I read history books, she said. People who were alive, yes, you can say I don't remember very much, but people, everyone, they know: life was better. Everyone had job, now everybody don't have job, looking. In Soviet times, university is free, now pay. Russia everyone have medical, like Sweden, like Switzerland, now no one have medical, pay money for everything.

Some of her talk had the ring of standard anti-modern complaints: in the good old days, everyone knew their neighbors (she seemed unaware that someone like me would immediately think of the Stasi, or the KGB, using people's neighbors against them). People used to help each other. Nobody went hungry. And some were more culturally specific. In Soviet times, she told me, You could drink vodka. Ten, twelve vodka and have no head in morning. Now you have three, four vodka and head is terrible in morning. She frowned and smiled at the same time, like a Russian Schopenhauer.

Surely there were some things that weren't so great about the past, I suggested. Stalin's secret police, for instance—

Stalin! she cut me off. Now, *they*, she said, tossing her head northward, they all say how bad he was. You know, they want the restitutions, what do you call it? Reparations? So they all pretend they don't like Stalin. But I tell you this: we all know, without Stalin—and she shook her head back and forth for emphasis, again puffed with pride—without Stalin we don't win the Great War. Stalin *made* Russia the power.

The idea that there are people in the former Soviet states who long for the good old days was not a complete shock. Change always creates nostalgia, and there were beggars in the streets, casualties of capitalism; whatever safety net was in place had gaping holes. The deco grandeur of these Black Sea towns (Odessa, Sevastapol, Yalta) that Vladimir Nabokov remembers from his youth is long gone, the paint and plaster peeling off into the street, some buildings just shells. But still, her overt Stalinolatry surprised me. Stalin's mass starvation of Ukraine in 1932 and 1933—when an estimated seven to eleven million Ukrainians died as he shipped the grain they grew back to Russia, executing those who had the temerity to steal some for themselves, and sending new Russian immigrants to take over their farms—would seem to militate against it. Certainly the Ukrainian skinheads angrily appreciating traditionalist music in Kiev know the story and had no desire to see any revival of Russian power, much less any new Russians coming across the border.

A WIFE IN KISHINEV

NOT ALL UKRAINE'S ethnic Russians, in 2009, cared about such things. In Odessa, for instance, I met a cabdriver named Nicolay who looked at me blankly when I asked him about it. Nicolay approached me at the airport where I had just returned my rental car. I had booked a flight for Athens at six the next morning, and needed to drop off my rental car before the agency closed. I was about to get the bus back to my hotel when Nicolay grabbed me. There was the standard haggle over the fare, except that instead of revising his price downward to meet mine, he increased the good-natured boisterousness with which he argued for the reasonableness of his original offer. Inexplicably I finally agreed with him, and we headed for my hotel.

He had some local music on the radio and I asked about it. He held out his hand toward the radio, palm up, in a kind of *What is this?* gesture, and popped the radio off.

Tonight I go Kishinev! he announced apropos of nothing, happily, with a keen gleam in his eye. Kishinev is the Russian name for Chişinău, the capital of Moldova.

Ah, too bad! I said, in part because his enthusiasm was a little infectious. I want to go to Kishinev, but I have run out of time.

Yes? Yes! he yelled, ecstatic, bouncing in his seat. We go, Thomas! We had exchanged names within minutes of meeting. Look! he said, reaching under the glove compartment, where, from deep within the plastic cover of the heating system, he pulled out his passport. He did this while screaming through Odessa's formidable traffic, like everyone else driving way too fast, aggressively.

Here is me, he said, pointing to his passport picture, turning to show me, sitting almost sideways in the driver's seat, facing me, and steering with his left thigh. Nicolay, he said. Or Nicholas, if want. And look!—he continued, flipping through page after page in the fattest passport I'd ever seen, with dozens of identical Moldovan and Ukrainian stamps to the page. See? Every day I go Kishinev! I have wife there! We go!

He hadn't looked at the road for minutes, but was managing about seventy kilometers an hour and somehow weaving between trucks. He paused, waiting for my assent.

I'm sorry, I said. I can't.

He faced front briefly and held out his hand in supplication to a bus he felt had cut him off. *Jeezaman!* he said to the bus, a word I wasn't sure was Russian, Moldovan, Ukrainian, or English. Okay, he said, slapping the dash to convey finality. We go tonight, Kishinev, three hour, tomorrow, back, Odessa!

I'd love to, but I have to go to Athens tomorrow, in the morning.

Athens, he said, trying to place it.

Afeeni, I said.

Okay, Afeeni! No problem! Today Kishinev, tomorrow Kishinev, Afeeni.

No, I can't do that, I already bought the ticket to Athens from here, Odessa.

This stumped him for just a moment, but then he lit up again. No problem! You change! Here is my house! he said, jerking the car hard left onto a side street, tires squealing. Sergay is here, sleep. He very good English, translate.

Sergay was his son, also a cabbie. But the road was closed, a big backhoe digging it up.

Fuck you! he yelled at the construction mess in front of him, yanking his car back into the traffic.

A block farther, he pointed to his own head—he'd had an idea.

This where I live, no traffic, bullshit, he said, swerving onto a side street, almost hitting a dog ambling across. He honked at it, held his upturned hand toward it over my knee. Jeezaman! he said disgustedly at the dog's effrontery. The street was potholed but empty. So you go, me, to Kishinev, he said, only a hint of question in the statement. Two hundred dollars only. Sleep little money, eat little money, girl little money, tomorrow, back, Odessa, Afeeni! He clapped his hands horizontally at this last word, the upper one making like a plane to Athens.

I'm sorry, I said. Six a.m. flight . . .

I was madly trying to remember each of his sentences, perfect poems that sprouted at the slightest provocation. When I asked about the changes since independence, he summed up what he saw as the problem:

Every day, business, people, China, people, China, business, business, business, fuck you! These last two words were directed at a forty-five-degree angle out the front window toward the general state of things. I started to type some into my phone while trying to convince him I couldn't come to Kishinev.

When I asked if things were easier before 1991, he shrugged.

Now? he said. Marlboro Red? In Kishinev? One dollar! Odessa? Four dollars! His needs, he insisted, were modest.

For me? he said, Little beer, little chichi, little cigar! Good! Korea car? he asked rhetorically, slapping his steering wheel. Good car! Small petrol!

Can you take me to the airport in the morning? I asked.

No, I go Kishinev, he said, sadly, since he had finally accepted I wasn't going with him. It would have been a huge fare for a trip he was taking anyway. I tell Sergey come get you, he said. Good English, Sergey.

POWER

I TRAVELED ON to Athens and then Lesvos, where I stayed with my American expat friend John. He's a musician, so I told him about the music I had found in Ukraine, including the omnipresent Ruslana, the Ukrainian singer who won the 2004 Eurovision Song Contest. She mixes Carpathian folk tunes into her technopop and goes the peasant look one better with weird comic-book outfits that are part cavewoman, part faux-medieval, part heavy metal, and part Madonna. John talked about klephtic music, which takes its name from the kleftes (Greek warriors who fought against the Ottoman occupation), another stream of folk music with overt political meanings. But he was most excited about Gogol Bordello, a band led by Ukrainian-born Eugene Hütz, which mixes Eastern European gypsy music with a dozen other influences. John's half-Greek, half-American daughter sang along as he played me a cut from their album *Multi Kontra Culti vs. Irony*. Then, from their energetic live album, he played 'Mussolini vs. Stalin,' a fun nuevo-gypsy tune with the lyric:

> *Mussolini was a-shavin', whistlin' Tarantella*
> *Stalin was keeping eye on barbeque*
> *When their fish line bell started to jingle*
> *Mussolini caught a-nothin', Stalin caught two.*

And Gogol Bordello had sent him to find Vladyslav Troitskyi, who started as a pure folk revivalist, but whose latest project had been influenced by Hütz. It was a group called DakhaBrakha Ethno-Chaos Band, which takes a retro-peasant-shirt-wearing, traditional-instrument-playing ensemble and mixes it with rock, hip-hop, art-school experimentalism, and an eclectic mix of urban world music. Troitskyi is determinedly putting the multi in the culti. Instead of dreaming of a pure ethnic past, DakhaBrakha, like Gogol Bordello, embraces the 'ethno-chaos' of today's world.

This sense of making do, of resigned muddling through—even when, as in the case of Nicolay, seeing your wife requires crossing two borders, both of them disputed—may be more widespread than the inflamed nationalism of the Kiev skinheads or that of my Russian translator in Sevastopol. For the moment, the Russian ethnic loyalists seem to be winning in Crimea and the Eastern Ukraine, and the Ukrainian nationalists in Kiev. But across the region, the collapse of socialism and the inequities of the capitalist transition have left old women in babushkas picking through garbage to survive, and veterans with their legs blown off by land mines begging in the streets. Ethnic Russians and ethnic Ukrainians alike may bask in ideologically fecund nostalgia, and like the American nostalgics that want to return to the America of their forefathers, their emotional fantasies simply make them pawns in games of real power, whether those of shock doctrine conservatives in the United States, of political cronyism in Ukrainian politics, or brazen Russian expansionism.

I don't want to go anywhere, my translator in Sevastopol said to me. I love Kryms'kyy—the Russian word for the Crimea—I don't love Ukrainya, I love Kryms'kyy. Krmys'kyy is Russia, not Ukrainya. She took a swig of beer and gazed into the near distance.

Well, I started to say—

It was also Polish once, yes, she said, acknowledging that things are more complicated than that, even if it wasn't where I was going. But then Russia, she *takes* it—and as she said this, she made a big gleeful sweep of her arm across the table, like a poker player raking in chips. She smiled proudly, even wistfully.

Some day, she said, Russia, she takes all her children home!

She was right about Crimea, as it has turned out. I wonder if she might have decided, since then, that she was otherwise wrong—that Mother Russia was never the mother she imagined, or, at least, that she was now a very different kind of mother. I often think of this woman, as Russia continues straining at its frontiers. And I think of Nicolay, as well. What has come of his border-hopping under the new regime? His needs were simple; I fear they might well have become more complicated.

SINHALESE, TAMIL, HINDU, MUSLIM

COLOMBO, SRI LANKA

IN 2009, when I arrived in Colombo, a three-decade civil war was still raging between the Sri Lankan government and a separatist group called the Tamil Tigers. The Tigers controlled the Northern Province completely, and were strong in some of the eastern provinces. Armed conflict—all-out war—raged across hundreds of miles, with the Sri Lankan army periodically advancing into Tiger territory only to be beaten back. The Tigers had also engaged, for thirty years, in sporadic terror attacks, planting bombs in Colombo, by far the largest city, and Kandy, the religious center. The war was fought along both ethnic and religious lines, pitting the Buddhist Sinhalese majority against the mostly Hindu Tamil minority. Seedy, ragtag Colombo, after all these years of war, had checkpoints every mile or two on every road. Police, army, and private security guards armed with heavy weapons were everywhere. My tuk-tuk driver was hauled over to show his papers every five minutes.

The tuk-tuk driver's name was either Julian or Julius—he nodded vigorously to both when I tried to clarify—and he was my driver every day I was in Colombo, always waiting when I left my hotel. I may have been his only fare for that ten days. Everything about him splayed: his always bare feet had bulbous toes that looked stretched out to hit an octave on the piano, his legs were always hanging out both sides of the cab, his conversation never stayed on track, he waved his arms like an Italian. He was, according to the racial categories of the place, a Burgher, of mixed European—mostly Portuguese, it looked—and Asian descent, and he spoke in a strong and poetic Creole that was often impossible for me to decipher. He had a crazy energy and was always concocting things for me to do, places he could take me. He had no particular opinion about the war. When I asked about the checkpoints, he explained that they were there because of the bombs, that the police were looking for bombs, which of course I knew already. He was the kind of guy who doesn't expect to ever, in any way, have an impact on politics, and so observed it all, when he did, from a distance. Each time we were pulled over, he explained it again—bombs—always with the same cheerful sense of inevitability. All his life the war had been going on, and it concerned him no more or less than the rain—like rain, it had some impact on his life; he had no impact on it.

Sometimes at the checkpoints I'd be asked for my passport, but I could tell they weren't really interested in me—the American wasn't going to bomb anything. I suspected they checked my papers out of pure curiosity or boredom. At most stops, men in two or three different uniforms—army, police, security service, it was never clear who was who—would be working together, perhaps, I wondered, to prevent mutinies or collusions. They all seemed so friendly, benign. How could they be at war? Where did they store the hatred?

Julius wanted to drive me to Kandy, even though it could be as much as four hours each way. He explained that he could pack an extra gas can. But I didn't think I could suck tuk-tuk exhaust for that long. When I told a breakfast waiter I wanted to go to Kandy, he said his cousin would take me in a very nice car. We agreed on a price, and the cousin picked me up the next morning. He was a very proper, clean-cut Sinhalese family man.

I asked him, as we crawled through traffic leaving Colombo, how the war with the Tigers would end. He looked straight out his windshield, not at me, but he didn't hesitate:

The Tamils need to go home, he said. Back where they came from, to be among their own kind.

KANDY AND THE BUDDHA'S TOOTH

IT IS TRUE that the Sinhalese have been on the island longer than the Tamils. The Sinhalese arrived from Bengal in the sixth century BCE, the Tamils in the third century BCE. It is also true that the British brought in many Tamil workers for the tea plantations in the nineteenth century. As far as I could tell, the Sinhalese didn't make this distinction—for them, the Tamils who had been there for twenty-three centuries were the same kind of foreign intruders as those that had been there for two.

The road to Kandy was interrupted every so often by semi-permanent army posts, stacked high with green sandbags, and the town itself had a post next to every temple and every important building. The Tigers had twice blown up Kandy's most sacred spot, the Temple of the Sacred Tooth. The temple, as advertised, protects a relic tooth of the Buddha, smuggled onto the island in the fourth century. It was bombed first in 1989 and again in 1998. Eight years later, people were again, or were still, jumpy.

The Sinhalese have a scary pride in their racial superiority to the Tamils, and Kandy is their sacred mountain, the keeper of the Sinhalese flame. The local restaurants feature traditional Sinhalese dancers and music, the museums display self-congratulatory exhibits on Sinhalese history. This is not a society interested in multiculturalism. In Sri Lanka's first post-independence government in 1948, the Sinhalese prime minister had Tamils in his cabinet. But in 1956, nativist Sinhalese S.W.R.D. Bandaranaike was elected Prime Minister, calling himself the 'defender of the besieged Sinhalese culture.' He purged the government of Tamils and introduced an act restricting service in the government to Sinhalese. Hundreds of thousands of Tamils emigrated. Others fought.

KANDY, BEING A TOURIST MECCA, is full of touts.

Hello! Remember me? From the hotel? a man on the

street said as soon as I walked away from my driver. My hotel was back in Colombo, of course.

No, I don't remember, I said, smiling.

Really? the man asked, smiling back, with a friendly twinkle in his eye. I could tell from his curly hair that he was of mixed heritage. He seemed bright and not at all sleazy, despite the obvious dishonesty.

Will it just go on forever, this war? I asked.

He shrugged, hands out, as if to say, How can a poor man like myself know such things?

The second tout who approached, a few minutes later, said, Hi! He waited for me to respond, and then said, hopefully, I am from your hotel? He made a vague gesture toward the center of town. He looked Sinhalese, although it was not always easy to tell.

Hi, I said. We were standing near a stack of green sandbags, behind which three men in uniforms sat, with guns between their knees. I asked him the same question: Will this war go on forever?

No, he said. The Tamils don't belong here. The British brought them here. One day we will defeat them and they will go home to India.

The Indian state of Tamil Nadu lies directly across the Palk Strait. Indian Highway 43A heads east, and having crossed a bridge, ends at the tip of Rameswaram Island; Sri Lankan Highway A14 heads west, crosses a marsh and ends on Mannar Island. The two are separated by less than thirty kilometers of water.

The Sinhalese trace their ancestry to Prince Vijaya, who sailed down with 700 followers from what is now West

Bengal and conquered the central, western, and southern parts of the island in 543 BCE. Those 700 have become fifteen million. They make up 75 percent of Sri Lanka's population, and excepting the three provinces that have a Tamil majority, the Sinhalese make up 90 percent. Sri Lankan Moors—Muslim descendants of Arab traders who also speak Tamil—and people of mixed European and other ancestry, like Julius, make up the remainder. The tension between the Buddhist Sinhalese and these other groups dates back thousands of years. The Indian Tamils that invaded in the third century BCE ruled the island as recently as the ninth and tenth centuries, albeit briefly. The Indian Tamils that now live in the central highlands do not descend from them, but from the workers brought in by the British from Tamil Nadu for the coffee, rubber, and tea plantations. They have 'only' been in Sri Lanka for one hundred to two hundred years; sending them 'back' makes as much sense as sending three-quarters of all living Americans 'back' to some ancestral homeland.

A shopkeeper, where I had stopped to buy water, and who until this subject came up had been very sweet and simpatico, turned vicious when I brought up the subject.

They are animals, he said. They live like animals, they should die like animals.

As many as 40,000 did, indeed, die like animals just a few months later, as the army pushed into the north and finally, for the time being, quashed the rebellion. There is now a Lessons Learnt and Reconciliation Commission at work—the reconciliation commission having become the signature institution of a fratricidal culture.

A third tout approached, smiling. Hello, he said. Remember me? From the hotel?

UP A TREE

A COUPLE DAYS after returning to Colombo, again forsaking Julius and his tuk tuk, I took a series of local buses south, along the sea, an endless stretch of coconut palm beaches sprinkled with small towns, to quaint Galle, at one time Portuguese and still full of colonial filigree, at the bottom of the island. On the way back, around one hundred kilometers south of the capital, I hopped off the bus and wandered into the village of Dodanduwa, set on a large lagoon. A man hailed me and tried to sell me on the idea of taking a ride on a raft. He was wearing a sarong. He looked tired, with a sad-sack air about him that made me want to buck him up, so I said okay.

I followed him down a path, through some trees. My mental warning system began to sound. *Okay Tom, not entirely smart, walking into the woods with a stranger.* But it quickly opened onto the lagoon, where a couple of guys were sitting on a raft made from two plastic canoes and some rough boards, lashed together with faded blue nylon rope. They looked like they knew exactly how dreary an idea it was.

I said, Hello, waved, and they said nothing.

Very nice ride, the man in the sarong said.

I said, No, thank you, not ready to get into multiple negotiations about fares, and not in the mood for taking a chance on their less than seaworthy craft. I started to head back to the road.

My shadow followed me, and said, Come see a beautiful Buddhist temple.

I didn't trust his judgment after the raft idea, and tried to suggest, gesturally, while he continued wheedling his case, that we were parting ways, walking backward with a sad smile, shaking my head, saying Thank you, no, thank you.

It's very nice temple, he said, sleeping Buddha, standing Buddha, not in guidebook.

I stopped. *Not in the guidebook?* This I liked.

How far? I asked.

Very close, he said. Just down this road. He pointed behind him without looking.

Okay, I said, why not.

This way, he said, with a courtly sweep of his arm, though still with the fatigued face.

We started walking down a road, having a little chat. His name was Sunil. He was born there in Dodanduwa. He was better at speaking English than understanding it. The road was decaying asphalt with a house on either side every hundred yards or so, then every two hundred. Then the road crumbled into wet dirt, the houses stopped, and the jungle grew close. It got very dark, fully canopied, with occasional glimpses of what I assumed was the lagoon on my left.

The dense foliage opened up briefly as we passed a small copra mill. An antique gas engine chugged and turned a loud, belt-driven shredder. Coconut shells were shoveled in one end, which sounded like spoons in a garbage disposal, and the shredded copra flopped out of the front. Two women shoveled the copra onto a mat and hauled it across the road to dump into piles, presumably to be picked up later. It was hot work, and the women looked like they had spent a lifetime on the manual labor rack and three or four days in the clothes they had on. They agreed to a photo, not because they cared, but because it gave them a few seconds of rest. They worked hard, every day, it was clear, and the fact that a random tourist had shown up, and was taking their photo, and was showing them the photos—none of this was interesting enough to warrant a smile.

Then the jungle closed in again. We had been walking for well over a mile.

Where is the temple? I asked.

Just here, he said, pointing up the road.

Just around that corner?

Yes, he said.

A old man, maybe seventy-five, maybe older, came by on a bicycle, his sarong hiked up above his knees, and my guide and he exchanged what seemed to me to be a conspiratorial wink and short laugh, making me nervous. The idea kept popping into my head that I was being led into a mugging. Something about Sunil's furtive dourness had me on edge.

Another mile or so later, we seemed to be walking forever. It was hot and humid, and I had gone on automatic. I wasn't happy, but also wasn't ready to let all this walking go for naught. We came to a short stretch of sunlight, and I thought, *what am I doing?*

Look, he said.

Through a break I could see a large tree, copiously hung with what looked like oversized avocados.

Fruit? I asked.

Bats, he said, nodding.

Excuse me? I zoomed in with my camera. They were bats.

Bats! I said. They were enormous. And promiscuous—there were thousands of them.

Yes, bats, he said. I looked at him, wanting to share my amazement at hundreds of ten-pound bats hanging in a midday tree. He avoided my gaze. Why? And why still so sad-sack? It looked, I decided, like guilt. What was he feeling guilty about? No wonder I was on edge.

Bats, I said. He started walking on; I stood.

I think I'm turning around, I said, pretending some exasperation.

He said, again, Temple right up here, soon. I hesitated, but I followed.

The vegetation closed back in, and a couple hundred yards into the darkness once again, I saw something large move in a tree on the right.

What is that? I asked, pointing.

He looked and shrugged.

Nothing, he said.

As we got closer, I could see: there was a man, fifteen feet up a tree, standing on a branch.

We were now several miles from town. Was I paranoid to think I was being ambushed?

I pointed to the man and said, What is this?

Nothing, nothing, he said, pretending the man wasn't there.

There's a man in that tree.

Oh, yes, he said, and proceeded to have a conversation in Sinhalese with the man in the tree.

I kept walking. The man in the tree seemed amused. Laughed. What did that mean?

My guide shuffled, in his Droopy Dog way, to catch up with me. A half mile later I stopped and said, okay, forget it, we're too far, I'm turning back.

He pleaded with me. Please, please, soon, he said, please, beautiful temple, right here. The worried dent between his eyebrows looked permanent.

I'm not sure why, I'm really not, but I relented and trudged on. The jungle was darker than ever. The man in the tree, was he coming? What was he waiting for?

AND THEN, we turned a corner, and there was light. And some kind of structure. As we got closer I saw a couple of boy monks in orange robes, ten years old, sweeping the end of the road with straw brooms, at the gates of a temple.

An extensive temple complex, stepped up the side of a hill.

It was beautiful, fantastic. A mammoth Buddha reclined in one room, its feet twelve feet high. Many others full of brightly colored standing Buddhas, sitting Buddhas, bodhisattvas, and mandalas. Outside, along the stone stairways, were a series of statues, made of what looked like papier-mâché, also brightly painted. They depicted sages and saints, many in inexplicable and horrible scenes—a man holding his own severed head, two men sawing through the crotch of another beheaded man, or perhaps it was the same man, farther along in his unfortunate story. The statues varied in height, some life-sized, some smaller. Some, like a woman with the immense fire-spitting face of an irate truck-stop waitress, were eight feet tall. She was holding a ten-foot pole stuck in a tall tub—making butter? A mortar and pestle? Grinding some little person to death? She was like the scariest second-grade teacher in all of history, glaring down at the world.

My guide showed me around, stating the obvious with a solemnity meant to cement his tip, and ushered me into the main room of the monastery. An older monk, the abbot, I supposed, came in on cue, and my guide did his version of a formal introduction. The monk ignored him utterly. To me he said what seemed to be welcome, but not in English (my guide: He says welcome). The abbot was very grave, but at the same time charming and solicitous. He showed me a picture of his predecessor, a painting on the wall of a man who looked exactly like him—the same bald head and saffron robe, of course, but also the same glasses, the same shape to the skull, same round face, same age, same apprising eye. He pointed to a guestbook, and invited me to sign.

The guestbook had been frequently handled, with an old-fashioned, thick board cover, each vellum-thick page lined with columns for one's name, address, and donation amount. Beside the book was a donation box. Each of the people who signed before me had left a donation, and it looked like each of them had had a schoolboy-forged zero added to the amount. Everyone had apparently left one or two dollars, all made into a clumsy ten or twenty dollars, a skinny zero sometimes squeezed in before a period. Nobody seemed to be falling for it. The abbot watched me put two dollars in the donation box, snorted contemptuously, and left in a huff.

WITHOUT A PADDLE

THE MONASTERY was on the lagoon, as it turned out, and my guide wanted to take a raft back. Much faster, he said. It did feel like we had done a big loop to get there, so that crossing by raft might be faster. I asked how much.

Anything. What you want.

Like a couple dollars?

Yes, he said, No problem. We walked down to the lagoon, and the guys we had seen back in town were waiting in a small inlet, clearly having rowed down to meet us. The younger of the two was in the back of the portside canoe, the old man in the front, each with a paddle. My guide climbed into the backseat of the starboard canoe, and I started to get in the front, but all three of them motioned for me to sit in the center, on the slats lashed together, the seat of honor.

The boatmen pushed off with their oars against the bottom and turned the raft around. Instead of heading across the lagoon, though, we headed into a mangrove thicket.

Hey, I said.

Yes, my guide said, very nice.

The swamp was thick with dead and live plants, each tree's outspread roots plunging into the water on a fan of angles, and vines and half-fallen trees crisscrossing just above our heads. They formed a maze of dark tunnels, just large enough for us to pass through. The trees seemed alive with threat, and in fact they were: as we passed under a large branch, I saw an eight-foot lizard lounging, menacingly. I turned to look at the boatman and he studiously avoided my gaze, as did my guide.

The swamp got thicker, and darker, and what was that on the right? A bright blue piece of flotsam—another tourist's jacket? If I decided I had to make a break for it, could I? Could I swim in this water? Were there other lizards in it? What else? Would I get caught in a maze of roots and vines? Covered in leeches? I was getting a little panicky—paranoia and claustrophobia, a bad combination.

And then, out of the gloom ahead, I heard voices. *Oy, I thought, here we are. The endgame.* I couldn't swim out, obviously—no matter what was in the water, I wouldn't know which way to go. There were three against me on the raft, and it sounded like at least three more ahead. I was at their mercy. An overload of fight-or-flight adrenaline was beginning to make me queasy.

AS WE CAME around the corner, though, the voices turned out to belong to some local hipsters in their father's boat. They looked at me like the patsy I was, and didn't return my hello or my wave. I felt like an idiot, afraid of phantoms, but I told my guide I really had had enough, I needed to catch the last bus back to Colombo.

He seemed, what, hurt? He said something to the boatman. They paddled on, unchanged, except for being slightly more grim.

A half dozen turns later, we were back into the lagoon. The old man in front had started huffing and moaning with the labor. It took another half hour to get back to town, and I felt terrible for him, as he whimpered a bit with each pull of his oar. I promised myself to give him a big tip, maybe five bucks each for the three guys, in a place where the average daily wage is still half that.

The local economy gets to you, once you inhabit it, and you know what is generous and what is stingy, and what can make a person's day or week. I'm always generous, off-the-local-charts generous, leaving tips three or four times what their neighbors would be able to manage. But much more than that feels obscene, almost humiliating. When I was young, I made the mistake of answering when a Moroccan man asked me how much I made, which at the time was very little by American standards, and I had had the good sense to shave 30 percent off of that. The number, nonetheless, hit him like fire hose in the gut. I watched his sense of his own achievements crumble.

So, yes, five dollars each seemed like the right call—enough to make for celebration, not so much as to insult or shame. As we approached the little dock where my guide had originally tried to sell me a raft ride, the boatmen, in a clearly coordinated, practiced way, without speaking, turned the raft around to back in. Then, suddenly, they stopped, and held us twenty feet offshore. The pilot pulled out a small wooden board on which was painted, like a menu: ½ hour $30, 1 hour $50.

I looked at my guide. He was looking away.

You said two dollars, I said. He shrugged ever so slightly. I leaned over and tried to hand him a five-dollar bill, saying, Here, you pay whatever you want to them, the rest is yours. He wouldn't take the bill, so I stuck it in his shirt pocket and started taking off my socks and shoes, stuck my camera inside one of them, and hoped that the water wasn't too deep.

When they saw I was going to swim they made a ruckus and backed us in the last few feet to shore. They docked, jumped out, and blocked my way, the main guy pointing to his price board and yelling at me in a language I didn't recognize. My guide, I saw with the kind of slowed-down clarity danger allows, was adept at looking like he was trying to help both sides at once, blocking my way while beckoning me forward and looking concerned for my safety. There was a lot of shouting, none of it in English. I held my shoes and camera like a halfback, lowered my head, and pushed through. Jittery and ashamed, I walked a block, then sat down to put my shoes back on at the edge of town as the sun was starting to set.

MY GUIDE ran after me, saying, I'm sorry, I'm sorry!

I said, Look, that was terrible. I would have given you all a lot more money if you hadn't lied to me and kidnapped me and tried to extort me.

That wasn't me, he said, that was the boatmen! What can you do? Muslims!

Muslims. Neither Tamils nor Singhalese. Nor Burgher. Muslims, who had been ethnically cleansed by the Tamils in the north. The true despised minority.

And it is a very good temple, he added. And a good ride.

Yes, I said. But you lied to me about everything. I was starting to come down from the adrenaline rush, nauseated, shaky.

But I had to lie to you, he said. You wouldn't have come with me if I told you the truth, how far it was.

He was right, I wouldn't have.

If you had come on the boat first, he said, no long walk, no problem. You wouldn't get on boat.

But, thirty dollars? Fifty dollars? I said, aggrieved. I knew it was a cab ride in Manhattan, a couple of Martinis in a bar downtown, but it was also half a month's wages for hard labor in Sri Lanka. In my anger and my shame, even the old man's moaning now seemed like stagecraft.

It was just a suggestion, he said, quietly.

But they Shanghaied me! I said. I took a certain pleasure now, as a kind of retaliation, in using words he wouldn't know. They wouldn't let me go!

Muslims, he said. Terrible. They lie, cheat. I gave them the money you gave me, and they said they had no change. They lie to me too. I get nothing.

Sad-sack, I thought. Then: liar! I wondered how much he actually gave them. I suspected maybe nothing.

Look, I said. It is a bad business model. I would have told everyone to come looking for you. Other tourists, to come to this town and ask for you. I write, I told him. I publish. I could have helped you.

I was laying it on a bit thick, still coming down. He stood there contrite, his hands open at his sides in weak supplication.

I gave him another five bucks and walked onto the bus back to Colombo.

JULIUS

ON THE RIDE BACK I thought about the beheaded statue holding his own head by the hair, the head looking out at the world. He was Buddhist, I assume. Sinhalese? The man being sawed in half—I had seen this kind of statuary once before, in rural southern Thailand. Southern Thailand, like Sri Lanka, is a place where Muslims and Buddhists are at odds; one of many where they are, in fact, killing each other. The sawed man is a stock image of Buddhist hell, as are dozens of other tortures—people on racks, people having huge corkscrews twisted through their torsos, people with limbs sawn off, and so on. That Thai monastery had also not been in the guidebook. I had stumbled upon it while driving around aimlessly, wandering onto smaller and smaller roads. The Thai monks had built seventy of these horror scenes, and kept making more, and repainting the ones that were there, to ensure the blood remained bright red. What kind of meditative practice was that?

When I got back to the hotel, Julius was upset. Why hadn't I let him drive me to Galle? He must have heard I had asked where to get the bus. I apologized, needlessly, as it turned out—nothing could keep him down. He was ready to get back to work.

You want gurs, broda? he asked. He was once again relaxed. He lay back, in his familiar pose, in the front seat of his tuk tuk, legs spread, his astounding toes hanging out both sides of the cab.

Gurs?

He saw my confusion.

Yes, you want gurs? He did the international sign for woman, the two hands sketching symmetrical curves in the air, and the international hand signal for fucking.

Girls, I said. No, thank you, I'm going to my room.

Boys? he asked, ever optimistic.

Desire is the cause of all suffering. That and being sawed

in half or beheaded or shot or punctured by shrapnel or kidnapped and killed.

No, thank you, Julius. I go sleep now. Funny how pidgins are contagious.

Sleep! Naw! Too early! Man! Broda!

I looked at his hopeful face and wondered: what images of hell, what ideological nonsense, had made me assume I was about to be kidnapped or mugged? I thought of Søren Kierkegaard writing that people travel to see rivers, mountains, and exotica: 'garish birds, freak fish, grotesque breeds of human.' These wonders dazzle them, he says. 'They fall into an animal stupor that gapes at existence and they think they have seen something.'

Had I seen something?

Gurs? Julius suggested again, never one to take no for an answer. But I was too lost in wondering about my day to answer, standing there next to his tuk tuk, looking down at his stupendous toes. Boys? he asked, more quietly.

I handed him the cost of a ride.

You're right, I said. I should have had you take me to Galle.

I went into the hotel.

STALIN AND THE POLICE

BAKU, AZERBAIJAN

A DOZEN BLOCKS DOWN the hill from the Avis agency in Baku, a large black Mercedes plowed into the side of the car I had just rented, smacking me sideways to a dead stop. I sat holding the wheel like I was still driving. I wasn't going very fast, maybe forty kph, down the cobblestoned street. He must have been doing sixty or seventy. I assume I stepped on the brake at impact. I ended up ten feet farther in the direction he was going than he did. We both were still in the intersection. I had been driving for all of two minutes, and the car was totaled.

I took pictures and then standers-by helped me push the car to the curb. The Mercedes—I suppose they are well built, after all—looked fine, a bit of a crumple in the bumper, its front license plate on the ground. My car had both passenger-side doors and parts of the front and rear panels crumpled in, as if he had hit me in the car's mathematical center. The side windows were shattered and the windshield spidered. The right front wheel was at a forty-five-degree angle. The passenger side mirror and some other pieces of metal were on the street, which we picked up and piled on the piked hood of my car. The Mercedes driver stood to the side talking on his cell phone. He was a tall, good-looking salt-and-pepper guy in his fifties, who waved and smiled at me while still talking into his phone—no worries. And I agreed. I had the super insurance, no deductible, and it was an easy case—he clearly rammed me, not a judgment call, really, simple physics. I had ended up still in the intersection, but partly on the far curb, all the momentum of our meeting going in the direction his car had been driving, none in mine. He had probably been on his phone when he hit me, and he must have been going fast to do that kind of damage. So we took each other's information, which he seemed surprised I wanted to do, and waited for the police. Nobody but me spoke English, so the only word we all understood was *polizei*. In ten minutes a friend of Salt-and-pepper arrived, and they put their heads together. It occurred to me he had lawyered up. A half hour later the police arrived, two officers. They took my car registration and the insurance card and my passport. A second police car showed up, this time with three men, and photos and measurements were taken, reports filled out.

The Mercedes driver and his lawyer had a long conversation with the lead investigator—he was clearly in charge because he was the only one without a clipboard or camera or tape measure—and then he came over to me, made a long speech, and motioned that I should get in the police car. I pointed to the Avis sign on the car, to the Avis contract his assistant was holding, and back up the hill to where the Avis dealer was—why don't I walk back to the Avis dealer? They speak English, I said a couple of times. They would come and collect the car, and take care of everything, since it was all insured. He nodded that he understood each part of what I was saying. I said, good, and reached for the contract. He wagged a finger at me, shook his head. No.

I was escorted to the police car by one of his flunkies. We were going to the station. They repeated everything to me in Russian, which helped a little, but still not a word of English. I pointed to the Mercedes driver, and he smiled at me and waved again, reassuringly. The policeman let me understand he was coming too, but he got in his car with his attorney. I escaped the flunky long enough to grab my things out of the rental—I had already checked out of my hotel and had my bag with me—and we all drove to the station, which turned out to be not a precinct house, but a motor vehicle crimes center ten or fifteen kilometers away, in a run-down block building on the sleepy outskirts of town. There was nothing else in the neighborhood but a body shop and what looked like a couple of warehouses. We parked and walked into a buzzy lobby, with dozens of petitioners milling around, all awaiting their fate.

I had been in Azerbaijan for a total of ten hours, eight of them asleep after a long series of flights—Los Angeles to New York, New York to Frankfurt, Frankfurt to Tehran, Tehran to Baku. It had been twenty-eight hours on the road, so when

I'd hit my hotel's sheets the night before, I had passed out and didn't wake until first light. In the morning, I had coffee, packed my bag, threw it on my shoulder, and walked the few blocks to the Avis office, where I rented this compact Opal. I had started down what I knew to be a road that would take me to the highway out of town when the sharp smack sent the car shuddering sideways. I had had no particular itinerary—Baku is on a peninsula that juts into the Caspian Sea in the far east, and I was hoping to pass into Georgia on the western border, but that was the extent of my plan. I was therefore under no time pressure: I had no reservations for the following night, and nothing calling on me. So I was happy to let this drama play out, intrigued to see how the wheels of justice ground in Baku.

WE STOOD in a hallway, twenty or thirty of us. There was no line, and no apparent movement anywhere. Every once in a while, someone in a uniform would come out of an office, walk to a door at the end of the hall, knock, go in, then walk out again a couple minutes later and return whence they came. Twenty or thirty pairs of eyes tracked them the whole way. One cop sat at a desk in this waiting area, shuffling papers and writing things on them, and now and again a forlorn petitioner would approach him, bowing, before being waved away. Salt-and-pepper and his attorney continued in conversation away from me, and they each took calls on their phones. After forty-five minutes, a cop came up and ushered them into the office at the end of the hall. I started toward the office, too, but was told by the cop at the desk—so he *was* paying attention!—to sit back down. I waited for a few minutes, thinking, *they must question us each separately? Okay, makes sense.* I waited another twenty minutes, and then started to feel something was fishy. I walked over, ignoring the cop at the desk, and knocked on the door they had entered. A young policeman opened and, without waiting for an invitation, I walked in. The police chief—he was surely the chief, with his stately paunch, his bald head scarcely concealed beneath a few long comb-overs, and his oily demeanor—was shaking hands goodbye with Salt-N-Pepa and his attorney, laughing heartily like good pals. None of them looked at me as the two left. After they departed, the police chief went back behind his desk, sat down, and turned his attention to a television mounted on the wall. A very calm policeman sat at a desk against the back wall and never looked up from his papers. His considerably more nervous partner occupying the front desk, the young man who had opened the door, looked stricken when I walked past him toward the chief.

THE AZERI BOSS HOGG

HELLO, I SAID, and without looking away from the TV, he took a puff on his cigar with one hand, and with the other motioned me to go back toward the young cop. The young cop, apprehensive, came over to get me, and offered me a chair in front of his desk. He sat, took out a piece of paper and a ruler, and started to draw, very slowly, a four-way intersection, the road about two inches wide. The television on the wall, a fifteen-inch tube unit, played a sitcom with a laugh track, each of the characters cartoonish and clownish. Every once in a while, the police chief would laugh out loud, puff on his cigar, and cough. The sitcom was set in a police station—what are the chances?—and people were yelling at each other, gesticulating wildly, tearing at their hair. The production values were terrible, the acting extravagant. The police station in the show had a freestanding jail cell in the center of the chief's office. Every once in a while, someone was put in it and locked up. Then everyone would yell at each other and run around, until that prisoner was pulled out and another one thrown in. The TV police chief seemed to be the butt of most of the jokes. The real police chief laughed so hard he had a couple of coughing fits. The other two cops were trying not to pay any attention.

The young cop was very earnest, and when he finished his schematic, he asked me, again with no English, to show him what had happened, using two matchboxes as cars. I pointed to myself and flashed the box in my left hand, then said, Mercedes! and waved the box in my right. I showed my car heading down the street he had drawn, and then showed the Mercedes coming from the side street and smacking me sideways. He looked distressed. He showed me, in turn, a different scenario, in which I plow into the Mercedes. I say, No no no. I showed him the pictures on my camera of both cars, did my claymation reenactment again. His face was in a rictus. He wrote down what I had told him, then, taking about twenty minutes, slowly drew onto his map little pictures of our two cars at the intersection. Toward the end of it, the chief said something to him. He answered. The chief said something else. The young cop looked at me, down at the drawing, and back over to the chief, who was laughing again at the TV show, his feet up on his desk. A hooker had been brought into the station on TV, and appeared to be saying very funny things. The actor playing the police chief was acting furious. My police chief harrumphed an appreciative laugh, and lit a new cigar.

The young policeman took out a new piece of paper, and started drawing a new map of an intersection.

Whoa! I said, just speaking in English. What's wrong? I asked. What did he say? I pointed to the police chief, who pretended not to see me. I didn't expect an answer, of course. I pointed to the phone on his desk, took out my rental agreement, and found the number of the dealer. Here, I said, call this number, they speak English, they will translate. He looked over at his chief, in obvious fear of the man. It was hilarious when the TV police chief exploded in anger; here it would clearly be no fun. The chief ignored him. I pulled out my camera, and showed him the picture of my car, the doors stove in. I showed him the Mercedes front license plate on the ground. I then took the two matchboxes and moved his new paper out of the way.

Number one! I said, emphatically, like that would help the language gulf, scenario one! I am coming down the road, and—showing with matchbox number two—bam, Mercedes smashes me in the side. You see?

Instead of nodding, he glanced at his chief, and looked about to cry.

Scenario number two! Mercedes is sitting on the road and I—I made my matchbox move ludicrously sideways, making a screeching sound like my tires were squealing as they got pushed perpendicularly, and smashing the side doors of my car into the front of his car—I smash into him sideways! This is impossible! Impossible! I said the word again, once with a Spanish accent, then with a French accent, then again in English, all directed at the chief, thinking it had homonyms in many languages, maybe Azeri too. He ignored me, eyes on the TV.

Then he got up and, without looking at us, studiedly unconcerned, walked out the door.

Where is he going? I asked.

He mimed eating from a plate and shrugged. It's lunchtime. The silent cop in the corner, transferring his attention from his papers to the floor, got up and walked out. The young cop, apologetic, bowed to me, timorous, and followed him. I went to the door, and the whole station had emptied out, everyone apparently off to lunch. There was nothing I could do. I was in the middle of nowhere. They had my passport and the car's papers. I sat back in the office and watched the TV. I couldn't tell whether it was an extremely long program, or if they were having some kind of marathon, or if it was a video on a loop. The slapstick cop show went on and on. I pulled out my guidebook and started planning my route, in case I ever got out.

AN HOUR AND A HALF later, everyone returned.

Hey! I said to the chief, you might want to take a look at this. I held up my camera to show him pictures of the cars. He waved me off without looking at the camera or at me, flopped into his chair, and put his feet back up on his desk. He lit another cigar, and started watching TV again. The young cop bit his lip, moved his head slightly and slowly from side to side.

THE AZERI BOSS HOGG 189

I could almost hear him add, *Please, do not poke the bear.*

I felt bad for him, but we were now four or five hours in. It was time to try something.

What? I pleaded with him. What am I supposed to do? He held out his hand, palm down, the international sign language for stay calm. I sat back. A cop from out front knocked and came in, timid. He said a few words, the chief grunted, and a short round man in his sixties, in a wrinkled suit, bowed and scraped forward. He spoke to the chief until the chief held up his hand, still watching TV, and said a few words. The petitioner bowed and scraped backward out the door, the cop closing it behind them.

A half hour passed.

Another timid knock, this time a vivacious woman in her thirties, half Marlo Thomas, half Valerie Bertinelli, who made the chief hop up. He flirted a mile a minute, they double-cheek kissed, she flashed and swanned around, they laughed. The silent cop brought her some papers to sign. Then she tried to leave, but he kept slowing her exit with more flattery, holding her hand and petting it, following her to the door, until, after yet more double kisses, she managed to escape. Once she left, he returned to his scowl, his chair, his cigar, and his TV. I was stuck in a room with Boris from the *Rocky and Bullwinkle Show.*

Another half hour.

I said something about the U.S. embassy. Maybe they understood, maybe they didn't.

Another half hour. A middle-aged guy in dusty worker's clothes was escorted in. He bowed, reached in his pocket, and held out some money to the chief. This pissed the chief off.

He threw a temper tantrum, yelling and throwing his arms around, all the while pretending the money wasn't hanging in the air. The escort grabbed the worker's outstretched arm, pushed it down to his side, still clutching the bills, and ushered him to the door. But before the man left, I saw the escort take the cash.

Of course! A bribe. I took some dollars out of my pocket and held them up in the air. Is this what he wants? I said loudly. Money? The chief got up and blithely sauntered out of the room, making a silent-film point of not noticing my cash raised in the air. The assistant looked at me like I was making his day hell.

Right? I said. A bribe? Baksheesh? I wasn't sure if I was acting angry or if I actually was angry.

The nerve-wracked guy again motioned me to be calm, clearly far from calm himself. Glancing at the cop at the other desk, he reached under some papers and slid my passport and car registration and rental agreement toward me, pointedly sub rosa. I took them. He pretended to work on his report, I slipped them into my pocket, stood, stretched (stretched? Why?) and tried to discreetly slip the guy a twenty, because I was grateful to him, and felt bad for what he might face. He turned red, shook his head, and wouldn't look up. I pocketed it, grabbed my pack, and ambled through the door, walking briskly across the lobby into the free world.

Outside, it was hot. Forlorn petitioners were waiting and smoking. I couldn't see a taxi. I tried a couple guys. Taxi? They shrugged. I was afraid go back into the station to ask.

Eventually a bus came by and a number of people hopped off. I got on, gave the driver a dollar. He gave me change.

Once we got into a busy part of town I got off and grabbed a cab back to Avis, showing the driver the address on my rental agreement. My smashed-up car was in their lot. That it took me seven hours to get there didn't surprise them.

Welcome to Azerbaijan, the clerk said. She wasn't the same woman who was there in the morning when I had rented it.

I am sorry about your car, I said.

She was unconcerned. Insurance, she said, and shrugged.

LEARNING TO NEGOTIATE

BACK ON THE ROAD, a bit more vigilant now, I made my way out of Baku. The first fifty kilometers were on a highway, my map said, and I moved with the traffic, which was fast. Twenty minutes down the road a policeman pulled behind me with his siren on and blue light flashing. I pulled to the side to let him pass, but he slowed and stayed on my tail. I pulled onto the shoulder and stopped.

Remarkably, this cop spoke English.

You crossed a solid line, he said.

I did?

Yes, we have cameras. We can go to the station and I can show you.

I remembered, then, a short stretch of road, with temporary concrete barriers protecting a construction site, where the dotted middle line had been replaced by a solid line, and the road had narrowed. It changed from two lanes to what was really a lane and a half. I must have been over the line there, in my half lane.

Where the road narrowed? I said, describing it with my hands.

Yes! he said, with a big smile. A kind of, Can you believe it? Everyone falls for that! smile. 130 Euro, he said.

Really? I said. 200 dollars?

He shrugged and handed me a laminated menu of fines, in English. Crossing a solid line—he pointed to it—130 Euro. He had had this conversation before. His uniform was sharp, new, and ironed, the black leather belts shiny.

This, he said, touching my seatbelt shoulder strap. This is fifty Euro.

It is too much! I said.

Yes! he said, still smiling widely.

What could I do? I gave him 130 Euro. He gave me a receipt. He seemed to be having fun. It's a game he always wins, but he still enjoys it.

I DROVE ON, into the brown hills, and the road became a two-lane blacktop, no shoulders, with switchbacks as it climbed. The land was broad and empty. In the distance a shepherd walked his flock. Around one hairpin a lone butcher shop was perched on the side of the hill, two fresh carcasses hanging out front, peeled off, one assumes, from the wandering flock.

As I crested the rocky summit, the speed limit dropped to forty kilometers an hour for a sharp curve to the right, and as soon as I made the turn I saw a sign that said twenty kilometers an hour. Behind it a group of a dozen policeman had every car and truck pulled over. They motioned me over, too.

It was a literal speed trap. The sign was placed so that there wasn't time to see it and brake fast enough. Everyone who drove the road was busted.

This cop didn't speak English, he just filled out the ticket and handed it to me, pointing to the amount: 110 Euro.

I can't afford to be in your country! I said. It is impossible! I showed him my earlier receipt. He looked at, crossed something out on my ticket, and showed me. Now it was ninety Euro. Okay, progress. I handed him seventy Euro and he counted it, and gave me a don't-press-your-luck look. I acted like I didn't understand. He shrugged and waved me on.

Once it plateaued, the road was straight, for the most part, curving to cross streams, but otherwise a slight, straight ribbon through vast fields of sunflowers and wheat. Gypsy wagons sat on the edges of the field here and there, but there were no houses. These were collective farmlands from the Soviet era, and the farmworkers all lived in the small villages along the way, not on the land. Each gypsy wagon was a mini-boxcar on a farm wagon chassis, a six-by-ten-foot combined home, storehouse, and toolshed.

I stopped in the ancient city of Sheki, with its minarets and sultan's palace, in the hillside forest that stretched from there through Zaqatala and Balakan to the Georgian border.

I headed west on the highway again and, not fifteen minutes later, two policemen stepped into the road with flashlights and flagged me over.

Good, I said to the cop, tired enough that I didn't care whether he spoke English. Where is a hotel?

Hotel? he said.

Yes, I said. Show me a hotel and I'll pay a ten Euro fine.

Otherwise take me to jail.

Jail? he said.

They looked at each other and then back at me, and they lost the staring contest.

Twenty Euro, he said, and I pulled out a five and handed it to them.

It's all I have, I said, shrugging and starting my engine. They took it and stepped aside.

CROSSING THE RIVER

A FEW DAYS later I was heading south, and the map showed a dirt road traversing the flats to a river crossing at Aghdash. I'd been sticking to the smaller paved roads, up through the northern mountains, and it was time to explore the less traveled ones. It looked like I could jump off the road halfway between Oghuz and Nij and head straight south, before picking up the highway again to Göyçay. I had already been deep in the Azerbaijani countryside—with its falconers and farmers, shepherds and gypsies—but I wanted to get a little farther off the road and see what might turn up.

I made a right onto the dirt road, and it quickly became a tortuous washboard. Evidently, fifty or more years ago a great effort had been made to smooth it—the road was elevated five or eight feet above the fields, ruler-straight and level, and I suspect it may have had a hard surface at some point. But time had not been gentle. In the distance a herd of animals snailed across the plain, and, after a couple hours of crushing shudders on the road, I came upon a horse-drawn wagon trotting down a dirt path along the edge of a field, several boxes of vegetables ready for market in the back. It took me forever to gain on him, the road was so bad, and then it dawned on me that this was why he was below. Probably nobody used this nasty road anymore. I found a way to descend and drove down the farm path at the edge of the fields, parallel to and much smoother than the raised road. A mile or so in, I hit a ditch, and there was nothing to do but retrace my path until a ramp took me back to the gravel and its bridge. After that I could read the signs, see when people were dropping down to the dirt path, when heading back up to cross a stream, a bad stretch, a ditch. After three hours traveling on an otherwise straight line, I passed under a decorative metal arch announcing that I was entering Astranavoka Kandi.

A boy of about thirteen was on horseback, moving thirty cattle out of the gate. He was distinctly proud of his horsemanship, ostentatiously weaving his steed left and right like a show horse at a rodeo, making the herd jumpy. Once I passed that commotion, the town seemed completely empty. I came to the center—identifiable because there were buildings on all four corners of the intersection, and it was the only intersection. Buildings tumbled away from the crossroads in all directions for a couple hundred feet, then got sparser and stopped a couple city blocks out. There were maybe fifty or sixty households in all. None of them were businesses, or at least, none had signs. There were only two people I could see, each asleep sitting up in a small patch of shade, leaning against a building. One was on the northwest corner, with two goats snoozing next to him; the other was on the southeast corner, at the center of a flock of sheep, half of whom were also sleeping. The men were both grizzled, in their sixties or seventies, and from their body language—they faced away from each other, as if huddled against the ill wind from the opposite corner—I got the distinct feeling they hated each other.

I PARKED AND WALKED to the man on the northeast corner and said the name of the biggest town on the route I hoped I was still on—Göyçay. His eyes opened, drowsily, and he gave me a blank stare. I pointed south, and then to the east. I was pretty sure it was one of those two directions. Nothing. I thanked him and walked to the opposite corner, where the other old man had been studiously ignoring us. I went through the same routine, and he waved his hand, no, nothing like that here. South? No. East? No. West? No.

Meanwhile a crowd had started to gather, emerging from what had seemed to be empty buildings. Kids first, then young men, middle-aged men, then some women. I got my map out and showed them what I was trying to do. Maybe because many didn't read—except for the name of the town painted on the rusty arch in an unpracticed hand, there was not a single piece of text to be seen in the village—or maybe because they were not used to reading maps, it was hard for them to figure out where was where. I would point at a place and say VladiMIRovska, and they would all look at each other and frown and shrug, and finally someone would say VladimirOVska, and then they would all smile and nod and point north, back up the road I had come down. Eventually we agreed on the towns we were talking about. Göyçay was not pronounced like it looks, to rhyme with boy-kay, but Gyo-chuh. I knew that Göyçay was south of where we were standing. When we finally agreed on the pronunciation, they all pointed north.

A young boy shouted and got the crowd's attention. He pointed down the street at an older woman, wide abeam, babushka on her head, heading our way, swaying left and right the way some big people do. The crowd laughed in anticipation, and elbowed each other, and made it clear to me that I was in for a treat. When she arrived she looked straight-faced at me, and said something to them that made them all howl with laughter. I had no idea what it was, of course, and tried to act amused. This gave her new ammo, and she got off another shot. She gave away nothing with her face, a perfect deadpan. All of her teeth were capped in gold. Her one-liners kept coming, anything I said or didn't say, anything anyone else said, all were transformed into instant barbs. She had her audience in a frenzy of delight. I said, in English, that I was happy to be her straight man. Her riposte to this got her the biggest laugh of the day. The guy with the goats was actually crying, and the smaller kids were looking at me like they wondered why I wasn't laughing as hard as the rest. After that, she did a Rodney Dangerfield turn, and dismissed them all with a wave of her hand, like they didn't get her, didn't appreciate her, and went muttering her way off stage and back down the dirt main street, leaning left then right on her thick legs.

I took out my guidebook, and traced on another map what I wanted to do. One of the men, a guy of about fifty with an air of authority, threw up his hands in a that-does-it! gesture and got in the passenger seat of my car. Two of his friends, one about thirty-five, one forty-five, got in the back seat. Come on! they gestured to me. Let's go, enough already!

I got in and they motioned to drive down the road to the east. We left the rest of the town watching. A couple city blocks out, in an empty lot, there was a twelve-foot-high statue of Stalin framed by two thirty-year-old pine trees. *Holy shit.* I stopped the car—I still didn't know what we were doing, but I couldn't leave the statue without a picture. I snapped and got back in, noting how odd it all was, and turned in my seat to take in all three of my passengers.

Stalin! I said, and looked around at the men.

They shrugged, and I wasn't sure exactly what that signified, but I took it to mean, *we didn't care then and we don't care now.* I was struck by the placement: had there been a town square there, at some point, where this plot of grass was now, chewed down by the wandering sheep? I pointed at the statue, at the emptiness around it. They looked over at the statue, then back at me. They shrugged again. *We know some people have fun toppling them,* I imagined them saying, *but it's just extra trouble, and we don't even notice it's there.* It was easier to let the center of town migrate a few blocks over, to the crossroads, and just leave it be.

They waved me farther east. We drove half a mile and the road petered out and became a set of tracks through a field, possibly a remnant of a former road, maybe just a farmer's path home. It occurred to me not just that I was alone in a car with three strangers, driving into nowhere, but that there was something familiar about the scenario. I had put myself at the mercy of random people once again, and although it had always, so far, worked out fine, and although I wasn't particularly concerned, it did cross my mind that if this was the one that turned bad, the what-was-he-thinking question would be hard to answer. Because I really did have no idea why any of them, much less all of them, were in the car. I had no idea why I was driving across the stubble of a large harvested cornfield, and then across an unimpressive hayfield. It got bumpier and the tire tracks disappeared. They pointed me a little left, a little right, and then, after a while, the going was just too rough, and they motioned me to stop. I braked and the car settled between clumps of earth in the tall grass. I hoped I would be able to get it moving again.

THEY GOT OUT OF THE CAR, and started walking farther in the same direction across the field. This was my moment to escape, to turn around and flee, but how cruel and silly that would be if this all had a non-sinister explanation. I got out of the car and followed them. The sun was getting low, and the late afternoon breeze was brisk, the hay alternately flattened and shuddered by the wind. And then, cresting a small rise, I saw it, a deep gorge and at the bottom, a winding river. See? they said—and again, when people keep talking at you, eventually the seemingly random phonemes become patterned and you almost feel you understand the language—See the bridge? They pointed down below, a good mile away and a thousand or two thousand feet down, at what were clearly the remnants of a washed-out bridge, a road on the other side leading to where it used to be, some ruined stanchions in the middle of the raging river, and a road leading out, toward the rise we stood on.

Then we all did our version of the hand gestures appropriate to describing a bridge that had been washed away, and we all agreed that I had been rather thick not understanding that earlier, when they tried to tell me back at the crossroads, and we had yet another laugh at my haplessness, walked back to the car, and got it moving, although they had to get out and push it first. I dropped them off at the crossroads, and I started my long drive back across the washboard torture to where, ten hours after setting off on my shortcut, in the deep black of night, I approached the highway and wondered where I might find a bed.

MULTICULTURALISM IN IRAN

TEHRAN

TEHRAN IN 2010 was famously governed by a traffic engineer (Mahmoud Ahmadinejad has a PhD in traffic planning), and equally famous for its horrible traffic. Fortunately it had a seemingly infinite supply of irreverent, quick-witted cabbies who kidded around like somebody's funny Jewish uncle. They all appeared unflappable, and all knew about Irangeles, or Tehranageles—my home town of Los Angeles being the center of the Persian diaspora—even though some politely pretended they were hearing the nicknames for the first time. Most had relatives who lived around the corner from me. Some used to live around the corner from me themselves.

I was in Iran when the Green Revolution had just had its Obama 'Yes We Can!' moment, but had already sputtered out.

The repression in Iran, the kind that squashed the Greens, was infamous in the United States, and so I was surprised to find that the cabbies were far from shy about politics and religion. After a conversation with one about Bush-era policies, for which I offered my standard apology, I asked a softball question about his own government.

Ah! You mean our crazy president! he said, without a pause, and laughed. When he saw my surprise, he added, Yes, we are not stupid, we know he is crazy!

I said I was surprised he felt no worries about saying that. We were stuck in traffic, and he elaborately mimed checking the backseat, looking under the visor, in the glove box, as if nervously searching for listening devices.

They can't make us deaf and blind, he said. Everyone knows he's crazy. This is not news. This is hardly seditious. Like many Iranians, he had better English than most Americans.

Later, a different driver, also holding forth against the various powers-that-be, said: I don't like Khomeini, I don't like, I don't like any-meini, they are all just power-hungry like anyone, all trying to hide it.

The anti-meini cabdriver was taking me up to see the Shah's palace, in the north end of the city, and once we got out of downtown—eight blocks that took a half hour—it was an easy drive.

But it is okay, he said, as he dropped me off. The people will eventually win.

I had only been there a few days, but as rousing to my old idealist-communalist soul as his sentiment might have been, I had to wonder: *which people?* The people had won once before, in the Revolution of 1979, when the Shah fled his palace to live out the final year and a half of his life in exile. That Revolution had turned into the ayatollahs and Ahmadinejad.

MOHAMMAD REZĀ SHĀH PAHLAVĪ'S palace was designed by Mohsen Foroughi, Iran's most famous modern architect, and looks a bit like Avery Fisher Hall in New York. In 1968 Tehran it had perhaps been an exciting modernist statement; in 2010, it looked bland, sterile, and dated. One can imagine Jackie Kennedy showing it to a TV audience. Overlarge rooms, spare and severe. Uninviting furniture, made less for lounging than for standing next to at a state reception. Everything beige, off-white, brown.

The only rooms with real color were the kids' bathrooms. The wall tiles in both of them—yes, they each had their own bathroom, it's a palace, after all—were festooned with Disney decals: Mickey, Minnie, Goofy, Snow White, the Dwarves. They had been applied by the kids themselves it seemed, some at off angles, without design. The children of wealth and power, the inheritors of a dynasty, their heads had been full of the same images as kids their age in Sheboygan.

The Shah was installed by the British and Russians in 1941, immediately after they had deposed his father, who had been Shah since 1925. With his father forced into exile, his country occupied by Allied forces, and his oil fields controlled by the British, Pahlavī had limited power. When the occupying army left, a democratic election replaced the Shah with Prime Minister Mohammad Mosaddegh, who took steps to nationalize the oil industry. In the early 1950s, the CIA, at the request of the British (Iranian oil being a pillar of the UK's economy), helped organize a coup that threw Mosaddegh in jail and put the Shah back in control.

Pahlavī passed his annual performance review as the Anglo-Americans' man in Tehran with flying colors, a telegenic and charismatic leader who seemed unassailable; seemed, in fact, born to the role. As a kid, I had seen pictures of him, wearing a white military uniform—itself a Disney concoction, tall multicolored collars and cuffs, sashes, chest full of medals. He was a regular in the pages of *Time* and *Life*, and on the evening news. In the palace, similar photos were everywhere, especially in the Shah's office. They showed him hobnobbing with the full range of famous dignitaries: American presidents from Kennedy to Carter, Nasser, Sadat, Indira Gandhi, and other heads of state, along with the rest of the 1960s international pantheon—Sinatra and the Rat Pack, Elvis, Ann-Margret, and assorted movie stars.

None of those photos had the time-capsule impact, though, of the Disney decals. These kids, immersed in American popular culture, putting up *decals*—themselves a pop-culture technology of limited duration—splashy, brightly colored decals messing with Foroughi's autumn palette and clean lines, at the very moment when American and European youth were beginning to mess with designs of all kinds, and colonial and postcolonial kids were getting ready to bring an end the old order of the world. Something about the momentariness of it all, about the inability of the historical actors involved to see history's curtain descending, the glimpse into the most private of rooms, the casual cosmopolitanism, the hokey commerciality—all of it made those Disney decals, a few with an edge curled, dried out and fading, deeply sad.

OUTSIDE THE PALACE, there was no taxi queue, no obvious place to find a cab. I started walking in what I hoped was the general direction of downtown, until I came to a bus stop. There were five or six people waiting, and I said the name of my street and hotel, showing them a business card from the front desk, hoping someone would recognize it and give me directions. An older woman grabbed the card and a conversation ensued, and as new people came and joined in, it grew increasingly animated. An older woman said something to me in Persian, and I shrugged. Maybe? I said. A profound disagreement had developed, as far as I could tell, with people pointing in at least three different directions, and as the argument grew somewhat heated, some feelings were hurt, and one of the party was sulking, one declaiming, and several shrugging back at me. One quiet young man raised his eyebrow at me—he looked to be about sixteen, in a white oxford shirt and slacks, a conservative haircut, and an open and honest boyish face, only a few years past the decal stage. I smiled at him and raised an eyebrow back.

I can show you, he said quietly. At about the same time, a slightly older kid, in camo pants and an army cap and white t-shirt, maybe nineteen, who had recently joined the confab, said, in accented English, I know where to go to hotel, come with me. I checked in with the oxford shirt, and he bowed his head, in deference to the nineteen-year-old's age, and I turned to say thank you to the rest of the group, most of whom were still arguing with each other and paid no attention. The sixteen-year-old shook his head, suggesting no, there's nothing you can do, the nineteen-year-old agreed, and the three of us left the bus stop, making our way a few blocks farther south to a subway station.

I assumed they would tell me which train, which exit, and then we'd say goodbye, but they insisted on going with me. I tried to pay their fare, but they had passes. They asked me about Los Angeles, and my family, and I asked about theirs, and we all got on a train, and continued to talk as we traversed a few stations. The younger was a student, hoping to go into engineering. The older was in the army, and was on leave for the weekend.

Then the soldier said to me:

Court.

Okay, I said. Court.

Yes, he said, pointing to his chest, I, Court.

This was significant, what he was telling me, but I had no clue why. I looked to the sixteen-year-old. Yes, he nodded. It is true, he is Court.

A certain amount of polite yessing is necessary for linguistically limited communication. Yes. Of course, I said. He could tell I didn't understand. I tried to parse it. He is court? From court? Tennis court? From the king's court, he's royalty? Didn't seem likely. He is due in court?

I am, too, the young one said. We are both courtish, both court.

Kurdish! You are Kurdish!

Yes, Court.

We got off to change trains, and I kept telling them they didn't need to shepherd me, I knew where I was going now.

No, no problem, they said, we want to go there anyway. They were lying, and it crossed my mind maybe there was a tip implicit, which was okay with me.

HIPSTERS AND HOSPITALITY

AS WE WAITED for the next train, in a modern, very large, but fairly empty station, a trio of hipsters sauntered down to the platform, two guys and a girl, a classic trio of barely post-adolescent misfits—a tall, thin, striking ringleader with a goth girl and a chubbier, more pimply male sidekick. I had noticed—in Azerbaijan, in Tajikistan, and now in Iran—that in countries where women's hair is often or always covered, the boys have the fancy hairdos. Some opt for boy-band-like blow-dry sweeps, others prefer plastered, spit-curled bangs of the oddest assortment, more David Lynch or Fellini or Munchkinland than Paul Mitchell. The ringleader had a big swoop of bleached hair across his forehead, his shirt half buttoned, low-belted skinny jeans, and a bling-y belt. He walked like a runway model, making his presence felt. The girl and the sidekick found him very impressive, and looked to him for their every move. He launched into a loud conversation with me—loud enough that, had there been other people in the station, they would have heard him. The followers glanced at me to clock my reaction, then turned back to him like sunflowers.

He*ll*o, he said, with a Bruno-like pout, hands on his hips. *Where* are you *from?*

This might be fun, I thought, even as I noticed that my two Kurdish guides backed up a step and looked a little worried.

The U.S., I said.

America! he said, in a somewhat unreadable challenge. And how do *you* like my *country*? If he was being gay-dramatic, maybe this was Iranian camp. If he wasn't, it was belligerent. My guides had made subtle gestures suggesting the second, and had sidled down the platform, motioning me to follow.

I love Iran, I said. I think your country is absolutely fabulous, I added, with a little emphasis on the last two words, testing Theory #1.

Why do you think it is *fabulous*? *What* do you think is *fabulous* about it?

This was said with a sneer and obvious sarcasm, and with at least a solid tablespoon of anger, although still with a snide smile on his face. The sidekick and the goth girl were trying to smile, but having trouble. They were getting nervous, too, hanging on his every snarl.

I decided that I needed to issue my own challenge. The people, I said. I have found the people to be very warm, hospitable, charming, helpful—suggesting that maybe he wasn't doing his part.

Do you love *your* country, the *United States of America?* he interrupted, loud, steaming, saying 'States' with extra sibilance.

I love some things about it, I said. I dislike other things about it intensely.

His lackeys had not so much backed up as shrunk, and now literally stared at their hipster-colored sneakers.

You are being *evasive*, he said, fast. Do you *love* your country?

It is not evasive, I said. What you asked isn't an easy question to answer. Do you love Iran?

My guides looked distressed at a distance, cocking their heads for me to bolt. This gay guy had some crazy energy, and they wanted none of it.

Yes! I *love* Iran, he said, and was so worked up that—and I admit this may not be entirely fair—I kept thinking of a documentary about neo-Nazi groups, and how many oppressed and repressed, compartmentalized gay men were involved, shouting their hateful slogans. I *cannot* take a single *breath*, he said, loudly, melodramatically, without thinking about my *love* for *Iran*. And when I think about *America*, I *cannot breathe!*

Nice chiasmus, I thought.

AT THAT MOMENT the train arrived, and I was about to enter the same car as these three kids, but my guides did a pincer movement, pushing me onto the next car and walking me through a couple of others until we weren't being followed. I wanted their take on the swoop-haired guy, but couldn't get them to talk about him. Their English was more limited than his, and I'm not sure how much they caught. Then it occurred to me that being Kurdish around a rabid nationalist was probably even less fun than being an American.

I asked general questions about being Kurdish in Iran. Do people know you're Kurds? No, not by looking, they said, but when we speak, they hear the accent. And are you second-class citizens? They looked at each other and smiled. Maybe third-class, the soldier said.

The soldier's stop was coming up, and after offering to accompany me three more times, and my saying really, it wasn't necessary, I knew now where I was going, he said goodbye and stepped off the train. My other helper guaranteed me he was going my way, which I knew he wasn't. Hospitality runs deep in this part of the world, except when it doesn't.

As the soldier left, a young man got on, high shine on his shoes, pressed, fitted, high-end clothes, and a sharp haircut. He saw the kid and me talking and came over to stand by us. I stood out as obviously foreign. He said hello to me, and greeted my guide in Farsi, then without waiting for a response asked me where I was from. The U.S., I said. He found this very interesting, and asked me a couple of questions about my city and my work. I returned the questions. He was in business and let on in various ways that he was very successful. He asked if I was finding my way around Tehran okay. I said that my young friend was showing me back to my hotel. He asked the kid something in Farsi, the kid answered, and then without acknowledging that he had spoken, the self-proclaimed success stepped between me and the kid, literally cut him off, never referred to him, never looked at him again—cut him dead. It was extraordinary. The kid's accent had made him disappear. I'd like to say I was quick enough to have responded in a coherent way. But it had happened too fast, and I was still figuring out what to say when from behind the Persian's shoulder, the Kurd gave me the high sign. It was our stop.

We got off the subway and went up the stairs to the street. That man, I said, in the subway. That was because he heard your accent.

Yes, the boy said, implying it was not a big deal, just the way things were.

I followed the boy, but I was pretty sure he was leading us in the wrong direction. It was hot, Middle Eastern desert hot, and extra blocks were not to be taken lightly. I stopped and bought a couple of bottles of water and had to ask him three times until he finally accepted one of them. We talked about what he saw as his future, which he hoped would mean a college degree in engineering. He asked to look at my hotel card again, and stopped and showed it to a man standing in front of his suitcase shop. The man shrugged, and we kept marching on in the wrong direction. We finally got someone to agree with me about the direction and a mile later we were at my hotel. I knew that a straight tip was out of the question. I asked him to come in and have a cup of tea at my hotel, and he looked into the lobby with longing for a second, and said no. I tried the requisite three times and a fourth, then tried to contribute to his college fund a few times, and he cut me short.

It is important, he said, decisively. It is important that I accept nothing.

He was Strether, the literature professor in me thought, the renunciative hero of James's *Ambassadors*, whose sense of moral obligation makes him insist on getting nothing for himself. Why? I asked.

It is important for Iran, he said. And for the Kurd. I am happy to help you.

He bowed and walked away.

ISFAHAN

I HAD TAKEN MY TRIP to the Shah's palace playing hooky from a conference about multiculturalism, the first ever held in Iran. I had been invited to it based on an academic book I had written. Like anything academic in Iran, the conference was run by the government, with various ministerial and clerical dignitaries in attendance. The Kurdish question was not addressed in any of the talks. The scholars from Indonesia and the rest of the Muslim world were interested in general theoretical questions, and in questions that came up in their own, local work, not in anything on the Middle East. The Kurds were not yet an issue the Iranians were willing to talk about; in fact, when I asked people from other countries at the conference about it, many wanted me to explain what I meant. Most of the Americans attending were from religious schools, and they seemed to think it rude of me to bring it up. The Iranians simply ignored it, changing the subject or literally walking away.

There was an ayatollah at the conference, from the holy city of Qom, who was clearly a big star. He was followed around by a videographer, a still photographer, a male assistant, and a female assistant. I wasn't sure if a documentary was being made about him, or if he was so important that his entire life was being filmed. He was quite young to be walking around with such an air of authority, only forty or a little more, and he exuded money. His robes and headdress were thousand-count and brand new, his skin flawless, his big brown beard shiny and coiffed, and when he was handed a business card he executed a no-look pass to an assistant. He humbly accepted the adulation of many of the conferees, and was good at pressing the flesh or, in the case of the Western nuns, bowing indulgently, and engaging for several minutes with each. He had made his reputation, as far as I could tell, by being the first imam on the multiculti bus. His lecture was a hash of truisms and equivocations of the sort that a pressured undergraduate might have come up with in the United States twenty years ago. But he was sharp. I walked up to say hello, and we managed to talk for a few seconds before he turned to address another well-wisher and never turned back. He had smelled a rat. I had asked him about the Kurds.

The ayatollah was as unflappable as the cabdrivers, and he was a formidable character. He was well aware of his charisma, and, it seemed to me—even taking into account that I am Voltaire-strength anticlerical—that he knew he was full of shit. He was in the business of selling legitimacy. He was a zealot in multiculturalist garb, international legitimacy's multicultural pimp, and he had a pimp's dead eye for the mark. I watched him talk to an old British translator and spiritualist, oozing generosity toward him, doing a patronizing slow nod. The translator was thrilled.

AFTER A COUPLE DAYS I decided that I wanted to see more of Iran than the conference, and so I slipped my minders and took a bus to Isfahan, the city of song; then another to Shiraz, the city of poetry; and a third to Yazd, the city of the desert. The natives of each of these cities thought of themselves as the *real* Persians. In Shiraz, where the wine used to come from before wine was outlawed, people said the real Persia is the Persia of our poets. In Yazd, the driest city, 3,000 years old, famous for its architecture, its *bādgirs* or windcatchers, its adobe, and its ancient domes, people say the real Persians are the desert people. In Isfahan people have been saying

Esfahān nesf-e jahān ast (Isfahan is half of the world) since the eleventh century.

As I made my way around the country, I found that the two things most people agreed on were the importance of poetry and the importance of engineering. Everywhere, the tombs of the poets are pilgrimage sites, and people weep as they touch the marble crypts. Everywhere, people sing the old poems, publicly, in spontaneous groups. In Shiraz, at the Tomb of Hafez, a fourteenth century poet whose work every Iranian can recite, people buy verses from a man who lets his bird grab a slip of paper from a box with its beak for each person—a random verse, like a cookie fortune, just for you. People recite the lines, touch the stone and weep, and pray, enraptured, in a kind of pained, mournful ecstasy.

Everywhere, too, teens and young people asked me if they could practice their English. They all wanted to be engineers. They all hoped to attend a Western university, but even if they couldn't, they explained, English was the language of science and technology. One kid, who was walking with his sister in Isfahan—she also wanted to be an engineer—asked me a hundred questions, and then took me to meet the rest of the family, who were picnicking in Imam Khomeini Square.

This is so nice, I said. The whole family out, in the evening together. How often do you eat dinner like this?

Oh, six or seven times a week, he said. The square was full of families, a rock festival's worth, with youngsters running around, and the older people sitting on kilims. Thousands of picnics spread across what was, after Tiananmen, the second largest square in the world. Mosques sprouted on each side, each more eerily magnificent than the last.

Two of the brothers were already studying to be engineers. The oldest was very full of himself, two or three years and several important exams ahead of everyone else. He was ever alert for praise or snipes, but neither ever came; he was both captain and prisoner of his exalted place in the family. The other was a classic number two. He never spoke unless spoken to, never betrayed a sentiment that wasn't the entire family's, and was no doubt processing volumes of unspoken thought. The third brother (the one who had found me), his sister, and a still younger brother were all happy puppies, it seemed to me, well loved and cared for. The parents asked nothing of me, or of their children. They parented like shepherds, watching, calm but alert from the side. I asked the family if all Iranians liked poetry, and the whole family said yes, and several said, We must take you to the Bridge.

The seventeenth-century Khaju Bridge crosses the Zayandeh River and doubles as a dam. In the evenings under its stone arches, groups of people gather to sing and to listen. The approach was magical. The lights in the repeated tiers of arches reflected in the lake, and the sound of singing grew stronger as we approached. The singers take turns, a capella, until everyone joins in. In some cases there is a slight hint of a contest—a slam—but mostly it is pure appreciation. People hum or sing along, and exceptional performances cause tremendous excitement. On the upper level of the bridge, also covered, are shops and food, and passersby strolling, eating ice cream. But below is where most of the people are. The singing goes on into the night, and it feels simultaneously underground, like a beatnik club, and like church, like an observance of something fundamental, profound, serious.

The best of the bards sang with tears in their eyes, the crowd applauding wildly. It was like *American Idol* without the cameras or judges, on a dozen different stages, and the songs all reverently traditional. The communal emotion, the joy in this everyday ritual, was clean and sacrosanct—the Persian soul in communion with itself.

CAUGHT CHEATING ON THE VISA

AT THE AIRPORT, as I was leaving, the uniformed officials wanted to know where I had been. I said I had been at a conference looking into the question of multiculturalism. They weren't sure what to make of the word. They asked me if I had been somewhere besides Tehran. I said no. I'm not sure why—it just seemed like it might be simpler. They looked at me with some alarm. Is there a problem? I asked. Please come with us, they said. We walked down several hallways. Wait here, one of the officials said, and they walked off with my passport. Only a single soldier remained.

They left me in a cul de sac gate, at the end of a corridor, a gate that looked like it hadn't been used in some time. It occurred to me that it might not be used again until sanctions were lifted. I thought about all the tourist dollars and Euros and yen and renminbi that weren't coming into the country. And how starved so many people seemed to be for contact with the outside world.

After about an hour, I asked the soldier guarding me—it was just the two of us—if he knew what was happening.

He just shrugged, which may have just meant he didn't speak English.

How much longer?

Another shrug.

After a second hour had passed, and with the time for my flight approaching, I said, just to see if it would have any effect, This is outrageous. Taking my passport and making me miss my flight, outrageous! It seemed worth a try, to fake a little anger, on the grounds that my flight was about to board.

Yes, he said. It is quite outrageous.

I was surprised; not just English, excellent English. He was a young man, like most soldiers, still in his early twenties.

Really, though, I said. Is there a problem? Have they forgotten me?

He gave me a level glance.

I wonder, he said, without looking at me, and with no particular emotion. I wonder what would it be like for me in your country, if I arrived at the airport, and when I arrived I told immigration I would be one week in New York, and instead I was one week in many other cities, and when I was asked I lied, I did not admit to my other travels, and I was unwilling to explain myself, or say what I had been doing in your country? If I hadn't done what my visa request said I was going to do? If I was dishonest with the immigration police?

Ah, I thought, so they know who I am already. Interesting. And they know where I went.

What do you think? the soldier asked. Would I be detained for two hours, or perhaps more?

Yes, I said. But we are assholes.

He humpfed. Admittedly, it hadn't been much of a concession.

But really, I asked. Do you know what will happen now?

Don't worry, he said. Your plane is two hours late. You will be okay.

OCCUPIED TIBET

LHASA

SITTING IN AN UPSTAIRS CAFÉ in Lhasa, watching the pilgrims circle the Jokhang Temple, I noticed a boy on the roof next door, with an automatic weapon. peering down at the street. He wore the green camo uniform of a Chinese soldier, along with a helmet and a bulletproof vest. He was a sniper on patrol. During the hour I was in the café, he didn't move a muscle. He looked about sixteen, but was probably older.

I didn't know how many snipers were deployed around the town, but the new city and most of the old was crowded with Chinese soldiers. In the new city, armored personnel carriers drove by. In the old, groups of foot soldiers walked in formation, individual officers strode with purpose, and armed guards stood at doorways and gates. The army was keeping watch, enforcing a restless peace, and the endless pilgrims circling the temple with their prayer paraphernalia were confronted, every seven or eight minutes, with a small phalanx of five or six painfully young soldiers in full riot gear, plexiglass shields, automatic weapons, helmets, and visors at the ready, walking in formation against the pilgrim traffic. Always watching, waiting for revolt.

Behind them, a thousand miles of Tibetan plain run north and east, like a visual koan: one can advance farther and farther into the vast tableau, but the horizon never arrives. As the clouds lounge overhead, the broad plateau expands forever, the nomadic animals chew the earth, yurts park. Sometimes, lured by electricity, their owners abandon them and build out of stone, next to the railway.

The train from Xining moves at 120 kilometers an hour, they say, but in this vastness it seemed to crawl. Yak herds transform the emptiness briefly, and then disappear, apparently oblivious to the train as it slides by. Every hundred kilometers or so modernity clears its throat in the form of a gleaming concrete station, each threaded by aluminum and copper to the next for a thousand kilometres across the plain, like a necklace of the gods with tiny white concrete beads. The empty stations were kept Communist Party clean, and disquietingly attended to by ever-watchful Chinese police, even here, in the middle of absolute nowhere. One station reports its altitude: 5,068 meters (16,627 feet). Higher than any train in Peru, half a mile higher than the top of the tallest Rocky Mountain.

The five other bunks in my cabin and those in the next few were taken by a group of schoolteachers from Shanghai.

The English teacher was a moralist who found it unethical for people to keep pets while humans starve in the world. We talked about income distribution, about pets, about the dogs and cats becoming more popular with the new bourgeoisie. In Chinese, a cat says *mao*; I asked if it is *mao* as in Mao Tse-Tung. The ethicist frowned. The rest looked at their feet. Whoops. Too soon.

PILGRIMS

AT THE POTALA PALACE, that fabled, massive, plastered cathedral to nothingness, the pilgrims pray for deliverance and succor. They pray for the return of the fourteenth Lama, for the days before these Han Chinese moved in and took over, before the last days settled down like a smothering fog. They implore the spirits of all the Panchen and Dalai Lamas, asking them to send spirit messengers to confound the Chinese Army. They pray to a thousand Buddhas and saints that the Chinese will all go back to Beijing.

Of course that will never happen.

Many of the pilgrims have more pressing prayers. One couple from the country—obvious from the way they hesitated to speak to the monks, and bowed, and held their hats—carried an obviously sick child in their arms. They gave the monk in the room of the seven Buddhas their money. He discussed it with them, and I wished I could know what they were saying. Was he offering a tiny quid pro quo? Would their daughter live a few more days?

Many of the other pilgrims had come in from the country, too, but many were daily petitioners from the capital.

They walked briskly and threw money at the feet of statues, put it in boxes in front of shrines, dabbed spoons of yak butter into the lamps, in what looked like a practiced routine. The monks followed behind, swept the bills off the floor, emptied the boxes, and brought the crinkled pile of currency to a desk, where a monk straightened out the bills, bundled them, and recorded the amounts. In almost every room in the Palace, and every room in the Jokhang Temple, and in rooms in many other monasteries, a monk sat at a table, counting money, clapping batches of bills down on the desk, wrapping them in bundles of what, one hundred? Then they would count them again, flipping through the edge of the bundle with expert fingers, before adding it to neat stacks.

But the petitioners are so poor! I felt a rage like Martin Luther's. *Their baby is dying! Don't take their money! Send them to a hospital!* I wanted to nail my theses to the door of the Potala Palace. All my life I'd read about the superiority of Tibetan Buddhism, about how shallow we Westerners were who thought we knew the Four Noble Truths and the Eightfold Path, how contaminated we were by instrumentalism and materialism and desire, and how our yearning for enlightenment condemned us to chase our own tails through an eternity of fruitless misappropriation. But now I wanted to scream at Alan Watts and the rest: *Western Buddhism is* closer *to pure Buddhism.* Tibetan Buddhism in practice is a travesty, the same old religious con, trimming the impoverished suckers while the priests keep the nicest digs in town. The poor, yak-herding dolts take their entire tiny pile of disposable income and throw it on the floor in front of cartoon statues of semi-mythical saints, and the monks don't even look at them. The country folk are the marks. The monks just rake up the money, and put it in their tidy stacks, and enter it in their tidy books.

All around the Potala, and all around the Jokhang, the faithful trudged, prostrated themselves, prayed, twirled their charms, spun their bells, and burned great fronds of sacred herbs, the air as thick with smoke as Dickens's London, burning the throat and irritating the eye. People seemed intensely downtrodden to me, like they'd given up completely and now just practiced out of habit. I was reminded of the Ghost Dance cults of the 1890s in America, when the wars were over, and the Indians were fucked, and there was no going back, and they prayed and they danced and entered a trance and kept dancing. One assumes the Ghost Dance did for people then what the pilgrims' march in Lhasa does now, confirming some belief in an order of things that was not simply of this world, the world disappearing before their eyes. What the Indians got, for their troubles, were the Wounded Knee massacre, the massive redeployment of U.S. troops, and the death of Sitting Bull. The Tibetans can't hope for much better.

THE CHINESE TROOPS were everywhere, not just on the roofs, and not just in riot gear wherever worshippers sleepwalk in their circles. The army also regularly dispatched a flotilla of trucks, fitted with loudspeakers, blaring at anyone within earshot as they drove through the city. I asked a woman what they were saying.

They announce that the army is a beneficent force for life in Lhasa, she said. The army, the truck say, is friend of people of Lhasa and friend of all people of Tibet. She knew she didn't have to add comment.

In the street I saw another young Tibetan woman, a girl, really, in jeans, modern, wearing a pink and white trucker's cap. The legend on the cap was: WE FUCK THE FAKESHIT. I had no idea. I motioned to the cap, and asked, but she had no English and just smiled. I later saw the cap for sale around town. It struck a chord, and I knew that whatever subtleties I might be missing in the syntax, it was definitely anti-fakeshit.

As the soldiers patrolled the streets, weighed down with riot gear, they sucked up the thick, oxygen-weak air, particulate-rich from burnt offerings dedicated toward their expulsion. A young deer, not quite a fawn anymore, made its way into one of the upper courtyards of the monastery. It walked delicately across the cobblestones toward two Chinese officers, who seemed spooked. What is this? Some spirit animal, come to mock us? I imagined the officers temporarily confused about how to write the report.

THE CHINESE HAD BUILT, in recent years, directly across from the Potala Palace, a truly hideous monument to socialist progress, a sword-shaped affront to the Dalai Lama's former home. Its sole purpose is to remind people who is in power, but at this point it may be that every shopping center and apartment building and gleaming office building in the new Han Lhasa, across the street from the old Tibetan Lhasa, is the more powerful and thoroughgoing challenge.

The Tibetans find ways to protest. They mock the Chinese in song and dance, ridicule them with classic night club ethnic masquerade—one of the most popular shows in Lhasa includes a skit of caricatured Brahmin Chinese, in Mandarin garb, with pasted-on Fu Manchu mustaches, dancing around and playing pedantic, stuck-up idiots.

The Chinese soldiers remain stoic beneath the victory towers of medieval Tibetan armies. (Another shock: so many of the beautiful gold ornaments atop Tibetan monasteries are triumphal symbols of bloody battles won—the monks' ethos is historically no more pacifist than that of the Chinese soldiers.) The nuns tend their convent's flowers. The monks debate. They debate the meaning of life and death, of the deaths of thousands in the uprising of 1959 as the Dalai Lama escaped, of the untold deaths during the destruction of six thousand temples during the Cultural Revolution, of the 450 who died during protests in 1989, of the 400 who were killed in March of 2008. They debate the future of Tibet as if it hadn't already arrived, and make their food into magical shapes to ward off an enemy that's all around, staggeringly wealthy and heavily armed.

A lavish banner spanned the road to the airport, reminding all who passed: *The Developing Zone is Very Amazing!*

The pilgrims pray, and spin their golden wheels.

THE DOCTOR IN THE CASINO

DAR ES SALAAM, TANZANIA

THE GUIDEBOOK agreed with the State Department: do not go out at night in Dar es Salaam. And so, on my first night in Tanzania's storied leading city, I wandered downstairs in my hotel, looking for the restaurant, which turned out to be a few floors up. Downstairs, instead, was a casino. I walked in to see if there was a poker game (there wasn't, just machines) and fell into conversation with a substantial-looking man in his sixties. He was a doctor, he said, in general practice. He was well-known in the place, and several people came by and paid their respects while he was more or less talking to me. I was watching the crowd, trying to figure out what I was seeing. I thought maybe a couple of the women were prostitutes, which turned out to be true in at least one case, and the men, I had to assume, were a mix of locals and businessmen from elsewhere. The doctor was talking to a voluble man in his thirties, whose blustery, backslapping ways were being iced by the doctor's wise mien. The young man felt it; he was large, six feet two or six feet three, north of 250 pounds, but he looked boyish in the face of whatever the doctor was telling him. I couldn't hear any of it because of the bloops and blinks of the casino machines and the quiet confidentiality of the doctor's way of speaking. But I could see that the doctor was doing most of the talking. The young man had no back-up, no other chops beyond his hale-fellow shtick, and after a few minutes he wandered away, defeated.

I knew very little about the city. I was full of wonderment that I could walk around with the net worth of a village or two in my backpack—a camera, a cruddy laptop, a smartphone, a few hundred dollars, a passport, and some credit cards. Why didn't someone immediately bonk me on the head and take it all? The semi-pro camera itself, from Costco, was four times an average Tanzanian's annual income. The city was bustling with the begging poor, the non-begging poor, the sidewalk-entrepreneurial poor, and the grifting poor, as well as the shopkeepers and shoppers and church-goers and police. It is run-down, but cosmopolitan: one sees the influence of Arabs and Indians and the various European powers—Portuguese and English, mostly, but French and German too—and more recently the Chinese. People of every ethnicity and race walked by, which meant a white guy wandering around in sneakers and a silly hat with a camera didn't cause much fuss. At a hotel casino at night, even less. Only the prostitute perked up.

DAR ES SALAAM, TANZANIA

The doctor had been approached by another man, and again I got the sense that he was a personage. People were not approaching him like they were old friends, idly shooting the shit. They were deferential, and he was responding, in each case it seemed, to some need. He was dispensing wisdom of some sort. When he finished with this latest petitioner, I asked him how often he came to the casino.

I come to gamble because I find it relaxing, he said. I come when I am troubled about life.

I noticed he didn't answer the question, but I said, You seem so relaxed and well respected and content. It is hard to imagine you troubled.

But of course, you are seeing my surface, he said. My surface remains very calm. But we don't know a man when we know his surface. And when do we ever know someone's troubles when first we meet them? How long do you know a man before he reveals to you his pain? Certainly you don't think there are people who live untroubled lives, people who live without pain? No, of course you don't. You were in part flattering me, and in part condescending—no, no, it is okay, I am condescending to you even now. You wonder if *the good doctor* has a gambling problem, and of course, whatever troubles lead a man to vices like gambling, gambling simply makes things worse, doesn't it? Gambling brings its own kind of troubles. I know this, and I do not assume I am somehow above such problems. But I will not allow it to happen; I bring only what I am prepared to lose, one hundred dollars, no plastic, so I cannot get into that kind of trouble.

He was a bit of a monologist so the smallest prompts kept him talking.

How are you doing tonight?

Tonight? Tonight I won around a thousand dollars. Yes, a thousand dollars more or less. This will allow me to lose ten times, and ten times I will be able to forget all my troubles again. When I lose, I go home. And when I win, I go home. Meanwhile, my troubles are forgotten, either way.

I asked him about Tanzania, and how he felt it was doing, and he described what he saw as the main issues facing his society, among them the problem of corruption, about which he had much to say, culminating in the nicely orotund conclusion: Corruption is the great enemy of progress.

I told him, briefly, my theory that the United States is now the most corrupt country in the world. We have just managed to control all the small corruption, I said, in favor of big corruption. We have regulated the giving of bribes by statute, and government servants are only allowed to be extorted by wealthy corporations.

He found this mildly interesting but was unconvinced. In fact, he was unconvinced by just about anything I had to say. It occurred to me that he was a man in the habit of dispensing opinion, not accepting it—an occupational habit, I supposed.

We were very lucky, he said. Our first president did not want anything for himself. He did not want to collect wealth.

Nyerere, I said.

Yes, he said, Julius Nyerere. He said it like I was one of the less bright interns following him on his rounds, like he would say, yes, that is scrofula, implying that any fool could see that it was scrofula.

He went on as soon as he could see I was chastened: You can go to Nyerere's house and see, he died not a rich man. His house is nice, of course, but it is just a house, you would never know he was president. But! He is gone! We look around now and see. We don't want to be like our neighbors. We do not want to be like Kenya. We do not want to be like Uganda.

Or Rwanda or Burundi, I added.

Certainly, he said, not a man to be hurried. We do not want to be like Rwanda. We do not want to be like Burundi. We do not want to be like Mozambique. We do not want to be like Congo—and at that he raised an eyebrow. We do not, of course, want to be like Zimbabwe, and this got a higher eyebrow raise than the Congo.

Another distinguished-looking man had come in, wearing gold wire-rim glasses. Excuse me, my doctor said, and turned to him. The woman who had been smiling at me from across the bar took advantage of this diversion to sit closer and suggest I join her. I said no, thank you very much, I am very tired, and I must go to sleep.

I could help, she said.

I thanked her again, and said goodnight, and then thanked the doctor and said goodbye. He glanced over at me from his conversation—he had moved on, this time talking to a woman of about fifty—and looked at me like he had never seen me before in his life.

BUDDHA AND THE ENGINEERS

YANGON

YANGON, when the British occupied it, was called Rangoon. Rangoon had been one of those dream destinations for me, a stop on my childhood *Wide World Game,* when I knew nothing of Burma, when I had no idea why Burma-Shave was called Burma Shave, or if Burmese pythons were from Burma, no idea if Burma had been part of the Raj, or even what the Raj was. I hadn't read George Orwell. I didn't know who lived there, or whether it was jungle or desert, although the python suggested jungle. I just knew I needed to go.

The minute Aung San Suu Kyi—the Nobel-winning opposition politician who had been under house arrest for almost two decades—was released and announced that tourism should resume, that the boycotts she had encouraged to push for democracy should end, I went. It was 2011. I had avoided the place on her word, and when I heard I happened to be in Bangkok; I went straight to the Myanmar consulate and, as soon as the visa was ready the next day, went directly to the airport and grabbed the first available flight. It was on Air Bagan, which I didn't realize until later was on the list of businesses banned by human rights groups and the State Department, because of the owner's ties to the generals.

I landed half expecting something like the military receiving line that greets you in Phnom Penh, where a half dozen scarfaced guys in scary uniforms with scary expressions take their sweet time for no particular reason, one at a time, as you shuffle past them, each looking up at you and down at your papers suspiciously, while of course images of torture and murder play in your head. There seems no purpose to this hazing except to impress upon foreigners the deep bench the security agencies have.

But Yangon was the opposite. The flight's sixteen passengers walked across the tarmac while fourteen suitcases were dropped out of the hold and arrived at the minimal terminal thirty seconds after we did. Within minutes, our passports were stamped, and we were in the middle of the airport cabbie rush.

The first few guys had big personalities, and big elbows. One man a row back, though, had a kindly eye and a convincing command of English, and he grabbed my bag as we walked to his beat-up, but well-swept, Nissan. He was sweet and easy-going, and when we started to talk about whether I'd be needing a car in the coming days, he gave me his card. It bore his name, Myint, and above it, Tourist Services. Below was his cell number and 'B.S., Physics.'

I liked him, and we talked right away about Aung San Suu Kyi and the big changes in the air. My guidebooks had been full of warnings, saying that any and all political speech could be punished, that it was irresponsible to lure people into any loose talk that could get them in trouble, to tread lightly, to never bring up partisan questions unless someone else did so first. But my experience was the opposite. People on the plane, Myint, the people at my hotel: everyone was happy to talk politics. Everyone. The Lady, as people called her, seemed to be on the cover of every newspaper and magazine in the country. A transformation was underway, and although, as in any military dictatorship, especially one as wantonly violent as the Myanmar generals had been, things could be reversed in a day, at that moment people were almost giddy when politics came up, high with a sense of new freedoms and new possibilities.

Like many international pariahs, Burma is not on the credit card grid, and it is therefore impossible to rent a car. As Myint left me at my hotel, set between two huge movie theaters, one playing *Rise of the Planet of the Apes* and the other *Cowboys & Aliens*, we agreed he would pick me up the next morning. I went up to my room and looked out the window, trying to reconcile my vague imaginings of the country with the confused mixture of radical difference and the universal contemporary I was finding—the great swirls of gold sandalwood paste decorating almost all of the women's and children's faces, the men's longyi, and the songbirds for sale on the sidewalk—with the asphalt, concrete, movie-houses, and taxis that spread before me.

WHEN MYINT picked me up the next morning, he began dutifully ticking off the major temples. As we drove and walked, I asked him about the physics degree.

Ah, I love physics, he said. I love the theory, love the math.

I asked if he was looking for work in that field.

Here? he smiled. There are no jobs, not even consulting. The foreign companies, they use their own people. There is nothing except the university, he said, wistful.

I work at a university, I told him. Is teaching a possibility?

Well, my teacher encouraged me, and I started graduate work, but then I had a wife, and children, and I had to stop.

In the U.S., graduate students sometimes make money teaching, is that true here?

He laughed. My teacher—and every time he said those two words, it was with reverence, with the warmth of a devotee—my teacher is head of the department at Yangon University, and has been head since I was a student, 15 years ago, and for years before that. He makes $300 a month. I cannot support my family on his salary. And he is the most senior physicist in the country—a new professor? No, I need to drive the tourists. Because of my physics training, my English is good. My English is good?

Yes, I said, very good.

Tell me, please, if I make mistakes. I would like to continue to get better as an English speaker.

How does he do it, your friend, the head of the department? I asked. How does he get by?

He shrugged. Maybe he has other money. Maybe his wife has money, maybe he does get a little consulting work, like some of the engineering professors. He lives simply.

For lunch, we entered a restaurant I had encouraged him to pick. He had first stopped at one of the tourist spots, the sign outside reading, *Authentic Burmese Cuisine and Pizza*. I asked him to take me instead to a place he liked, a place where he ate when he wasn't burdened with tourists. He led me to a spot along a small river, a roof covering a concrete slab with half-walls here and there, more of a pagoda than a building. It was packed. We went up and he ordered some things at a central counter, curries, vegetables, rice, fried things, and went to sit and wait. Everything was fast, the staff running, the cooks in the center flinging, and rain started to fall out of the sky with monsoon heft. The waitstaff all had large fans, which they used to keep flies from landing, and they had uncanny skill. The fans sent massive gusts of air, aimed perfectly an inch off our plates, stupendously foiling an enemy both legion and wily, keeping the black invaders from landing, all while running food and replenishing tea. When necessary they'd execute a behind-the-back fan maneuver, alive to every fly in the joint. Myint didn't eat here very often, he said, because it was a little dear—the two of us had everything on the menu, it felt like, and rang up a $7 tab. He was perfectly aware it wasn't haute cuisine, but it was great: charred corn, samosas, curries, and salads, everything poised between India and Thailand. We were both extremely happy, savoring every bite.

We and most of the people in the restaurant watched the rain, a vertical river smacking onto the street.

TWENTY MINUTES LATER, the downpour eased and the lunchroom emptied. We headed out to a new temple, the opulent one built by the generals. Myint was a devout Buddhist and said a little prayer at each place we stopped, including this one. It is a hideous affair—not according to Myint, for whom there was no such thing as a misbegotten temple, and who thought it was one of the best things the generals had done, but objectively. An enormous marble Buddha had been hauled in from a distant quarry in Myanmar's equivalent of the Mars project, or *Levitated Mass* rolling in from the desert to LACMA. The engineering feat was memorialized in a series of murals in the entryways, showing the behemoth slowly making its way from the interior to the capital, the generals and leading monks watching over the process as benevolent stewards sent from the heavens, literally looking down from the clouds. The bland colossus was housed in a humongous cage of glass partitions that offered protection—from pigeons? Karen separatists? Some other dissidents?—while producing a glare that rendered the sculpture nearly invisible. The setting was a horrific riot of gaudiness. At Wat Pho and the other Thai temples I love the colored mirrors and tutti-frutti decoration, and I adore the wild tempera colors on the pyramids of Tamil Nadu, but I wasn't feeling this. Maybe I'm a sucker for patina, maybe this one just didn't have the age it needed, for me, to exonerate its aesthetic crimes. Or maybe, of course, maybe this temple was exactly as horrid as I thought it was. It looked like the 99-cent store had been hired to decorate.

I tried to draw Myint out about it, but he didn't find the massive frumpery of the temple kitschy or otherwise a problem. He did, however, object to the cost, with so many people hungry and needing medicine. As we left, I told him I was templed out for the day, and that I'd like him to show me some neighborhoods. Show me where the rich people live, I said. Show me where the poor people live.

Ah! I see, he said, with a knowing and satisfied smile. You want reality! He approved, in his quiet way.

Our first stop was a well-off neighborhood. The Burmese equivalent of McMansions had been spanked up on every other lot in recent years, each decked out with gratuitous columns and filigree, ostentatiously large and entirely lacking in architectural finesse. They seemed equivalent to upper-middle-class American homes, rather than those of the very rich. I began to wonder if the distribution of wealth wasn't as bad as I had read. Then Myint took me to a more upscale neighborhood, and here the money was even harder to see. Everything was behind walls.

Most of the generals are here, Myint explained. This the house of General Than Shwe. This house General Thura Shwe Mann. This Maung Aye. It was as if his English deteriorated talking about these people he hadn't ever been allowed to talk about to tourists before. But let me show you another house, he said. You came on Air Bagan?

He knew because not that many flights landed in a day. He pulled out of the neighborhood onto a main drag, and pointed to a large compound. Look, he said, look inside. That is Tay Za's house, Myint said. The man who owns Air Bagan.

As we drove slowly by, I could see, through the bars of an ironwork gate, an open garage housing a Lamborghini, a Bentley, a Porsche, a Land Rover, a Hummer, a Jaguar, a Rolls, a Ferrari—it was a twelve-year-old American boy's fuel-injected wet dream, motorhead heaven. Just passing by, we laid eyes on at least a couple million dollars' worth of automotive extravagance. An obscenity of cars.

The country's per capita income had jumped from $235 a year, or less than a dollar a day, in 2005, to $1100 a year in 2010. A Bentley still costs 350 times the average annual income.

Tay Za, Myint said, is good friend of Than Schwe, of Maung Aye, all of them. He laughed, not exactly bitter, although maybe bitter for a practicing Buddhist.

So many cars! was all I could say.

And in a poor country! he added, not with anger, but sadness.

The most flabbergasting fact was that Tay Za *wanted* people to see this collection from the road. He could have installed solid gates, like the generals. He could have had garage doors. In Myanmar, by the way, a used, five-year-old Toyota, imported, worth $5,000 anywhere else, can cost fully $30,000 once the myriad middlemen and intermediary agencies have taken their cut.

I said, I assume Tay Za didn't have to pay all the taxes and bribes. He smiled.

But where will he drive them? Myint answered. It was true, the roads were bad enough that getting up to fifty kph was strictly for the thrill-seekers, and usually ended with a squeal of brakes and a thud to the spine as the wheels hit lane-wide potholes. The Hummer and Land Rover could get around, but the Lamborghini and Ferrari couldn't have gone half a mile in any direction without bottoming out.

Tay Za, he explained, was the main money launderer for the generals. He was the man who allowed the generals to get around the web of international sanctions they'd been operating under for years. The head of a holding company that, among other things, deals with Russian arms importation, Za is involved in construction, property development, agriculture, transportation, shipping, mining, hotels, tourism, and timber, with some 60,000 employees in all. When the generals couldn't spend their money internationally, Tay Za spent it for them.

The generals—it's a redolent phrase, and never spells anything good. Nor do its regional variants, like *the colonels* in Greece or the *juntas* of Nigeria, Peru, and elsewhere. The Myanmar generals had been in power since 1962 and had the PR cojones to keep a Nobel Peace Laureate under house arrest for most of the last twenty years. It wasn't clear if a recent international incident, in which a foolish American swam across a lake to reach the residence of The Lady, had anything to do with the softening—it was an odd stunt, since it was quite easy to drive up to the door, as Myint pointed out when we drove by it. Aung San Suu Kyi's house is in one of the better neighborhoods, and everyone knows where it is. She comes from the first political family of the post-independence nation, and her father, Aung San, is considered the father of modern Burma, having negotiated independence from the British in 1947. The swimmer, we agreed, had no reason to swim the lake; he was acting more like a scary stalker than a freedom fighter. But he had, because of the high profile Americans pushing for his release, brought fresh attention to the regime's repression.

I probably should have let it go, but as we approached my hotel at the end of the day I brought up physics again, self-importantly thinking that maybe he didn't get a chance to talk about it very often. He spent a minute looking over my head, caught in a brief moment of dejection or anxiety, and then his Buddhism came to his aid.

This is what we do, he said. His head did a sideways nod, like half of the Indian head-waggle, just another reminder that Burma is jammed like a wedge between the subcontinent and Southeast Asia.

This is what we do, he repeated, with a small smile. We accept.

THE COWBOY AND THE INDIAN

Wandering down random streets in Yangon my second night there, I decided, on a perverse impulse, to stop in a large indoor-outdoor restaurant, a high-end place of the sort I tend to ignore on the road, with fancy lacquered woodwork, lights strung between the trees, couples on dressed-up dates and special-occasion groups being merry. As far as I could tell, I was the only solo diner, although unlike in much of Burma, I was not the only Westerner. Most of the diners were middle-class Burmese, but quite a few were tourists and international businesspeople.

I was handed an English-language menu, always a sign I have made a mistake, and was wondering whether to just grab a beer and leave when I heard a flurry of hellos and good-to-see-yous behind me. One was from a man unmistakably Texan, and another sounded South Asian, like an Indian who'd done graduate work in the United States—it was less Oxonian than many upper-class Indian accents.

Something in their manner caught my attention, though I couldn't immediately say what. They knew each other, clearly, but it was hard to decode the level of warmth in the textbook exchanges about the kids, the family. I started to think the Texan was selling, in part because he was asking most of the questions. I heard all about the Indian's family—his daughter was going to a fancy school, cost an arm and a leg, but worth it, he thought, because the girl had really taken to her studies really quite well, yes, and what? Maybe, yes, maybe the boy, too—no, at another school, and maybe, it is too early to tell; besides, he is a boy! And the young ones, well, we'll sort all that out later, he supposed. All this elicited sympathetic noises and further prods from the Texan. He didn't come up with much in the way of reciprocal personal details. He was definitely selling.

In the meantime, the waitress had returned. I asked if there was anything local, and with her eyes full of pity for my haplessness—why was I in a place that charged ten times local prices if I wanted local?—she suggested a fish dish. The Cowboy and the Indian, as I had started to think of them, talked to their waiter at the same time. I agreed to the fish, then went back to writing up my notes from the last couple of days, interspersed with eavesdropping when I could hear the couple behind me.

My dinner arrived, and it didn't look great. It looked international. I noticed that the Indian behind me had long since stopped talking, and it was pretty much all Texan now, all the time. It was business talk, about the *exceptional synergies* possible between their two companies, *asset externalization, running the numbers, minimal upfront investment, strategic optimizations*: the kind of talk that always makes me grateful I'm not in business, talk that always sounds to me like a late-model theology or a con. I ate absentmindedly and tried to focus on my notes.

Did an LB 10, the Texan said. Afterwards it's flowing at 500 psi. And they said it was a fail. The area was too small. Put a bad taste in their mouths.

Shoptalk has a strong voyeuristic allure, like a glimpse into the private life of others, though just what it meant in this case, I couldn't say. The Cowboy's delivery, all very offhand, just a guy chatting about business with a pal, rang false; his talk was directed, motivated—not like a bad actor, like a good actor, making an argument, an argument worth money, and, for some reason, I thought big money.

He got a high skin on it, the Cowboy went on. Even if you go one or two skins, though ...

It was killing me that I wasn't catching it all. The Indian was the buyer, and something nefarious was being sold. The Cowboy made a statement, theatrically down-low, about the Vietnamese government, but the details were agonizingly elusive.

When they went to low base one, the Cowboy said then (or was it Lao Base One?), they were having major problems immediately, it was a major disaster—the Texas accent and attitude helped minimize it, like it was just a metaphor, nothing unprecedented—but it only took a year, he said. They stayed on it. First people freaked, people got a bad taste in their mouth, like how do you make a business out of this? So we did a lot of research. There are 1,800 fracks out there ...

So. Fracking. I started writing down as much as I could catch. They went in and out of range because of the ambient noise, and everything was scattered with jargon. But I got that the Texan had just come from Iraq.

You do enough of them, he said, and you go for the mean. We don't want to waste time on these pilot holes, let's just frack 'em right off . . . conceptually, with zero damage . . . I just took all the data from Japonal . . . You're talking big feet.

Big feet.

I thought of Myint, and the fact that Burmese science graduates couldn't get jobs, while these international oil men, with their international degrees and international corporations, exploited the country's oil Resources and plotted the despoliation of its water resources over dinner.

The Indian, when he spoke, was much quieter, and had his back to me. I turned around to get a glimpse of them. I was surprised. I'm not sure what I expected from the Texan, maybe Jack Nicholson in *Mars Attacks*, maybe Rick Perry, maybe Foghorn Leghorn. Instead he was a wiry little guy, half the size of his voice, a ferret to the Indian's panda. I had imagined the Indian wrong, too; he was more PhD than businessman, checked shirt, nerdy, pear-shaped, tall, the Texan short and slight but always pumped and pumping—like a good well, it occurred to me. The two, together, were a snapshot of the new order, the Cowboy pushers and the Indian engineers of the international oil and gas empire.

They go around, the Cowboy was saying. They build a twenty-year platform—standard—and frack, too, is just part of S.O.P. The average completion is like 75 percent. If you look at what fracking did—it was the stuff at fifteen, nineteen, that got . . .

I lost him again in the surrounding noise of diners. Every once in a while the Texan would get loud—Yer the only one who noticed that I do that! Nontraditional sourcing! Ha, ha—but otherwise I was missing a lot. Say you have one hundred wells, the Cowboy said, leaning in like this was the clincher. If five hit, you're in profit, and our data shows production at eighteen, low, twenty-five, even.

The idea, as far as I could tell, was that it was economically profitable to frack every oil well as you drilled it. It didn't matter whether there were known gas reserves, or even counter indications. Nor did it matter what environmental damage was done, shooting those chemicals into the earth—nothing like that came up. Just make it standard practice, the Texan argued, and you come out ahead.

The Indian, when he finally talked, seemed interested.

My intuition tells me, he said, if we could find an assessment method, a fraction of the evaluation, we would buy into it. I kind of want to pick your brain about how.

This threw the Cowboy into high gear.

They, he said, referring to the other clients who had come around, They had the same concern, that they were going to get into a big resource commitment. A lot of unconventional stuff, of course they were worried. All you're really doing is turning low reserve wells into high reserve wells. You can run all the numbers and see how you're doing. It's a decent model. The only thing that changes is you get some data. There's not like there's some big simulation model where you can get all your answers. It's like phase zero estimates, ha ha.

All through this I was seeing images from Josh Fox's documentary *Gasland*, of people's kitchen sinks spouting flames, of farm animals' hair falling out, of people developing open sores.

The question is, the Indian said, why would we be willing to pay for that, and how would you assess if it was worth it?

They do traditional volumetrics, the Cowboy said, reassuring. Their model is much more connected. You don't get huge differences on volume, you get huge differences about the amount of capital. We look at it and throw it all away, we believe our work is better.

It was all English, and untranslatable into English.

To me it's very alien that—the Indian started to say, and hesitated—I don't know if I'm too old —

But the Cowboy jumped in and didn't let him finish. No, you're right, he said. That reserve estimate was not hugely wrong. In Vietnam, the government forces us to do evaluation that way . . . If they really want to increase the uncertainty on this . . . If you really want to do this, he continued, it would take three years. Fifty jobs gets you there, monitoring the mean . . .

It's not conventional, the Indian said.

If it works economically—the Cowboy just put it out there—then—

He let this hang, and I heard their forks hitting their plates.

I had brief fantasies of my own little Greenpeace intervention, walking up to the table, asking if they'd seen *Gasland*. I was furiously writing down the snippets of conversation before they faded. The waitress came over and asked if everything was okay. She looked like she was seventeen, and tired. I said everything was fine, and took some bites, realizing I'd forgotten to eat. The Cowboy and Indian were leaving. At the door, well out of earshot, the Cowboy was still selling, not letting go of the handshake.

I WALKED BACK to my hotel, past all the better food on the street. *Rise of the Planet of the Apes* and *Cowboys & Aliens* were still playing in the theaters on either side; I didn't, at the time, make any connection. The next morning, Myint's friend picked me up to drive to Bagan, the former kingdom that left behind 10,000 temples. Myint couldn't do the overnight trip. The friend handed me his card. Above his name, Chan, it said Tourist Services, and under his name, 'B.S., Chemistry.'

AMERICAN-SIZED IN BAGAN

AFTER WE HAD SPENT a couple days together, the forty-year-old Chan and I had relaxed into trading idle curiosities.

Bagan, I said, as we drove past pyramidal temple after pyramidal temple along the Irawaddy River. I wonder if that's where the word pagan comes from.

He shrugged. But it seemed to me that the temples of Bagan—thousands of them, scattered through the jungle, thousands of them, just a day's drive from either Rangoon or Mandalay, most of them with their plaster worn away over the centuries, down to the brick substructure, but still impressive, some the height of a person, some four or five stories, and many dozens of them taller still, the size of cathedrals—were the just kind of thing that could have inspired a name; such a colossal, inconceivable mass of memorial architecture forces contemplation about the nature of things, about the nature of belief and ritual, about the afterlife of death.

I just wondered if maybe the name was a colonial name, I said. Given to this region by the British. He again shrugged. He just didn't know.

The roads among the temples were dirt, and there were very few tourists, indeed very little signage, very little evidence of living people.

McDonald's? he asked. It is bad for health, yes? A few McDonald's restaurants had opened in Yangon and Mandalay.

Yes, I said, and it makes you fat. It would be a shame if everyone in Burma got fat.

I mimed the Michelin man, and he laughed.

Yes, we call it American-sized!

Now, like most Americans, I'd like to drop ten pounds, or maybe fifteen, and I'm not happy about those ten pounds, or the fifteen, not at all. But I usually don't feel grotesquely overweight until I hit Asia. There I catch myself in a mirror and I'm horrified. In a flash, I understand the body dysmorphia problems people have, the anorexic inability to see the body clearly. I see myself in an Asian mirror, or even a reflection in a window, and I get depressed, and want to starve myself, stick my finger down my throat, or get liposuction or lapband surgery. Anything.

Maybe he saw something in my face.

I'm sorry, he said, saddened. That was . . .

No, it's true! I said, shrugged, and did the Michelin man again. He laughed and relaxed.

Yes, I didn't know so many fat people until the Americans came.

The British and Germans, too, right? I asked.

Yes, but the Americans win, he said, and it wasn't a twist of the knife—more like the calm, unperturbed reflection of a man twice his age. The Americans always win, he added.

The pagodas stretch as far as one can see, and even from the top of the tallest, one can only see a fraction. Of the original 11,000 temples a fifth or so are still standing, the rest prey to the region's constant earthquakes. The city, with 200,000 inhabitants at the height of temple construction, had fallen to a handful of stragglers and all but disappeared until the tourism industry started gearing up in the last decade. That brought a few thousand people back, a millennium after its glory days.

You have to pay for medicine? he asked. Something about driving in a car allows for non-sequiturs.

Yes, although many people have insurance, I said. And that pays most of the cost.

Medicine is free in Canada, he said. And England, and Denmark. Here we have to pay.

His Hepatitis C required expensive drugs—it was his biggest worry.

WHAT IS MERIT? I asked. I knew the pagodas were memorials, built to honor a person when they died, and that building one gave the builder, the person who paid for the

AMERICAN-SIZED IN BAGAN

memorial, merit. We were still tooling around the dirt roads, every once in a while stopping to look at one temple that was exceptionally large, or had some distinguishing feature, like paintings on the inside wall.

It is what you get for doing good deeds, he said.

Yes, I said, but what is it?

It was too obvious to him to require further explanation, as if I had asked, what is air? Merit, he said. Like when you make an offering at the temple.

Is it important to you? I asked. He had studied chemistry in college; I wondered if science had secularized him.

Of course, he said. It is important for anyone.

It just means you are doing the right thing?

Well, yes. But when you do the right thing like put on your turn signal, you do not get merit.

So if I live an exemplary life, do I get merit?

Well, yes, but that is only because if you are exemplary, you are doing things, like making offerings, that give you merit.

And what does merit get me? I asked.

This he found funny.

Merit! he said.

WHEN I CLIMBED up or through the temples, Chan waited at the car. At the top of the Dhammayangyi Temple, a four-sided, stepped, red-stone structure that rose high above the stupa-studded plain, the idea of merit seemed even less meaningful. One could build a civilization like this, and then Mongols could come in and wipe it out, shut it down, just like that. As the sun set and a slight mist rose from the sparse jungle, dotted with meritorious, mysterious piles, time stretched, and my wonder was a mix of plenitude and death—I could almost see the pyramidal piles of brick slowly turning to dust, performing their dry, glacial return to the land.

I came back to the car, and he said, I think Bagan is a Burmese word, it was this kingdom's name. Pagan is different.

OK, I said.

Already, he added, 1,000 years ago and more, Bagan is just Bagan.

He has a degree in chemistry. He has Hepatitis C. He has trouble paying for the medication. He worries about his children.

IT IS FASHIONABLE TO KNOW
ABOUT JEWS

SIGHETU MARMAȚIEI, ROMANIA

THE DAY OF CEMETERIES, in the middle of the bloodlands, started peacefully enough. I was heading west, bound for Albania, when I saw the sign for a Jewish cemetery. I had spent the night in a hotel a mile south of the Ukrainian border, in a little town called Sighetu Marmației, in northernmost Romania. I was there for no particular reason, except that this was a region where the peasant lifestyle of the last millennium was more nearly unbroken, in some ways, than anywhere else in Europe, where the horse-drawn traffic on the smaller roads rivaled the automotive. There was a corresponding lack of capitalist energy—the people at the hotel shrugged when I asked if there was a room, said they thought so. When they did my laundry, I only asked afterward what

I should pay, and they shrugged again. It seemed they were doing a load anyway. No charge.

The capital, Bucharest, is the opposite—there's a Soviet lack of any service smile, but everywhere people are on the make: it has escalatored shopping malls, fierce marketing, the most extortionate cabdrivers in the world, and prostitutes that respond to *no thank you* with, *Why not?* pointing to themselves and saying, *What's wrong with this?* Halfway between, just a few hours north in Transylvania, in Sighișoara, people don't gouge you, though they could—it's the birthplace of Count Dracula and owns an astounding conglomeration of cobblestones, chapels, clock towers, and everything else that makes for a European hilltop tourist trap. Nonetheless, the locals are genuinely helpful, and they find the Bucharest experience distasteful. The guide at the chapel at the top of Sighișoara's many stone stairways turned his nose up when I said I had come from Bucharest. He asked how I liked it, nose still up. I said it was like France, except with pushier prostitutes and pimps. He laughed out loud and said, I am going to use this, like France with pushy pimps, I will use this! wagging his finger and smiling.

He told me many facts about his church, and those in the surrounding countryside, some of which had been fortified, at various times, by high walls. Partly because they were protected from marauders, and partly because their stone crypts remained cool, even in the summer, they were used to store food, especially but not only in wartime. He told me that, until recently, the church's basement was where most people kept their lard.

Or, as you call, bacon, he said. You see?

Yes, bacon.

And when the Turk came, he went on, he came to one church close to here, the people came into the church, for to be safe, and fight. And the Turks, they piled all wood in a circle, all around the walls, and started it with fire, to burn the people out, and do you know what those people did?

No, I said, seeing where it was going, trying to head it off at the pass.

Yes! he said. They took all that lard, or as you call, bacon, and they threw it on the fire, and do you know what happened?

No, that is not true, I said. This is a myth, a folktale.

No, this is true! Because, you know, the Turks, they all ran away.

No, I said, and I couldn't help laughing at the ludicrousness.

Yes! Because he doesn't like the smell, they are Muslim, you see?

Yes, I see, but, no, I'm sorry, that is not true.

Yes, very well documented.

He was a pleasant chap, and he could tell that story in a half dozen languages or more—I heard him do it in Japanese while I was still there, and he turned and winked at me in the middle of it. Sighișoara, for all its enshrinement and invention of the past, for all its crenellations and gothic touches, is clearly in the twenty-first century. Maramureș, as the area north of Transylvania is known, not so much. The peasants dry their hay on racks and build distinctive, very tall, egg-shaped hay mounds, using a central stick and a frame, ten or twelve feet high. Their horses are enormous drays, the largest horses I've ever seen, their hooves more like elephant feet than anything equine. Some of the men still wear the traditional *clopuri*, straw hats with a unique funnel brim. The broad, sturdy women wear scarves and print blouses, and shorter-than-usual peasant skirts. One can't help wondering how the lithe, Westernized teenage girls, in their skinny jeans and sneakers, will become them in a few short years. The very old women are also much in evidence, sitting on porches, walking cows, riding on the wagons. The wagons, with sides cobbled together from rough boards, are pulled by single or paired horses, which trot them down the highways. The shepherds carry tall sticks. The Orthodox churches are made out of wood.

Maramureș is famous for these wooden churches, eight of them UNESCO world heritage sites, and new ones are being built in quantity. They feel like gargantuan dollhouses, or popsicle-stick houses, made of hewed log sides with delicate wooden shingles, shake roofs, wooden steeples, and carved doors, window frames, and gates. Many of the wooden houses use the same siding and roofing, while others are covered in colored tiles, or highly detailed, painted relief stucco. The area was for long periods under Hungarian imperial rule, and there are still Hungarian villages, Hungarian place names, and a Hungarian look to the peasant clothes. Braids of drying onions, garlic, and peppers hang from porches, and the potatoes are dug by hand. The horses wear tassels from their bridles, bright red tassels hanging from below their ears. Some of the village houses have satellite dishes and most of the kids go to school, cell phones are everywhere, and the homemade wagons have rubber tires, but in most respects life seems to go on much as it did in the fifteenth century.

BIBI AND THE CEMETERY

ON THE OTHER HAND, the fifteenth century was nastier. By some reports, Vlad Tepes (aka Count Dracula), as part of his psychological warfare against the approaching Sultan Mehmet, impaled 20,000 of his own men, women, and children on pikes and planted them in Mehmet's path. The surrounding centuries have their own gruesome stories, one in which 25,000 people have their eyes poked out as some kind of retribution. Many involve the slaughter of Jews and Roma.

Then, of course, the twentieth century, with its massive, industrial-sized horrors, making Dracula seem demure by comparison. Driving out of town, I spotted a small sign bearing a Star of David, and a little farther down the road, I could make out what I assumed were the Romanian words for synagogue and cemetery. I followed the arrows until I saw another small, slightly rusted sign, and then another, before I finally arrived at an old sheet-metal gate in a stone wall. I opened it and I went in. There were hundreds of graves, maybe thousands, with soft stone markers, most of them weathered to illegibility. The grounds were thickly overgrown and haphazardly hacked back, making it look like a haircut a kid gave himself with blunt scissors. The stones jagged at every angle. Some were broken. There was a small building I took to be the synagogue and a smaller one that might have been a crypt.

A man came in and said, English?

He introduced himself as Tibi, the new superintendent of the cemetery. He was a quiet man in his early seventies; he asked few questions but answered all of mine. There had been either 8,000 or 80,000 Jews in the area—his English wasn't always as ready as he wanted it to be, and numbers, especially, were a problem. When he was telling me how many people were buried in the cemetery, he gave up and just scratched the number with his key into the back of a gravestone. Interesting curatorial decision, graffiti.

I said, I assume you are Jewish?

Yes, of course, my mother was Jewish. She passed away last year.

I said, I'm sorry.

Thank you, he said. My father was Hungarian.

And of the Jews who lived here, how many survived the war?

I don't know. Not many. Some went to Israel.

Some of the old markers that could still be read were inscribed with only a person's name and their dates. On some, the death date of 1944 was followed by the single word, Auschwitz.

But there is no body, then? I asked Tibi.

Of course, no body. He shrugged. Just the stone.

He said it as if it were unimportant. I suppose some tradition had to be invented.

And this crypt? I asked, approaching it.

These are the rebbes, he said.

He handed me a piece of paper from a small stack, with Hebrew printed on both sides. He then bowed, and left me alone in the crypt. As I looked around I saw tin boxes integrated with each of the eight raised graves, each with a slot in the top. It seemed that people had folded up the pieces of paper and stuffed them in the boxes. I wasn't sure what to do, and I couldn't read the Hebrew. I folded mine and put it in my pocket.

As we were leaving, he said, five lei, for the community.

I said, yes, of course, and gave him the money—five lei was around two dollars.

He pointed at the security camera above the gate, and said, For the community, safe. I wasn't sure what he meant—that the money paid for things like the camera, or that I shouldn't worry that he might be just shaking me down, because our transaction was being filmed.

I LEFT TIBI and followed another set of signs to an Elie Wiesel memorial. Born in Sighetu Marmației, now by far its most famous son, he grew up in a modest house on a corner lot, which has been converted to a small museum. The building contains a somewhat half-hearted, or at least half-finished, attempt at recreating a couple of rooms as they existed before the War, with the rest given over to display cases. The pictures from the 1930s, of summertime families and friends in their bathing suits, people posing with siblings and spouses, are indistinguishable from the family photos of my relatives in Maryland in the same period—middle-class Jews with good lives, wide lapels, and neat hair. These were Wiesel's family and friends and acquaintances, his townspeople.

Another room, though, contained pictures of men in long beards and long rough coats and dark hats, women in scarves and peasant dress, their big farmers' hands holding on to cloth bags containing all they were permitted to take with them as they were herded into boxcars. These do not look like Americans of the 1930s. These are Europeans, they are from the country, and they are about to be murdered. So were most of the middle-class Jews of Sighet. One case displayed pictures from April and May 1944, of Maramureș Jews being loaded onto trains bound for Auschwitz, just eight months before it was liberated. This was the feverish end of the attempted extermination. Of the 35,000 Jews in Maramureș in 1935, just a few thousand escaped or survived the camps. The rest died, almost all within a few short months, at Auschwitz.

Wiesel and his family were sent to the camp in those months. His mother and youngest sister were immediately killed.

Some of the questions I had asked Tibi were answered in the displays, one of which outlined the number of Jews in each of the local villages in different years—it was 8,000, not 80,000, in Sighet; the Jewish population in Maramureș was very stable at 35,000 from 1910 until the Holocaust. In 1948 there were 3,072 Jews. In 1992, there were 48.

Another case displayed letters from and to the American consul; I couldn't quite follow the exchange, and asked the young woman minding the museum for help.

SNOBS

SHE, I WAS SURPRISED to hear, was not Jewish. She was an attractive woman in her late twenties, had dark hair, and, well, she looked Jewish enough.

No! she said, I'm Orthodox.

Oh. I assumed —

Yes, she said, many people do. But, no, I am Orthodox Christian.

Her parents and grandparents had all grown up in Sighet and its villages.

I asked her other questions about the exhibits. How many of the Jews deported to the camps in 1944 survived?

Around ten percent, she said. But most of them did not return here. Understandably, they went to Israel or the U.S.

And how many Jews live here now?

She had the same number as Tibi: 100 or 110 in the Jewish community.

But, she added, you only have to say you are Jewish to be in the Jewish community. She said this with a slightly disapproving mien. Even, she said, if only one relative somewhere was Jewish. Maybe only fifteen people are completely Jewish.

So when Tibi says—do you know Tibi?

I know many Tibis, she smiled.

The man who takes care of the graveyard, I said.

Yes, well, he is new, he doesn't actually take care—well, he is at an administrative level; no, I don't know him. He is new to that job.

Well, he says his father was Hungarian. When he says that, can I assume he doesn't mean Hungarian Jew?

No, if he says Hungarian, she said, it is not Jew. Jewish means Jewish. Everything else means not Jewish.

What, I asked her, do the local people think about this house?

Well, she said. Some are ignorant, they don't care. But, how can you say? Many different things: some are from the villages, some are from the city and are educated, and they know what this is, some are snobs, some are communists, some are nationalists, all kinds . . .

Wait, I said. What do you mean, snobs?

Well, it is very fashionable, now, to know something about Jews. She smiled; she had said it like she was saying it was fashionable to know about orange wines—part in the know, part mocking.

I made a noise, but couldn't quite figure out the question; the programs in my head were all updating at the same time. Fashionable? I asked.

Yes, fashionable, she said. For certain people, yuppies. It is what makes them feel smarter. To know.

And what about in 1944, what did people think, as their neighbors were rounded up?

Again, the city is different from the villages. In the villages, Jews were, well—back then, people said, you know, they were barefoot, they were dirty, the children were dirty, they smelled—all the clichés, but for many people in the villages those clichés were the reality.

The clichés were the reality?

Yes, she said. Think of it, these are peasants living with the livestock, in the mud. You can say 'dirty' is stereotype, but dirty is also true.

But your grandparents? What did they think?

Two of my grandparents were Jewish, two were not —

Huh, I thought. And what did they think? I asked.

Well, I will tell you, but oral history, she said, it is, I don't know the word—

Problematic? I suggested.

Yes, problematic. My grandfather, who is eighty-four, he says he remembers an old woman, and at the train station, she died, from fear, from heat, from exhaustion, but when I ask him about it, he can't really say why he was there, how he got there—yes, my father's father, he was not Jewish, and he was a boy—why would he be at the train station? He may just remember hearing about it. He may have seen a picture. We can't know. Sighet is a history bomb.

Bomb?

Yes, a history bomb. This whole country is a history bomb.

And the communists think it shouldn't matter? Is that right?

The communists, yes, they have other issues.

And the nationalists, I assume, are no friends of the Jews?

She smiled. You must understand, she said. Every year, two hundred Orthodox Jews arrive here from Israel, together. And you can imagine, in a small town like this, so many—and they are very strange, the clothes, the beards, the peyots you know the peyots?—and the hats. If you say you are Jewish they talk to you, but otherwise, no. The local people, they find them very strange. You can imagine. But, after all, they are foreigners, and people here are peasants, really. Yuppies, educated people, they love Jews.

All around where we stood, from the Golden Dawn in Greece to the North African banlieues of Paris to Jobbik in Hungary and neo-Nazi parties across Europe, anti-Semitism seemed to be gaining ground. So much didn't compute. There was no anti-Semitism, she was suggesting, just reasonable distrust of foreigners; she wasn't Jewish, but two of her grandparents were; yuppies loved Jews, or at least knowing about Jews. What is the history bomb? That nobody's testimony was trustworthy, not even one's own family's? Not even one's own?

I asked, when I was leaving, if I could take her picture, and she said yes. She smiled self-consciously, and then looked up at my camera confidently.

But be careful of the nose, she said. It is a very Jewish nose.

NOTES FROM THE ALBANIAN DIASPORA

TIRANA, ALBANIA

ALBERT, HIS NAME WAS, and he stopped me as I was walking through the lobby of my hotel in Tirana one evening in May, 2012, after dinner. He asked me something I didn't catch, and in response I winged it with a Yes, hi.

He offered his hand and we shook. He looked a bit like Harry Dean Stanton, a lifetime of L&M cigarettes etched into his face, with the same ambiguous age—sixty-something, seventy-something?—and the same slicked-back hair. He may have used a bit more Brylcreem than Harry.

Where, where are you from? he asked.

America.

I know, that's what I asked you—were you American—and you said yes. What city?

Los Angeles.

Ah! California! San Francisco is the most beautiful city in California.

Yes, maybe —

With the beautiful bridge! And San Diego is also more beautiful than Los Angeles.

So you have been to California, I said.

No, but, you know, I see. Pictures, news, movies. Santa Barbara is also beautiful city, more beautiful than Los Angeles. I can name all the states and their capitals. I lived in Greece many years. I speak Greek, Serbo-Croatian, German, Spanish, English, Italian. I wanted to come to U.S. in '92, '93, I gave money to lawyer, not much, two hundred dollars, pfft, gone, Mafia!

He mimed spitting.

The hotel was in the middle of the city's Soviet-style monumental center. Next door was a giant plaza dedicated to a flamboyant bronze statue of fifteenth-century national hero Sheshi Skënderbej on horseback. Sheshi was a new arrival here; for decades the square had been watched over by Stalin. Gardeners had puttered around to little effect, making no headway against the architecture's brutal aesthetic privation. In midday, the sparse flat offered no protection from the merciless late-summer sun. As Harry and I talked it was getting into early evening, and the air was finally beginning to cool. Still, Harry had a slight sheen on his forehead, and I probably did too.

The problem with Albania? he said. I don't know! The people are sick. In the head. There is something wrong with them!

But it's better now, without Hoxha?

These guys, he said, meaning the politicians, they only—he mimes blabbering on—they lawyer, they talk, just talk, they fuck, they lawyer, the politics! It is, it is—he searched for the word.

He kept his face very close to mine, too close. A prodigious stench of cigarette and drink was overpowering the deep garlic and wine of my own meal. He gesticulated, looking both ways and leaning in, confidential. I noticed that I was breathing through my mouth. A number of the hotel workers, as they walked by, wondered if this was a situation.

Corrupt, I offered.

Yes, corrupt, yes, but more, more than that. Dirty.

I think, I said, trotting out my favorite hobbyhorse, that the U.S. is the most corrupt country, in terms of total dollars, in the world. We like big corruption, corporate corruption, not small, individual corruption.

Yes, he said, dismissively. You have the Elephant for the rich people, and Donkey, Obama. And everyone takes the money. But we have 70, 80 political parties. They all take the money, and the two big ones, they take the most. One pretends to be democracy, one pretends to be socialism. But really, it is nothing. It is nothing, this new democracy. Just change of ownership.

HOXHA'S MUSHROOMS

I HAD ARRIVED earlier that day from Macedonia, across several mountain ranges. I had already seen enough to conclude that Albania's new owners were managing the place even worse than the old. Stripped carcasses of industrial buildings haunted the smaller cities. A once impressive rail line across the country was in ruins, its hundred-foot-high concrete stanchions still preserving the grade across canyons, but its tunnels, with their nicely finished stone fascia, were gathering dust, staring with hollow eyes at miles of weedy, rusted track.

The country looked like a museum of itself. Tiny concrete monuments to the madness and genius of Enver Hoxha were everywhere. As Americans contemplated backyard bomb shelters in the 1960s, Hoxha presciently assumed that wars would remain non-nuclear for some time, and so embarked on a program of 'bunkerization.' He decreed that people had to build individual conventional-bomb shelters, and 700,000 half-buried bubbles of reinforced, poured concrete were built to withstand any conventional bombardment of the day. The idea was that people could shoot out of them in case of invasion. Hoxha had come to power in the chaos left by WWII and maintained Kim Jong Il–like total control until his death forty years later. He had closed the country to international travel, and ruled through a cult of personality, information control, and terror. He fought wars of words with his neighboring dictator, Tito; he broke with the Soviet Union because Khrushchev was a reformist; he broke with China because they allowed Nixon's visit. He was the last true believer. While he was alive, he never ended his country's state of war with Greece.

The story goes that he forced the designer of the tiny domed structures to prove their safety by standing in one while it was shelled from all directions by tanks. It's a horrific image, an engineer's worst nightmare, or anyone's really—death exploding overhead, only one's own designs for protection—until one realizes that the structures must have been tested many times before Hoxha was presented with the final version, at which point the whole story starts to seem unlikely.

Making every civilian effectively a soldier in an impervious gunner's nest had the side effect of making the populace feel perpetually under attack and protected by Hoxha's foresight. The at once archaic and futuristic mushrooms, so invulnerable that no one can manage to get rid of them, sit now as inconveniently shaped storage spaces in people's front and backyards. They are complemented by larger hilltop artillery bunkers hanging forlorn and abandoned on strategic hillsides, like materialized versions of the terminally suspicious vista offered by novelist Ismael Kadaré—depressed concrete sprayed across the land, as if Hoxha had marked every piece of property and every promontory in the nation with his own paranoid and paranoia-inducing vision.

I asked Albert if I was right, if things were actually a bit worse now.

Yes, things are worse in some ways, he said. Thirty percent have no work. With Hoxha, everyone was working, everyone. Albania, workers? They make ten, twelve dollars a day, workers in America, one hundred dollars a day. These people in government, they talk democracy, but in heart, no democracy. Ideology. Mafia.

He talked like a manic association test, nonstop, emphatic. I had given up trying to interject. He really didn't need any help. He was seventy, I decided, maybe more.

You know the big problem here? Pollution, he said, switching topics with abandon. Everywhere, the streams, the air, the sea—you see it—the bags of garbage everywhere. This is big problem.

He wasn't wrong. Piles of plasticized trash scatter the landscape. Albanians' relation to garbage is odd and seemingly contradictory. They will meticulously sweep and wash a family grave in a small country graveyard, trim the weeds around it, festoon it with new plastic flowers and a picture in a shiny standing frame, and yet leave behind a pile of picnic detritus, plastic bags, bottles, rinds, bones, and the old, faded plastic flowers not two feet away. People flop bottles, wrappers, bags of miscellaneous crap, anything out of their cars and trucks, anywhere. It's one of those 'over the wall' cultures.

It's true! Albert agreed. People, Albanian people, inside, it is all clean, but *shooit!* They throw things out the window. They clean house and throw dirt in street, in next yard. Their garbage is always problem of somebody else. I like American people, I meet them I say hello, they are good here—he pokes his heart—They have good ideology, good mentality, but the politics, no good.

Since he had rejected my version—endemic corruption—of what was wrong with our politics, I said, Why no good?

In 1991, he said, people came here, I met congressmen, big people, okay, not biggest, but middle-level political, congressmen. But after 1992, 1993, they don't like, they don't come back, '96, '97, they don't like, then '98, '99, everyone gets guns, starts shooting. Finally, Kosovo, they stop, and— he shrugs—2000, 2002, 2003, things—he mimes rising water—are getting better, not good, but better. But still, the congressman, he doesn't come back.

He shrugged, dejected.

Thus: what is wrong with American politics is that the congressmen who were interested in Albania lost interest. The year that the Soviet Union collapsed, 1991, was also the year that Albania shook off the Hoxha regime (which after his death in 1985 had been steered by his henchman, Ramiz Alia) and began its current experiment in dirty democracy. The 1996–97 reference is to one of the most spectacular Ponzi schemes in history—a Bernie Madoff–level con, if not even more severe. Aided and abetted by some of the most important Albanian politicians, 80 percent of the adult population invested in a pyramid scheme. People sent back money from overseas and mortgaged their homes in a get-rich-quick frenzy, all for a promised 20 percent minimum return. Some $1.2 billion later, the so-called investment collapsed, sucking most people's money out of the country in a matter of months. The ringleader escaped to Switzerland. Over a billion dollars in a country where the only airline has a total of three planes, the planes an average of twenty-three years old, owned by foreigners. It was in this context that Kadaré asked: 'Can a country's people be better than its planes?'

COMING FROM ST. LOUIS

THE OTHER REASON people lost interest in Albania is that, without a totalitarian state scaring everyone shitless, it turns out not to have a particularly pliable workforce. More than one person called it This Doing Nothing Country. In Berat I met a couple more returned émigrés, a father and adult son who still lived in St. Louis, just back on a vacation. They looked like hick Midwesterners, the son large, slack-mouthed, cowlicked, and T-shirted, the father a pudgy, nerdy bank teller in a checked shirt and high belt. It was all very Missouri except for the father's bling—a rapper's ransom of gold watch, gold chains, gold bracelet, gold rings; his American wealth conspicuously displayed on his unlikely person.

St. Louis has a large Albanian community, they told me, 500 families. It was large enough that these two hadn't needed to learn much English in the fifteen years they had lived there. The son didn't say much, and I suspected the father was talking to me in part to show off for his brother, who was with them, and who understood not a word.

I have been America three presidents, the father said efficiently. Obama, Bush, and Beel, he said, bending back a finger for each. For me Beel was best president.

Do you like Obama? I asked.

Look. Republicans is for rich people, he said, echoing Albert.

They both liked my thumbs down for Bush.

Bush-*shit!* the kid said.

But for me is Beel, the father said.

I asked how they liked St. Louis.

America, yeah, I like, the father said. But too much working.

Now the kid was ready to join in.

Yeah, he said, excited. Everyone is working, working all the time, and tarred. *Ahm tarred,* he said, impersonating the average American whining. *Ahm working, working, tarred, working!* Always they tarred and working, bush-*shit*! he said, with real feeling, part glee, part anger.

Too much working all the time, the father agreed, bestowing on his son a nod of approval.

The Albanian brother had the lost look of someone who knows he doesn't understand, and not just the language. The three of them were an Albanian Dreiser novel. The hapless character: the big lug of a kid, doomed to gaze from afar as the rich, the smart, the lucky, and the beautiful enjoy a life that leaves him alternately sullen and enraged. The successful character awaiting his fall: his father, flashing gold—you could tell, looking at him, that he felt those chains swinging at his chest, always, the heft of his watch, always. You could see his body's awareness in the way he held that arm, the tension in his short, rounded torso. The rings, the bracelet, the necklaces—he felt them all, and he was buoyed by the image of the envy he imagined them arousing. I saw him moments away from some dreadful Hurstwood blunder. Every once in a while, he would touch the bracelet on his wrist, touch the watch, keeping the dream-self alive. And then the sweet, bewildered brother, gone gray, wondering: who are these strangers? Why does my brother wear these gold chains? What good do they do him? Why is my nephew so unhappy? What right does he have? The old world and the new world, so unequal to the task, each in their own way, so equally mired in discontent, so equally capable of self-regard and self-loathing.

The seven o'clock call for prayer reminded me that Berat, this stone city on a hill, was in Muslim Europe, and when the second mosque's muezzin sounded, I realized that my room was right at speaker height and nearly equidistant from the mosques, one just a little louder. Competing versions of Islam were at work, the bitter rivalry played out at every call to prayer. The less-loud mosque sounded like it was being mocked by the other: *Allah akbar!* followed immediately by a staticky *ALLAH AKBAR!*, for all the world like a big brother taunting a younger.

CROSSING THE MOUNTAINS

IN THE HOTEL HALLWAY in Tirana, I had asked Albert about Islam.

Ach, he said, pawing at the air in dismissal. Nobody cares. Mosque, church, pah. Where do you go now? You have car?

Yes, I will go to the coast tomorrow, and down to Apollonia, I said.

You have four-wheel?

No, just a small car.

Pah, he said, disappointed. No good. You need four-wheel to see real Albania.

Albania has terrible roads, most of them switchbacking across mountain ranges. One day, far from the beaten path, I came across two cops with a roadblock. They had a driver in a twenty-year-old sedan pulled over, one leaning in the driver's window, the other the passenger's window. The driver-side cop flagged me down, presenting the standard poor-country puzzle—am I expected to pay a bribe, or not? He didn't speak English but asked me, with gestures, where I was going, and I told him I was heading for a town called

Belsh. He wagged his finger twice and motioned me to turn around.

No, I said. Look. I pointed at my GPS, which showed a road leading to Belsh. He shook his head, like he had seen this nonsense about a road to Belsh before. I like bad road, I tried to mime, but it was hard to get across. I pointed one last time up the road, imploring. He shrugged and shook his head one last time, suggesting, with the slightest nod, that the discussion was over. I thanked him and turned around. He was right. Even the good road, the one he sent me down, was pitted with gigantic potholes, hard to traverse without bottoming out, average fifteen kph.

On the main road into Tirana, partway up a steep pass, I ran into a mountainside traffic jam caused by a wedding party, the cars festooned, people in wedding clothes, all parked in the right lane along a hairpin turn, forcing uphill and downhill traffic to take turns. The hood was up on the fanciest car in the stalled procession, a large, ten-year-old Mercedes, maybe rented for the occasion. The people inside were glum. A couple of men under the hood had their fancy sleeves rolled up and were arguing about the engine. Wedding guests milled about as bored kids threw rocks over the cliff. I drove around them, eventually, and then around a few herds of sheep, and continued on. For the next twenty kilometers, a series of other cars decorated for the wedding raced past me to the rescue.

That's the kind of country it was. A place where your limo breaks down on the way to get married. The basic business of life was hard, and it didn't stop for weddings. In other places, everyone adapts, moves on, heads on to the church, leaving a volunteer behind to mind the car. Not in Albania. I could read it in the simple body language of the fuming bride, sitting in the heat without moving in the bridal chariot. She was arriving at the church in that Mercedes, not in anything else. There had been a dream, and nobody was giving it up.

Francine Prose's Albanian protagonist, Lula, in *My New American Life,* says, 'The Balkans had no expression for "win-win situation." In the Balkans they said, No problem, and the translation was, You're fucked.' Lula, like Albert, was an optimist. Albert was emigrating again.

I am going to Singapore, he said. Seven hundred Euros plane, I take two thousand dollars, and I look. I see. I think I can work there. You know Singapore? It is very nice, a city-state. Here, Albania, work three hundred dollars a month. With supplemental work, *supplemental* work, four thousand in year. In Singapore, five thousand dollars in one month.

He shrugged, case closed. He had a home temporarily. He was seventy. He was talking to an American in a hotel. He was going to look for work in Singapore.

PEOPLE JUST LIKE ME

KISHINEV, MOLDOVA

EVER SINCE running into Nikolay, my manic cabdriver in Odessa, I'd had an urge to go to Kishinev, Moldova, and a deep curiosity about Transnistria, Moldova's breakaway province and charter member of the League of Unrecognized Nations. The League's other members are Southern Sahara (which maintains its independence from Morocco), Abkhazia, South Ossetia, and Nagorno-Karabakh (the Armenian enclave in Azerbaijan). I had met a Moldovan girl once, years before, in Greece. She had the deep sexiness of the total brat—pouty and self-possessed, her flashing black eyes full of contempt. No telling how that might have helped form my expectations of the place, but they were immediately disappointed. The plane landed on the bumpiest runway I had ever experienced, shoddier than the bush strips in Africa. Kishinev, or Chişinău, looked like the worst neighborhoods of all the former Soviet capitals had been reassembled in one place. Characterless, historyless, charmless, depressing. My cabdriver wouldn't talk to or look at me. The hotel desk clerk's eyes never left his paperwork. The room was old-school Intourist drab, and breakfast featured the buffet that time forgot. Dreary, anemic eggs, hard bread, warm milk that clotted in my instant coffee, processed cheese.

The people in Kishinev were like the least attractive Russians— sullen, depressive, brusque, and utterly incurious about strangers. Missing were the crazy bearded old men selling books on the street, the Orthodox priests, the young, hip gangster-types or molls, the plutocrats in $300,000 cars. Just morose waitresses, surly desk clerks, bored officials, and bovine policemen, all pasty white—none of the Kazakhs, Mongols, Uzbeks, Chechens, and Tatars that give Moscow its cosmopolitan flavor.

I WALKED THE LENGTH and breadth of the city. It had the proto-capitalist trappings of Russia, the hair salons and dress shops with amateur hand-painted signs, the literal hole-in-the-wall sundry shops where only a window opened onto the street, the occasional upscale place that served cabbage rolls and pierogi. Whatever might have been distinctively Moldovan had been bulldozed a half century earlier and replaced with concrete blocks. At the far end of town an enormous brewery still had its old brick walls and silos, and an inviting sign announcing it had been established in 1873, but there was no tasting or showroom. I wandered into the yard through the truck entrance. Workers passed by without responding to my hellos, and I wandered back out.

Thus did my transparent eyeball theory—the idea that I loved travel for the way it allowed me to disappear—crumble. In Moldova I was, I realized, truly invisible. I could pass for Moldovan, and it occurred to me that I—just another white guy—might even have looked a bit surly myself, such was my mood. Maybe I was jet-lagged? I started fresh and clean the next day, though, and got the same reaction. I tried striking up conversations, but, lacking more than a few words of Russian, and meeting absolute disinterest, I gave up. I hopped on a bus for Tiraspol, the capital of Transnistria.

TIRASPOL, TRANSNISTRIA

THE BUS had a fourteen inch TV from 1985 up in front, and the passengers spent the trip staring glumly at a live-audience, Technicolor variety show. A blond 1960s-curvaceous model in a tight full-length dress danced in a sea of dry-ice smoke, singing an overlush EuroVision entry, backed by a dozen similarly shaped brunette dancers. She was followed by a duo: two guys in their late sixties singing a disco-beat folk song. The camera cut repeatedly to the audience, who were sitting at booths and tables, like the Copacabana in the 1940s, all brightly lit, drinking champagne and applauding, rocking out politely for the cameras. One of the two hosts was a blond man of about thirty, with a Beach Boys hairdo across his forehead and capped teeth. The other was an older man in drag. On came a young Madonna impersonator, flanked by four male dancers in suits.

Many of the passengers were smoking. We picked up and dropped off people every few miles. An older woman got on and sat next to me, soaked in enough perfume to remove paint, a nightmare of grandmotherliness. She ignored my greeting. On TV the hosts had been replaced—although it seemed to be the same show—by people who may or may not have been Kato Kaelin and Ricki Lake. My eyes watered from cigarette smoke.

After a few hours across nondescript industrial farmland, we approached the border. At last! Here would be some romance, some danger. A military station, complete with camouflage drapings and thick netting, flying the Transnistrian flag, occupied the center of a roundabout. That's more like it! In this crazy ICBMed, drone-filled, nuclear-submarined world, here was a group of insane soldiers with rifles, holding at bay some enemy that never comes, like Japanese in the trees of the South Pacific in 1958. Here was something different.

Transnistrian officials boarded the bus and checked our papers. They were appropriately stern, but didn't seem to find it odd that an American was coming in on a local bus. They were consummately bored. The people did not, as they often do in Russia, seem cowed by them. They officials left, and we rolled on to the forgettable bus terminal.

The people in Tiraspol were Russian or Moldovan, I couldn't really tell the difference. They were indistinguishable from the people of Kishinev. The town looked much like Kishinev, and I remained a nonentity, completely uninteresting and unremarkable to everyone I saw. They avoided me like I was a homeless person in Manhattan trying to strike up a conversation, and in an unrecognizable language. They pretended I wasn't talking. They looked past my request for a picture. The children made no sign they saw me.

The last hopes for my theory, the idea that travel liberated through invisibility, evaporated. I had never been so invisible, anywhere, and I felt not freed but bereft. I didn't like it. Not a bit.

HALFWAY TO PETRA

AMMAN – AQABA HIGHWAY, JORDAN

HALFWAY between Amman and the ancient red city of Petra, on the desert highway, sits a large, brown-brick rectangular restaurant and souvenir shop called The Midway.

As I pulled off the highway in 2014, only a single car was parked out front. This never bodes well, but I was hungry. I opened the car door and was nearly floored by the searing 115-degree heat. A Jordanian family came out, got in the other car, and left.

Inside two guys seemed to be in charge of the miles of product shelves—the place was the size of a large American supermarket—but were seemingly content with the lack of customers, and made no move to help me. An older guy disappeared into a back office, and a kid hung out in front, near the dozen or so tables and couple of booths. I asked him if I could sit anywhere, and he directed me to one of two red leatherette booths.

Can I get something to eat?

Yes, this is restaurant.

Great, is there a menu?

Eggs? he asked.

Excellent, I said, and he went back into the kitchen. I got up and walked around, browsing through endless tea sets, some quite beautiful inlaid vases, small tables, rugs, tooled trays, chess sets, lamps, decorative swords in jeweled scabbards, souvenirs, bric-a-brac. Everything was of surprisingly fine workmanship, only partly obscured beneath a layer of dust. I turned over a glazed ceramic bowl, and it was priced at 120 Euro. Everything else I checked was also twice what I would have considered paying.

Not five minutes later my young waiter emerged with a tray, on which was balanced a plate of sizzling omelet, scoops of hummus and baba ghanouj, and slices of raw cucumbers and tomatoes, along with a basket of pitas under a cloth, a small bowl of olives, and a pot of tea. He set it all out in front of me and began to slide into the seat opposite. Then he caught himself, and started back up.

No, please, I said. I would love to talk.

We spent an hour or so chatting about his life and views on the world. He started to look less like a kid, and more like a young man of twenty-five or even thirty, the small lines around his eyes betraying at least some days of trouble. He had lived in Europe for a time, he said. Since there is little work for young people in Jordan, many try their luck elsewhere. I asked how he had been treated; I had talked to a young Syrian in Greece, I told him, who had been beat up at a bus stop by right-wing nationalists.

Yes, I don't like Greece, he said. Greece is very bad for Muslims. I like Germany very much. Italy, Greece, Spain, no, no good. But Germany, very good.

What about America? Did you try to go to America?

Jordan no can go to America. I want to go to Burkina Faso.

No kidding! I said. I've always wanted to go to Burkina Faso! Why?

I have friend there—it is good place to work. Muslim.

COSMOPOLITANISM

THE SYRIAN WAR was raging not many miles away and I asked what people here thought of it.

Jordan—he meant 'we Jordanians,' and he said it with the full confidence that he was speaking not just for himself but for all reasonable people—does not like the King Assad. No! He kills own people, women, children. My brother dies in the war against Assad.

His brother had gone to join one of the rebel groups and died in the fighting, near Damascus. I said I was so sorry, that that was a terrible thing.

He shrugged.

Three millions Syrians in Jordan, now, he said, two millions in Iraq, one million in Turkey. It is war without end. And everywhere there is war. War in Iraq, war in south Yemen, Afghanistan, war in Somalia, in Eritrea. War in Nigeria. War in Congo.

You know a lot about the world, I said.

He shrugged again.

I watch television, he said. I pay attention.

Did you grow up here?

No, my uncle owns this shop. I grew up in Zarqa—you know?

No.

Near Amman. You know al-Zarqawi? Yes, with bin Laden? He is from my hometown. I am al-Zarqawi—means from Zarqa. Killed by Obama.

I was going to ask you if you liked Obama.

No.

Barack *Hussein* Obama, I said.

Yes, this I like! he said, smiling. But he is not from here, he is from Kenya.

No! I said.

Yes.

What do people in Jordan think of the U.S.?

Half the Jordan people think America is very bad. That America hates Muslims. Some, like me, know it is place with many people, and some like some things, not like some things.

And the wars in Iraq and Afghanistan, do people they think it is for oil, or against Muslims?

Because America hate Muslims.

Really, not just half think that?

No, all Jordan people think this. Already one million dead in Iraq. What else do we think? Do you go to Iraq? he asked. Other places?

No, not on this trip. I have been to Egypt—he nods—Israel—he raises his eyebrows.

Israel, don't like Muslim.

Where we sat was almost on the border; another thirty kilometers north was the Dead Sea. He could see I was waiting to hear what he had to say about Israel.

I know, he said, America brother to Israel. Israeli people, not bad, but Netanyahu, and Netanyahu people, very bad. Israel get big. Through all these wars, Israel get big. Now, United States afraid of Israel.

No.

Yes. Did you go to Iraq?

No, I would like to. I've been to Tunisia—nod—Turkey—nod—Dubai—nod—Azerbaijan—no opinion—Iran—very dubious face —

You like Iran? he asked.

Yes, I said. It was very interesting. People were great.

He looked almost shocked.

What, I said, as a prompt, not a question.

Really? he said.

Yes, why?

Iran people very bad. Iran is Shia. You know Shia, what is?

Yes, of course.

Well, he said, as if it was explanation enough for his disdain, then you know, Shia hate Muslims.

I was stumped—I tried to imagine him telling some Tea Party numbskull that the Iranians not only weren't Muslims, but that they hated Muslims. It would be like someone saying, You've heard of Catholics? They hate Christians.

He was a nice kid, a bright kid, a cosmopolitan kid, and sat across the table from me in the easy, accidental camaraderie of the road—passing strangers with no call on each other, and no beef with each other, mildly but honestly interested in the person on the other side of the plates and utensils. He must have felt my despair at the intractability of human conflict.

Yes, he said. I know, very bad, Iran.

No, I said, no. It is like you said about America—there are people in Iran who hate, there are people who want peace. He wasn't buying it. We looked at each other, strangers once more.

THE NEXT DAY I drove north, and spent the day skirting the Saudi, Iraqi, and Syrian borders. As I scanned the hills and desert in each place, I couldn't see anything except the same ground as on the Jordanian side. Along the Iraqi border, the desert was blank on the Iraqi side, blank on the Jordanian side. Along the Syrian border the low hills were dotted by olive trees on the Syrian side, dotted by olive trees on the Jordanian side. There was no smoke, no sound of artillery, no hint that anything was amiss. At the Syrian border crossing at Ramtha, the customs station, built in the 1960s, had been closed down so long that, where cars and trucks used to get inspected, trees were growing out of the macadam. Fifty kilometers north bombs were falling, a hundred kilometers south IEDs were exploding. In the deserted streets of Ramtha, children circled in the quiet on rusty bikes.

THE WOMEN AND THE KING

LOBAMBA, SWAZILAND

EARLY IN THE DOCUMENTARY *Without the King* (2007), we are shown the April 1986 coronation of the new king of Swaziland, one of his father Sobhuza II's 210 children by 70 wives (by some reports; others make it 125 wives and 800 children). The new eighteen-year-old king, Mswati III, is already technically wearing the crown at this point; his father, who had reined for eighty-three years, died in 1982, and his son was selected as the next king then, at the age of fourteen, with the understanding that the country would be run by his mother and aunt as regents until he reached eighteen and finished his courses at Sherborne School in Dorset, England.

He gives his coronation speech in the National Stadium in Lobamba, dressed in traditional leopard-skin loincloth and the appropriate accessories, his thin, hairless chest and beautiful young face almost tragically innocent. His accent reveals his British education, and he speaks with gorgeous solemnity. It is a powerful moment: a young man literally taking on the mantle of his father. Whatever we do or don't know about Swaziland—the tiny country wedged between Mozambique and South Africa—it's in Africa, after all, so we can guess the problems that await him: massive unemployment and poverty, and a people about to be slammed by the HIV/AIDS pandemic, already suffering among the highest rates of infant mortality and lowest life expectancy on the planet. We know, from the title and the opening frames of the film, that he is Africa's last absolute monarch, a king who will not just rule his country, but also appoint Prime Ministers, control the military, invalidate by fiat any law passed by the legislature, and decide by his will alone the fate of his people.

In the face of this grave burden, the young king speaks eloquently and feelingly of Swaziland's future, and of the grave obligation he has assumed. Although my experience is short, he says into a large microphone, and I am new to this task, I have in my predecessors an example I can follow, in sanctity and confidence. I will work, he says—sounding partly like a new king, partly like a schoolboy delivering an essay, because he is almost painfully young—to strengthen the bonds of friendship that already exist between this kingdom and the international community.

Without the King looks at the first twenty years of King Mswati III's reign, and it is an awful journey. It follows a depressing, almost clichéd trajectory, in which absolute monarchy corrupts absolutely. His opulent lifestyle—palaces for all his wives, American and European universities for all the children—and an economy dominated by nepotistic monopolies have kept the common people from enjoying any of the country's progress. Inevitably the result has been growing unrest, violently repressed, in that familiar fate of absolute rulers, wherever they rule.

Twenty-five years after he gave that speech, I happened to see him in that same stadium, again in his leopard-skin loincloth. A great deal more material is now required to cover those loins; his regal girth now flops as he walks, and he sweats in the heat. Except for ceremonial occasions, of course, he wears Western dress. When I saw him he was presiding, as he has since becoming king, over the single most important ritual occasion of the year: the annual Reed Dance, in which all the virgins of the country dress in traditional grass skirts so that the king might review them and pick his next bride.

THE REED DANCE

I HAD CROSSED THE BORDER at Namaacha, eighty kilometers of parched Mozambique scrubland from Maputo, where the immigration post saw very little traffic. I went through painlessly, getting a rote stamp in my passport, and headed toward the capital. Twenty-five kilometers in, a lone solder with a drop gate stopped me and checked my papers. You are here for Umhlanga? he asked, and I must have looked confused. For the Reed Dance? he explained, and I said I would love to see the Reed Dance, when is it? It is today! he said, gleefully, like I was an idiot, a lucky idiot, which is how I felt. Where? I asked. In Lobamba! he said, like it was a silly thing to ask, since everyone knows that. I charged down the road, my map in one hand, my guidebook in the other. I rifled through it as I drove, looking for more information. The two-lane blacktop ran through productive farmland, huge sugarcane fields, and eventually passed a vast refinery, with tractors crawling at various tasks and many large trucks. It was a modern operation, not like the sugarcane oxcarts of the Dominican Republic, and, more pertinently, not like the rural desolation of next-door Mozambique. I was once again in a new kind of Africa.

The roads were good, and I flew toward the dance. As I got close, I could see groups of people, including many girls in versions of the traditional dress—a grass skirt and nothing on top save some necklaces and a sash—holding their wooden machetes, some with families, some unattended groups of girls in different age-clusters. I could get no sense of where the dance was being held, since these groups were heading in many different directions—some arriving, apparently, some leaving. I pulled over and asked, Umhlanga? and was pointed down various roads until, in a large clearing, I saw buses of all colors and conditions parked in a sloping pasture, and a few policemen directing traffic. I made a reasonable guess, and followed some tire tracks across the field toward a couple hundred parked cars.

What looked like a stadium loomed into view, and a policeman waved me on. As I approached the arena, policemen looked in at me and waved me farther—because I was white?—until I was close to the entrance. I parked and started walking up the last bit of hill, and I could hear music. Thousands of people walked in both directions, some heading home, some heading in, families with girls from the age of three to sixteen or eighteen in their Reed Dance outfits, people snapping pictures, a holiday atmosphere.

As I got closer to the entrance a large motorcade raced by, a dozen sleek black limos and gleaming escorts. I looked at the man next to me quizzically, and he said, without any inflection, Mugabe. The next day I would see the Zimbabwean dictator's picture in the local paper, looking much more relaxed than the king, reviewing the dancers from a luxury box.

There was something as old as colonialism in the experience of watching ten thousand half-naked young women dancing topless in the sun, as the king and his retinue, half of whom were also in traditional dress and holding spears with feathers and leather shields, ran past them in a slow trot, the king's belly sweating and bouncing. Shortly after I arrived, he had taken to the field for the annual accounting of his droit du seigneur. The girls and young women were in long irregular rows snaking around the center of the field. On the far side a goatherd moved his animals obliviously across the land.

The sense of timelessness the ritual might have cast was disrupted by my fellow watchers, tens of thousands of laughing and chatting middle-class Swazis in bleacher seats, and by the knowledge that in the central VIP box the vicious killer Robert Mugabe sat with the crème of Swazi royalty. Scanning the lines of young women in the field, I saw a few in big Gucci-like sunglasses chatting on cell phones, women who, dare I say it, were not straining to look particularly virginal or traditional. Many of the five-year-olds were in skirts made not with grass, but with bright, tutti-frutti strips of plastic. And it was hard not to notice, running backward in front of the king and his party, an army of photographers and videographers and security, whose technology was all thoroughly up to date.

And then it was over. The king returned to the VIP box, which I assume had some special tunnel out, and the girls on the field and the people in the stands started on their ways home. A number of the girls asked me to take their picture, and of course I did. Noticing their lack of any shame or conventional Western modesty gave me a disconcerting sense, again, of being linked more to the colonial adventurers of the past than to the present moment. Once I started taking pictures, people lined up. The thrill of having one's picture taken had finally made sense to me. People want to be acknowledged without being known—that's why being quasi-invisible in Burma was so much better than being completely invisible in Moldova—and what better way than with a photo, which captures something, but cannot possibly capture who we really are. Mothers pushed their youngest daughters toward me, the teens ran up on their own. What better way, especially, if the photo is one seen only briefly on a stranger's camera, a moment frozen each time, a moment of a life that will live then with the stranger, the ghost of some dim psychic need that can never be fully understood, any more than the moment itself?

WOMEN'S WORK

AT DUSK I went in search of a room. I turned in at a sign for a bed and breakfast, set back on a large plantation, feeling foolish. What were the chances of an empty room in this small town on the day of the Reed Dance? The B&B was actually a grand farmhouse on a pineapple and vegetable farm, and I was in luck: they did have a room. The place was run by a white woman and her husband, originally from Zimbabwe, she told me. She was a third generation African whose family had originally been British. She was an elegant, upright woman, like the mother in a classic Western. She said the Reed Dance is always only announced a few days ahead of the actual event, so people don't have time to come.

They have to discuss it with the astrologer, she said.

Really?

Yes, several astrologers have to agree on the propitious date.

That seems like something that could be done in advance as well, I said, given that the stars and planets are fairly predictable.

She smiled. Yes, well, I suspect that the king has numerous reasons, personal and political, she said, for wanting things to remain up in the air. You see his friend Mugabe made it in time. I suspect they know long before they tell. And like any ruler whose legitimacy is questioned, he finds large gatherings of people rather troubling.

I saw a film about the king, I said. He seemed so promising when he was young.

It's an old African story, she said. Sadly. So you know he

no longer takes new wives at the Reed Dance, that it is purely ceremonial?

Yes, I said. The film said he wanted to become a global statesman, a continental leader, and that he needed to stop the old customs so he would be taken seriously, that he couldn't bring multiple wives to the White House or the UN.

Yes, she said, I'm sure that was part of it. But I think he had to make a change anyway. His father, the king, you see, had chosen wives in a way that was, well, I suppose it is the old European way—marriage as a form of political alliance—and almost all his wives remained living in their original villages. It was very smart, really; he had an ally in every village in the country, and he could visit with them, get a sense of any problems, keep an eye on everything. If any village had some trouble, he would marry its most powerful woman, give her more power, and bind her to him—buy her off, in a sense. He knew, of course, that women ran the villages—

Is that so?

Oh, yes, Swazi men are quite useless.

Useless?

Yes, well, we'll talk more at breakfast. I'm sure you need to find your supper, and I can send you to a wonderful spot. But to finish this thought—the king *fils* made an enormous error: he tried to make a compromise with tradition. He married fewer women—kept himself to one a year, rather than his father's three or five—and he brought them home, to the palace. By the time he brought the first few home, his European education was wearing off, I suppose, but not before he had instilled some of its values in his first wife, who is actually a remarkable woman. She insisted that he build each of the new wives a separate palace; she didn't want them in her house. Then the new wives all wanted what the first wives had, and so he ended up having to build them each their own palace as they arrived. Not only did the old system of governance break down—he had no eyes and ears in the villages—but it was a strain on the treasury. The old king left his wives on their dirt floors back home and lived here with his concubines, whom he could dismiss if they got pesky about a palace. Everyone knows about the wives and their palaces, too, and the poor naturally feel some envy. Where he used to make the villages part of the royal circle, he now makes endless covens of unhappy women.

I smiled at this, and she raised her eyebrows briefly. She was worldly enough, and kind enough as a conversationalist, not to mention that none of this was funny to her.

So, at any rate, she said. The king's marriages never had much to do with the Reed Dance. I look forward to chatting again at breakfast.

She offered me her hand.

I WENT OUT to the restaurant she recommended. It was set on a beautiful piece of land, the tables on a lawn outside. I was glad to see at least a few black customers among the white couples and families eating. I relaxed into the evening, flipping through the hundreds of new pictures on my camera, deleting the duds. The food was fine, and I had some wine. A young black woman came by and asked, since I was alone, if I wouldn't care to join her and her aunt at their table. I looked over and her aunt smiled.

Absolutely, I said. That's very kind.

They were exactly ten years apart, they told me, the niece nineteen, her aunt twenty-nine. They were both married to white men, one Australian, one Afrikaner.

Swazi men are useless, the niece said.

That's the second time I've heard that today.

I can make it three, said the aunt, and they laughed.

The aunt's husband was a salesman, they told me, and on the road a lot. The niece's husband owned a very large farm. Both were older, the aunt's by fifteen years, the niece's by more than thirty. The aunt was in love. The niece didn't second that.

We talked about many things, the Reed Dance, the future of Swaziland, the king, a bit about my work, my life.

We have to go now, the niece said, I'm afraid.

We stood and exchanged parting pleasantries.

This place, the aunt said, it is very nice, and sometimes we like to come here, but we would love to show you one of our favorite places, wouldn't we? she said to her niece, who agreed with a smile. Will you meet us tomorrow?

I OF COURSE ACCEPTED, and told my landlady about it the next morning at breakfast.

The colonial splendor of the house, with its white French doors opening onto a well-kept, lush garden in the back, its cool shade trees, and my host's gently patrician manner—it felt like Connecticut.

The landlady motioned for me to get my meal from the buffet while she talked. She stood slowly sipping her tea, holding the saucer in one hand, the cup handle between thumb and two fingers of the other. She waved off my suggestions that she sit.

I told her what I had learned from my new friends.

They are the lucky ones, of course, she said. Their husbands must be understanding and progressive if they are let out of the house like that. Some of the white men who marry blacks are just terrible, like old slave owners, worse than the Swazi men, who, although they can be horrid, are more useless than they are malicious.

Useless, I said. You used that word yesterday, and my new friends did last night, too.

Yes, I'm afraid it's true, she said. I suppose it sounds like a harsh thing to say, but it is, generally, quite true. They come by it honestly, I'll say. Theirs was, not too long ago, a hunter-gatherer-warrior culture—the women did the agriculture and all domestic labor and all manufacture, the men hunted and fought. Now, of course, the men don't hunt, and they are not warriors, and so you see your problem: everything else they might do has always, from time immemorial, been considered women's work, and so they won't touch it. The men have been made literally redundant—they find anything that reeks of women's work abhorrent, and there is nothing, or almost nothing, that they don't consider women's work. My husband simply won't hire them. We have—she did a quick count in her head—some thirty people working for us, between the farm and the bed and breakfast, and only one man in the lot, a mechanic from Zimbabwe. The Zimbabweans, and the Kenyans—they have a good work ethic. But every time we have hired a Swazi man we have been disappointed.

My new friends, I said, have asked me to dinner tonight, again, at a place they feel more at home.

My goodness, she said, in that British way.

What?

Well, I don't suppose—I shouldn't be suspicious.

But you are.

Yes, she laughed slightly, I suppose I am. Be careful!

Am I in danger? I asked.

Well, one or both might be shopping for a new husband, perhaps a trip to America? No, that's horrible for me to say. She paused, sipped her tea, and didn't in the slightest seem to think it horrible for her to say. She looked me in the eye. But it is quite plausible, she said, don't you think?

Well, the aunt is supremely happy, I said—my host looked at me like you might a slow child, but I went on anyway—at any rate she described a wonderful marriage. So it would be the niece; she said she was nineteen, but I'm thinking, from all they said, that she is twenty-two or twenty-three.

Married how long?

Six years.

Yes, and so perhaps the husband is already looking for a new schoolgirl. Some men are like that, you know, down here, like old sultans, using the whole country as a harem. Disgusting! Ah! Excuse me, I can hardly think I'm saying such things!

I assured her I appreciated her frankness, although it wasn't clear to me at what level of etiquette we were playing.

I hardly think, I said, that she'd want to trade in one guy who's way too old for her, just to get another.

She gave me that look again. I marveled at the eloquence of her pauses, like something from a BBC period drama. And

I was starting to be amazed at how long she managed to nurse one cuppa.

You can't really imagine, she said, how dire it is for women here. I go to the hills to try to help a little—you see the hills over there? she asked, pointing across the veranda, across the lawn and pond, to the far hills. The people in the hill villages are very poor, and, as you must know, AIDS has obliterated an entire generation, left an entire generation of children motherless, to be raised by their grandmothers. It is an inexplicable cruelty, that the men spread the disease and the women die of it at twice the rate—although I suppose that is not entirely fair, as the women are not exactly innocent in all of this. But these villages are now so misshapen. The working age men and the older men are all gone, dead or hanging around in the towns and drinking, and the working age women are all dead. The villages consist of overworked old women—grandmothers and great grandmothers—and thousands of orphaned children. And so these friends of yours, who can afford to eat at restaurants, they have escaped two horrible fates, you see—they are alive, and they have made it to modernity. The villages are as backward as —

She hesitated, and glanced at me, read something in my look.

Yes, I know, Mrs. Bwana decries the backward races! It sounds terrible to you. But let me give you a single example. In one of the villages that I try to help—I bring them foodstuffs, medicine, some household items that I gather up at my church—there was a darling boy of about ten or eleven, an albino, and I'm not sure you're aware, there is a belief here that albinos have special properties, that they possess *muti*—that is the word for medicine or magic, or anything that medicinal or magical powers—and just killing an albino is said to help you win an election, win money, cure a disease, remove a curse. And so last week, four men came in a small truck, with guns, and they grabbed this darling *child*, and in front of the whole village, who were screaming and pleading with them to spare the boy, they hacked off his head with a few blows from a machete, followed by his hands. Then they ripped out some of his organs, left the rest of his poor, bleeding body on the ground, and drove off!

Horrible, I said, a couple of times, because what else could I say?

And not that it is important, she added, but he was a favorite of the village, a boy everyone loved. Not that that is important.

And these men, they were from a different village?

I don't know. The villagers would probably not tell me if I asked. But we can assume they were from the city. They had a truck. And guns, I'm told.

People still believe in this, what is it?

Muti.

Muti. People in the city still believe it?

Yes, and why not? she said. You might as well ask if people believe in God or science. This is their worldview, this is how they grew up. But whether these murderers were looking to better their luck—and yes, *horrible* is the word—or whether they were in it for the money—there is a trade in albino body parts, you know, how is *that* for horrible?—I have no way of knowing. We have no way of knowing —

She trailed off, looking out into the garden. Then she turned to me, and looked me in the eye.

I do still love it here, she said, with some passion. I was sorry when we had to leave Zim. But now this is home. I wouldn't live anywhere else.

AN OFFER

MY TWO NEW FRIENDS texted me the address of a restaurant in Manzini, about fifteen or twenty kilometers east, and in the dark I had some trouble finding the place. I don't know what I was expecting, but it wasn't this. It was upstairs in a shabby building on a somewhat forsaken strip of highway, isolated except for the trucks roaring past. There was a small neon sign and a few cars in a dirty parking lot. The interior was that of your average small-town pizza place. The two women jumped up and called to me when I walked in the door, and I recognized them despite the fact that they both had on very different wigs than they'd been wearing the night before. (I hadn't realized, until that moment, that they had been wearing wigs the night before.) They were thrilled to see me, and called to the bartender to bring me a beer—they had started without me.

Perhaps it was the conversation with the landlady, perhaps I had just been oblivious and missed obvious signs the first night, but it was now clear that the aunt was pimping for the niece, not like an actual madame, of course, but like a mother in a Victorian novel trying to marry her daughter to the visiting peer. She praised her intelligence, and talked about how beautiful she was—they were both, in fact, quite beautiful—and whenever I asked a direct question of her, she found a way to bring the conversation back to her niece. Yes, she helped run her husband's business, the aunt said, and her niece had a dream to enter business, too, it turned out: she wanted to open a beauty salon. Her husband was too jealous to ever let her do such a thing, though, and so she had no way, in her current situation, to pursue that dream. Yes, it's true, the niece said, that she might just leave, and go to South Africa, or maybe to London even. She was saving her money.

I told them what my landlady had said, about their husbands being very progressive, or I would never have met them like this, two nights in a row. They looked at each other and laughed.

Well, my husband, the aunt said, he is traveling a lot, as I said, and we met later in life. And he understood that he was marrying an independent woman. So, progressive? I suppose. They looked at each other again and laughed some more.

No, he is, said the niece, compared to my brute.

I must have looked surprised, because she waved her hand.

No, no, he's not like that, but he is very old-fashioned, and he wants his wife home all the time, like a pet.

But you are out now, I said. Again.

They laughed some more.

Well, my aunt is very sick, she said, and she needs me! The girl had a great, open, infectious laugh, and I found myself thinking that she was, whatever else, very charming. As I was thinking this, I glanced over to see the aunt appraising me.

What exactly did they want? I wondered. For me to buy them a beauty shop in London? In Los Angeles? We ordered dinner. I decided to talk more about their husbands. I asked about the farm the niece lived on (cattle, fodder), how long her husband had been there (thirty years), where he was from (Australia), whether this was his first marriage (she laughed, He is sixty-five years old, it is not his first marriage!), and in various ways tried to suggest that I was interested in her current life, not in providing her a new one. The aunt got the point, after I went through the same questions with her, and stayed neutral and interested in everything.

At the end of the night, I paid the check, and in the parking lot the niece handed me her phone number (it was the chaperoning aunt who had texted me before, as was only right), told me I was a very good man, and looked down at her shoes, which I realized, when I looked back up to see her giving me a wide-eyed, imploring stare, was designed to get me to look her up and down. She knew the effect that usually had, and she was dressed for the kill. She gave me a hug that was almost chaste, but significantly not. I can show you the rest, she said, Of my favorite spots, if you'd like.

God. Somehow it didn't sound like a bad romance novel—she managed to keep the sexual half of the double entendre less pronounced than the nonsexual.

I thanked her. I thanked her aunt. They thanked me for taking them out to dinner.

I'm leaving early tomorrow, I said, for Lesotho. But thank you both so much.

You have my number, the niece said. I like you.

I looked over at the aunt, who gave me a look that said,

no pressure, up to you, my friend, but it will be your loss! She had one eyebrow slightly raised, like she was more curious than committed to an outcome. It was only later that I wondered what, in this particular case, she actually did want.

I HAD HOPED, when I got up in the morning, to continue my conversation with my landlady, but it turned out she had left for the hills with some foodstuffs for the villagers. One of her maids tended to my breakfast. I felt a deep regret, much deeper than I expected, that I would not see her again.

COMING HOME

YES

EVENTUALLY, I SUPPOSE, we all want to find out where we are, to stop roaming the earth, to be still, to be somewhere that feels not like the end of the road, but at the center of something. The great fantasist Jules Verne penned *Around the World in Eighty Days,* but he also wrote *Journey to the Center of the Earth.* However strongly I feel compelled to explore the ends of the earth, I am, like anyone, perpetually drawn back to the center, into the family circle, into my lover's arms, into the lives of my friends, into less fleeting, hardier intimacy than the road allows—into the normal flow of love and work that sustains everyday life.

I thought I might, in the course of telling these stories, while worrying through my many thoughts and feelings about my lifelong wanderlust, arrive at some conclusion about what it all means. But my thoughts proceed in the same mode as my travel—I get lost. I revise my sense of things with every step, surprised by what I find, unsure about my own agency, never knowing where I will arrive next, certain of nothing, finally, but my enormous good fortune in being able to go on, to find myself in yet another beguiling, remote, exhilarating place, or another distressed, desolate, depressing one.

I thought, earlier in my life, that my omnivorousness might someday be satisfied, but it clearly will not be, and I can't say this makes me unhappy. I am as driven to roam as I ever was, and as much a glutton for the new as I was in my teens. Only tonight, before I came back to a hammock on a riverboat in French Guiana, after spending hours on a canoe in the cool, early-dark evening on the Kaw river, I was as stirred as I had ever been surveying the *Wide World Game's* hand-drawn map. As I sat and wrote these last words of the book, I was already hatching my next adventure, into the interior of Suriname.

For several years I was quite sure that my theory of the transparent eyeball—the idea that travel allowed me a respite from self and self-involvement—was the final chapter of my search for the meaning of wanderlust, that in the egoless void of the road I found some peace and a pure sensual, experiential relation to the world, that the quality of my attention, once the road pushed my ego out of the way, once I was no longer performing a role, no longer managing the impression I made, no longer worrying about what I needed to say in my next meeting or what I said wrong in the last, was profoundly more intense, more engaged, and thus more edifying and fulfilling than my normal, anxious, self-involved daily grind. But that theory was dealt a near fatal blow in Moldova and Transnistria.

But not completely fatal. My sense of self certainly does undergo a transformation on the road, one that, I have come to see, may be partially imaginary, but is nonetheless enabling. It helps me feel that I am entering into these new worlds without preconception, entering more on their terms than on my own. Perhaps it is only to myself that I am invisible when I travel, perhaps I stick my head into my travels like an ostrich, and everyone else sees the rest plain as day. It doesn't matter. It works for me.

For a while, I doubted my sense that I was educating myself. People who have spent years in the places where I spend days and weeks scoff at my touristic impressions. I know what expertise is, and I know I don't have it—I am not an expert about a single place I describe here. And yet, as I look back, it is clear I have learned a thing or two about the world from having traveled through it, and as I read the news each day, I always understand what I hear or see in a qualitatively different way if I have visited the spot in question. I know, finally, what I know, and that is a good thing.

And I'd like to know more. So I'll keep going.

OBSERVANCE: ARGENTINA, GUATEMALA, LAOS, INDIA, MY DESK

THE PEOPLE MARCHING the streets in Buenos Aires in 2014, on March 24, the Day of Remembrance for Truth and Justice, were very well organized. They were there to memorialize the victims of political violence, to protest neo-liberalism, and to proclaim their commitment to Peronismo, from both the left and the right. Captains held them back at intersections before giving them the order to move forward. Along the sides of each set of marchers—groups from political parties, unions, farmers' co-ops, universities—people used bamboo poles to keep the marchers from straying in or out of their loose formation. Billboard-sized banners carried on a half dozen poles were stabilized by stay ropes as they made their way unsteadily down the avenues. Almost everyone wore the matching T-shirts of their group, blue here, yellow there, green, red, white. The drummers made a lot of noise, and there were some troupes of dancers in the parade, but nobody was unruly—people had done this many times before, and everyone knew the ropes.

The many onlookers lining the sidewalks knew their part, too, and didn't try to cross through the parade or interrupt it. The Argentinians were honoring their dead, demanding justice for the disappeared, and when they marched, they left at home their daily struggle for bread and fulfillment, and banded together to call, together, for a better life. They were, for the hours during which the parade wound through the city, immersed in a complex set of collective emotions—many of the stages of grief, but also the elation that comes when political actors hit the streets and find thousands and thousands of their compatriots, when for the time being, they are united, looking both forward and back, on the brink of their own history. Friends met and hugged. Many people danced with tears in their eyes. The great Spanish philosopher Miguel de Unamuno once said he thought the best thing people could do for the future was to all come out into the streets and communally weep, that this would heal and regenerate tattered social bonds. The Argentinians come close to fulfilling his dream.

The Holy Week parade in Guatemala is much the same. As in Argentina, thousands of people and brass bands take to the streets in a thoroughly coordinated effort, in which everyone knows their job, and everyone has been given some task in the annual procession, as they have been every year since they were very young. In Guatemala they carry massive floats, like heavy, oversized coffins hoisted by groups of twenty, forty, or more. Somber mourning and intense joy mingle in the streets.

In Bali, the seemingly spontaneous parades celebrating obscure religious holidays don't have any particular organization, but people walk slowly, and someone—maybe just the person in front?—decides where it leads and when it stops. As a species, we know how to parade.

THE MORNING WALK of the monks in Luang Prabang is slightly different. For one, it happens every day, 365 days a year. For another, it has a very practical purpose, not a political or commemorative one. A thousand monks come out of the town's sixty-plus monasteries with their empty food bowls, walk for a mile or so in a circle, and come back with their bowls full. And for the most part, nobody is watching. My first morning, I was the only one.

The monks came out of my monastery at first light, well before sunrise. It is a paradigmatic image, the brochure image, the poster shot: against the deepest blue morning sky, the orange robes appear, the only sound the slight swish of two hundred bare feet on their daily errand, behind them the aged temple, backlit by dawn.

Along the road, women—every once in a while a man, but almost entirely women, and almost entirely older women—set themselves up on little stools or folding chairs or a pad on the ground, with a bowl of rice, or other prepared foodstuffs. Some set up right in front of their homes, others come from down the street or across town. As each monk walks by, a woman pinches a small amount, the size of a grape, and drops it into the monk's outstretched bowl. The monks don't stop, all is done in motion, and there is no thank you, no how do you do. Five or six of the women will be lined up, and each monk receives a few grains from each, and then they walk to the next batch of waiting feeders and go through the same motions again. Some of the lines of women are neighbors, or friends—they know each other, at any rate. But it isn't a klatch. People are quiet and deferential as they wait the twenty minutes or so for the monks to arrive, and then as they offer them food for another half hour. This is a religious ritual, performed with reverence.

Well—the appearance of reverence, anyway. The monks look slightly bedraggled, actually, and intent less on matters of the spirit than on getting through the daily chore of putting together breakfast. They are at various levels of mindfulness, one assumes, and the feeders, too—some more, some less engaged with the moment. The almsgivers, whatever else they are doing, are accumulating merit, and so self-interested; for many of them, too, this is a daily chore, and even the most committed must occasionally lapse into absent-mindedness. The amount of religious emotion and devotion during any one of the thousands and thousands of handoffs that are happening all over town range, as far as I could see, from nil to some.

As my own mind wandered, I thought about infectious disease, and then got a little obsessed with the distribution system: instead of the very paltry offerings each woman gives, I started to wonder (in ways that I'm sure are not particularly Buddhist) why the women couldn't each give a ladleful, and cut the time and distance by a factor of ten or twenty. For that matter, why can't the women just come to the front door of the monastery and drop off a casserole and be done with it? Of course, this would destroy a beautiful ritual, and impoverish the town's daily life immeasurably, but given my pragmatic culture, I can't avoid doing the calculations.

I also cannot watch large groups of monks without thinking about celibacy, and what it means to choose it as a young man. And about what it means to recuse oneself from the world more generally, and then come into it only and ever as a supplicant. Many of the novices are just there for an education, and won't stay once they hit eighteen or so, but what of the older monks? Do they yearn to be free of the discipline? Of course they have the comforts of doctrine, and the beauty of ritual, and the peace that must at least occasionally passeth all understanding. But as I watched—as the sky lightened from deep violet to luminous cobalt to vibrant sapphire, as the saffron monks trudged back home—it occurred to me that among the religious emotions in evidence, conspicuously absent was joy.

REFUGE. The novices enter the monastery, and it is the opposite of journeying out into the world. But it is in some ways the same, since the open road is its own sort of refuge—isn't that why we call vacations escapes? When traveling, I leave my world behind, my world of troubles and strife, my world of achievement and defeat, of labor and tears. And, like monastic recusal, it does not come without loss, without its mortifications of the flesh. This is why, in India, people looked on me with pity—poor man, no family, all alone, wandering, exiled from the world!

But they are wrong to pity me, as I am wrong to pity the monks.

Because I am happy on the road, my home away from home, just as the monks must be once they finish their daily rounds, when they can stop the everyday getting of daily bread, and remove themselves from the quotidian once more, return to their world away from the world. When they can, once again, get lost. Sitting down at my desk, or in my hotel room, or in my hammock, to face the page, I am, for the moment, at the end of the road.

For the moment, that is, I am at rest. I feel secure—in part because always, wherever I sit down to write, the unfathomable road, yet again, stretches out in front of me.

ACKNOWLEDGMENTS

Thanks to Steve Cullenberg, Chuck Whitney, and Ellen Wartella for making much of this travel possible, and to my fellow fellows at the Los Angeles Institute for the Humanities, where I first presented some of these anecdotes. Thanks to audiences at UC Riverside, New School for Social Research, Goddard College, Rancho Mirage Public Library, Broad Stage, Los Angeles Times Festival of Books, Emerson College LA, and Prairie Lights Bookstore. Earlier versions or portions of some of these stories have previously appeared in print: the chapter on Ukraine in *Black Clock,* the chapter on Iran in *Santa Monica Review,* and the chapter on Albania in the *Iowa Review.* Thanks to editors Steve Erickson, Andrew Tonkovich, and Harry Stecopoulos for their help with those pieces. Thanks to early readers Juan Felipe Herrera, Janet Fitch, Seth Greenland, Jon Wiener, Melanie Jackson, Paul

Mandelbaum (once again), and Laurie Winer (as always). To Albert Litewka—il miglior viaggatore—and the rest of my fellow travelers. To Jonathan Hahn, for giving me the time. To Jesse, Yarrow, Cody, Guillermo, Mayela, Ken, April—you are the reason I come home. Well, you and El Dub: still, after all these years, the lightness and the light.